THE MELTING POINT

ADVANCE PRAISE FOR *THE MELTING POINT*

"*The Melting Point* is a riveting and clear-eyed account of U.S. military engagement in the Middle East and Afghanistan between 2019 and 2022. It is a must-read for anyone interested in understanding the dynamics of the Middle East; the contest between the U.S. and Iran; the U.S. and ISIS, al-Qaeda, and the Taliban; and the general calculations of U.S. power. It is a tribute to the values of an open society that a top general shares his experience not only with civilian leaders, but with the general public—the ultimate authority in a democratic society."
—Dr. Paul Salem, President and CEO, Middle East Institute

"Gen. Frank McKenzie is the embodiment of the meritocracy that is the U.S. armed forces, an institution like no other in the United States. Over four decades General McKenzie commanded at every level and served in ever more demanding staff assignments—in peacetime and in combat. He came to understand, as all senior officers eventually do, that what drives decisions on one side of the Potomac River is often vastly different than what takes place on the other. There are endless lessons to be gleaned from this superb work, and it is well worth the read and study by policy makers on both sides of the river."
—Gen. John Kelly, USMC (Ret.), former Commander, U.S. Southern Command, Secretary of Homeland Security, and Chief of Staff to the President

"A superb, exceedingly forthright, and compelling reflection by an exceptional military leader who strived to accomplish tough missions in hard places against determined enemies—as wavering support in Washington repeatedly undermined the effort on the ground. A must-read for political and military leaders and a very instructive chronicle for all Americans as we assess our important role in the world."
—Gen. David Petraeus, USA (Ret.), former Commander of the Surge in Iraq, U.S. Central Command, and Coalition Forces in Afghanistan, former Director of the CIA

THE
MELTING
POINT.

HIGH COMMAND AND WAR

IN THE 21st CENTURY

GEN. KENNETH F. MCKENZIE JR., USMC (RET.)

FOREWORD BY GEN. JAMES MATTIS,
USMC (RET.), 26th Secretary of Defense

Naval Institute Press
Annapolis, Maryland

Naval Institute Press
291 Wood Road
Annapolis, MD 21402

Library of Congress Cataloging-in-Publication Data

Names: McKenzie, Kenneth F., author. | Mattis, James N., writer of foreword.
Title: The melting point : high command and war in the 21st century / Gen.
    Kenneth F. McKenzie Jr., USMC (Ret.) ; foreword by Gen. James Mattis,
    USMC (Ret.) and 26th Secretary of Defense.
Description: Annapolis, Maryland : Naval Institute Press, [2024] | Includes
    bibliographical references and index.
Identifiers: LCCN 2023053490 (print) | LCCN 2023053491 (ebook) |
    ISBN 9781682474495 (hardback) | ISBN 9781682474525 (ebook)
Subjects: LCSH: McKenzie, Kenneth F. | Generals—United States—Biography |
    United States. Central Command. | United States—History, Military—21st
    century. | United States—Foreign relations—Middle East. | Middle East—
    Foreign relations—United States | BISAC: HISTORY / Wars & Conflicts /
    Afghan War (2001–2021) | HISTORY / Middle East / Iraq
Classification: LCC E897.4.M384 A3 2024 (print) | LCC E897.4.M384 (ebook) |
    DDC 355.0092—dc3/eng/20240215
LC record available at https://lccn.loc.gov/2023053490
LC ebook record available at https://lccn.loc.gov/2023053491

♾ Print editions meet the requirements of ANSI/NISO z39.48–1992 (Permanence
of Paper).
Printed in the United States of America.

32 31 30 29 28 27 26 25 24   9 8 7 6 5

All maps were drawn by Chris Robinson.

Dedicated to

Col. Walter B. Clark, USA,
The Citadel, Class of 1951

Col. John W. Gordon Jr., PhD., USMCR,
The Citadel, Class of 1966

That melting point of warfare—the temperament of the individual commander. When the moment of live ammunition approaches, the moment to which all his professional training has been directed, when the lives of men under him, the issue of the combat, even the fate of a campaign may depend upon his decision at a given moment, what happens inside the heart and vitals of a commander? Some are made bold by the moment, some irresolute, some carefully judicious, some paralyzed and powerless to act.

—*Barbara W. Tuchman*, The Guns of August

CONTENTS

MAPS

FOREWORD

Gen. Frank McKenzie is a Marine's Marine whose character and experience prepared him very well for his duties at the head of U.S. Central Command. He has the competence, caring, and conviction that great leaders must have. Frank and I worked together closely during our time in uniform, and he has ably shouldered the patriot's burden during decades of devoted, competent service.

While at Central Command, General McKenzie led several military operations of great importance, any one of which would have marked him as one of the most consequential commanders of his generation. This book is a thoughtful and clear-eyed look at his tenure, leavened by his trademark humility and his appreciation of history.

Starting with the title of this book, drawn from a phrase in *The Guns of August* by Barbara Tuchman about the mindset of commanders during World War I, we know that we are in the hands of an author who is both a student of military history as well as one of our country's most respected warriors, a man of thought as well as action.

Ms. Tuchman's book highlights a truth known by General McKenzie and all commanders: that whatever beliefs, experiences, prejudices, temperament, hubris, or apprehensions a commander has will contribute to success or failure on the battlefield as well as the fates of nations. There can scarcely be a more consequential set of responsibilities for any leader. A commander must be a sentinel, a guard against complacency, and a challenger of assumptions and conventional wisdom. All this and more can be said about General McKenzie.

Even the most confident commander must summon humility as he considers the mission. Homer described the Trojan War as wild and confused, a storm of dust and smoke, hoarse screaming and bloody swords, cacophony, and irrationality. Commanders who search for the orderly battlefield that unfolds according to plan quickly find that it doesn't exist. General Ulysses S. Grant had criteria for leaders, which boiled down to humility; toughness of character, so one is able to take shocks in stride; and the single-mindedness to remain unyielding when all is flying apart but enough mental agility to adapt when their approach is not working.

Looking at the commanders of World War I as Ms. Tuchman's book did, how closely was Germany's defeat linked to the beliefs, actions, and choices of General Helmuth von Moltke, the chief of the German general staff? His uncle and namesake had also been chief of the German general staff before him, so expectations were high. But he underestimated the strength of the allies, assuming incorrectly that France and Russia would not be able to mobilize their armies quickly enough to be a serious threat to Germany. He also overextended the German forces, rendering them unable to fight the two-front war that emerged when Britain declared war on Germany. The speedy victory Germany imagined eluded its grasp, and within a few months of the Battle of the Marne, the Western Front had settled down to the murderous and static trench warfare that lasted for almost three years. Moltke was relieved of duty and, humiliated, died a broken man less than two years later.

History is replete with examples of military campaigns whose failures inevitably reflected on the commanders: Napoleon's invasion of Russia in 1812, the Battle of Gallipoli in World War I, the Battle of Stalingrad in World War II, and the Battle of Dien Bien Phu in 1954 during the First Indochina War, to name a few. In each case, commanders who had planned and hoped for a successful outcome saw the crushing defeat of their forces and lasting damage to their names and reputations.

Any modern U.S. commander can only be humbled by studying these military leaders of the past who approached their arduous duties with the best intentions but whose names and reputations have been damaged or ruined based on the decisions they made in the moment. General McKenzie's book provides us with an honest, forthright, and clear-eyed assessment of his own time in command—describing decisions that were sound and have stood the test of time, as well as some outcomes he wishes were different. Written from an American combatant commander's unique vantage point, as the leader responsible for integrating military operations across a tumultuous zone, his is a vivid portrait of leadership in action.

General McKenzie takes us inside several historic moments during his tenure—the coward's death of Islamic State of Iraq and Syria leader Abu Bakr al-Baghdadi as U.S. forces closed in on him, the successful strike on

Qassem Soleimani, which was a crushing blow to Iran's strategic capabilities, and other operations designed to thwart the aims of Iran and its proxy states.

He also writes about our drawdown in Iraq, the rocky transition from the Donald Trump to the Joseph R. Biden administration, and the chaotic final withdrawal from Afghanistan. On each major challenge of his time in command, he explains what happened and why with his trademark candor and forthrightness.

General McKenzie was the ultimate theater-level commander of U.S. forces in Afghanistan, and the withdrawal from Afghanistan illustrates the duality and complexity of being a commander. While the collapse of the Afghan government was certainly not the desired result when the withdrawal began, the courage and hard work of several thousand servicemembers under difficult and dangerous conditions to evacuate 124,000 Afghan nationals were surely a source of pride. However, it came at the terrible cost of thirteen U.S. servicemembers and more than one hundred Afghan civilians killed at the attack at Abbey Gate, and General McKenzie never faltered in his (correct) belief that Iran remains the most profound threat to regional security and stability, the country supplying weapons and other support to proxies across the region who engage in acts of terror, to say nothing of their nuclear aspirations.

General McKenzie and all of us will surely feel a searing regret about those losses for the rest of our lives as well as about the Afghans left behind to face life (and death) under the tyrannical Taliban.

General McKenzie knows that you can train and equip our men and women in uniform, but they must also have a fighting spirit and a clear vision of what they are fighting for and know that they are on the side of right. Imbuing them with that spirit is one of the many jobs of the commander, which he did extremely well despite political confusion at home that would have daunted a lesser man.

Before he was Israel's prime minister, Yitzhak Rabin was a revered military commander who led forces in the 1948 War of Independence and the Six-Day War in 1967. Shortly before he was assassinated in 1995, he said this about his time as a military commander:

In that moment of great tension just before the finger pulls the trigger, just before the fuse begins to burn; in the terrible quiet of that moment, there's still time to wonder: Is there no other choice? Is there no other way? And then the order is given. The inferno begins.

Our people have chosen us. Their eyes are upon us. Their hearts are asking: How is the authority vested in these men and women being used? What will they decide? What will we arise [to] tomorrow? A day of peace? Of war? Of laughter or tears?

A child cannot choose his father and mother. He cannot pick his sex or color, his religion, nationality, or homeland. From the moment he comes into the world, his fate lies in the hands of his nation's leaders. It is they who will decide whether he lives in comfort or despair, in security or in fear. His fate is given to us to resolve—the leaders of the world.

General McKenzie has felt the heavy burden of Prime Minister Rabin's words. He has seen the success of the U.S. military in defending freedom around the world and the mortifying results of campaigns gone wrong. He has also had to notify more than a few parents that their son or daughter wouldn't be coming home from war. His book is a timely reminder of the challenges of command, and his final chapter of broader reflections is particularly insightful. For future generations who want to better understand what it means to be a leader, this book will be invaluable.

James Mattis
General, U.S. Marine Corps (Ret.), and Twenty-Sixth Secretary of Defense
Richland, Washington
May 15, 2023

PREFACE

As the commander of U.S. Central Command, I oversaw some of the most important—and controversial—operations in modern U.S. military history. I had direct operational responsibility for the strikes on Qassem Soleimani and two successive leaders of the Islamic State of Iraq and Syria, the many months of deterrence operations against Iran and its proxies, and our methodical drawdown in Iraq. I directed the execution of our noncombatant evacuation operation in Afghanistan and our final withdrawal from that tortured country.

This is largely a first-person account of my time as a four-star general and my service as one of the eleven U.S. combatant commanders. It's not all-inclusive. I spent three years as the commander, U.S. Central Command, and this isn't a day-by-day recounting of that time. I've attempted to capture some of the highs—and lows—of my time in command.

I have found that writing—and every word in this book is mine—is a useful release. My experiences have given me a unique perspective on how national decisions were made and how they were implemented. My views were those of a participant and a key actor, not an observer. I'm proud of what Central Command accomplished during my three years of command. I've tried to be clear and straightforward about what we did well, and where I fell short. The men and women of Central Command—in Tampa and in the theater of operations—are among the finest our nation has to offer. It was the greatest honor of my life to join them in defending our nation.

There are three themes that intertwine throughout this book. The first one is the importance of the primacy of civilian control of the military. It has become a widely perceived truth that this control has been eroded over the past few years. I don't believe that to be the case, and I believe I speak with some authority on the matter. Before Central Command, I spent almost two years as the director for strategy, plans, and policy on the Joint Staff, where I was the senior uniformed planner and strategist for the United States. I then served almost two years as the director of the Joint Staff, one of the most consequential three-star jobs in the U.S. military, a position where I interacted daily with senior civilian leadership both within the Department of

Defense and across all of the branches of our government. The civil-military relationship isn't perfect or frictionless, but then, it doesn't have to be—and probably shouldn't be. It is, however, more durable than many believe, and it is supported and embraced by the military to a degree that some critics do not choose to recognize.

The second theme is the uniqueness of being a combatant commander. Combatant commanders participate in the development of policy, albeit as junior partners. They are also responsible for the execution of that policy once civilian leaders have formulated their decision. This is a unique position, and it is very different than the role of a service chief or even the chairman of the Joint Chiefs of Staff. None of these officers are in the chain of command, and they have no ultimate moral responsibility or authority for execution. Only the combatant commander stands astride the boundary of decision-making and execution. The title of this book was chosen with that thought in mind. It is from Barbara Tuchman's observation in *The Guns of August* about "that melting-point of warfare—the temperament of the individual commander."

Finally, the third theme argues that leaders do matter, and the decisions they make have a profound effect on what happens on the battlefield. Not everyone is a leader, and not everyone gets to make decisions. In an age when expertise is devalued and hierarchical organizations are routinely bashed, leadership in and out of uniform and the ability and willingness to make decisions still matter a great deal. While this book talks primarily about military leadership, the lessons go beyond and have universal application. I made good decisions, and I made some wrong ones. I've led well, and I've led poorly. I've tried to talk about all of this here.

This book is dedicated to two men who had a profound effect on my development as a man and as an officer. Col. Walt Clark was a hard-nosed, no-nonsense infantry colonel who was the commandant of cadets at The Citadel when I entered. In the many years since that time, we stayed close, and he and his wonderful family have been a big part of the McKenzie story to this day. His death in 2010 while I was in Afghanistan created a big hole in my life. Bill Gordon taught me several classes when I was a cadet, and he lit the fire of intellectual curiosity within me, something that has remained.

I don't know that a professor can offer a more significant gift to a student. Down through the years he has also offered wise counsel and friendship. We have stayed close until this day.

I couldn't have done anything without my wife of more than forty years, Marilyn. Finally, I'd like to thank my agent, Andrew Wylie, for introducing me to the business of writing a book. I have enjoyed working with Naval Institute Press.

In this book, I've used some language from an article that I wrote in 2023 about the threat of Iran's drone program. That article, "Striking Back: Iran and the Rise of Asymmetric Drone Warfare in the Middle East," was sponsored by the Washington Institute for Near East Policy.

The views expressed in this publication are those of the author and do not necessarily reflect the official policy or position of the Department of Defense or the U.S. government. The public release clearance of the publication by the Department of Defense does not imply Department of Defense endorsement or factual accuracy of the material. Any errors of commission or omission are mine and mine alone. All of the proceeds from the sale of this book will be donated to the Marine Corps–Law Enforcement Foundation, the Semper Fi and America's Fund, and The Citadel Foundation.

Kenneth F. McKenzie Jr.
General, U.S. Marine Corps (Ret.)
Tampa, Florida
June 2023

1

HOW IT ALL BEGAN
ALARUMS AND EXCURSIONS

*The soft parade has now begun
Listen to the engines hum.*
—Jim Morrison, *"The Soft Parade"*

For me, the 2019 graduation weekend at The Citadel marked the beginning of a crisis with Iran that would define my time at U.S. Central Command (CENTCOM). It would prove to be the core problem I confronted as a commander. It was a beautiful Friday afternoon in early May in Charleston, South Carolina. My wife, Marilyn, and I were at The Citadel, where I was to deliver the graduation address the next day. I had been in command of Central Command for a little over a month. This was a particularly meaningful occasion for me, since it marked forty years since my own May 1979 graduation. The Citadel is the state of South Carolina's military college. Dating to 1842, it has managed to blend a liberal arts academic tradition with a military structure—the South Carolina corps of cadets. The Citadel and its slightly smaller cousin, the Virginia Military Institute in Lexington, Virginia, remain the only two purely military colleges in existence in the United States. In 1979, out of a graduating class of almost 489, 40 cadets were commissioned into the Marine Corps. Gen. Glen "Bluto" Walters and I had been the last two members of the class of '79 on active duty until 2018, when Bluto retired as the assistant commandant of the Marine Corps to become the president of The Citadel. I was now the last man standing from our class. He had clearly flourished during his short period of time at the helm of the college, and the signs of his leadership were evident everywhere on campus.

One of the most important events of graduation weekend is the parade on Friday, where after the corps of cadets marches on to Summerall Parade

Field, senior cadets leave their companies, march across the parade ground, and then take the review for the last time as cadets. The junior class takes over the regiment, and so the torch is passed. It's a moving ceremony. For the seniors, it marks the last time they will ever march in formation at The Citadel. Like all ceremonies that mark a passage of growth, it emphasized departure for the seniors and new responsibilities for the juniors. It had an element of bittersweetness. I was struck by the passage of time—the beautiful, lush greenness of Charleston in May was no different from what Bluto and I had experienced back in 1979: the cadets looked the same, the pretty girls, the proud parents and friends; it all had a timeless quality. As I sat there, I could even picture the ghosts of girls I had once known and loved when I was a cadet, now long gone. Directly across from where we sat, across the wide verge of the parade field, was Summerall Chapel, one of many things on campus named for an earlier president and one of the formative leaders in the history of The Citadel. I well knew the biblical quotation carved above the broad wooden doors, "Remember now thy creator in the days of thy youth." In various tableaux and bronze plates affixed to the outside wall of the chapel, several steps up from the street and covered by an arched overhang, were the names of The Citadel's "patriot dead," to use a phrase from one of those plaques. There were many of them, going back to before the Civil War.

The Citadel had been very good to me. I was at best an indifferent student as an undergraduate, but I did leave the college with three important academic achievements. First, I learned I could write, and write well, even under extreme time pressure. That was a quality that saved me during many late nights before papers were due in my classes as an English major. It would prove even more useful in my profession. Second, I developed an unquenchable thirst for reading, beginning with works in my major, but then taking an omnivorous approach to virtually any subject. Finally, and most importantly, I developed the beginning of a process about how to think critically. This was such a large part of my education at the college that I could remember the moment when the shades began to come off: it was spring 1976, and I was taking a final examination in a course called "History of Naval Warfare," which was taught by Marine Corps Reserve Maj. Bill Gordon. He was an engaging, energetic teacher, a graduate of the college in the fabled class of 1966, with a Duke doctorate under the tutelage of Theodore Ropp and significant combat experience in Vietnam. The question his exam posed was about the U-boat campaign carried out by the Germans in the Atlantic during World War II. What set the question apart was that it invited the student to consider institutional impacts on the development and employment of submarines by the Germans and antisubmarine warfare by the Allies. It was a broadening question, and it lit a spark in me that has influenced my thinking ever since. I don't want to overstate this—I'm confident that nobody in the class of 1979 (including me), or anybody who taught or led us during that time, would have seen in Cadet McKenzie in May 1979 whatever it was that led along a long and winding trail to being a general in the Marine Corps and the graduation speaker for the class of 2019—but it began a process that has continued for me until this day.

I sat next to Bluto in that warm, lovely Charleston weather, talking quietly about friends and classmates. It was a profoundly fulfilling moment for us both. As the corps of cadets began to march on, the crowd of several thousand fashionably attired family members and friends cheered and clapped. Marilyn and I were seated with Bluto and his charming wife, Gail, at the center of the reviewing area, the place where everyone's eyes were naturally drawn. We were both wearing what the Marine Corps calls "Dress Blue-White Alpha, with large medals and Sam Browne belt." It is both a uniquely visually compelling and uniquely uncomfortable uniform to wear. It features a black blouse with a high mandarin collar and white pants without pockets, with a large, heavy patent leather belt at the waist, with a loop over the right shoulder. For both Bluto and I, it would have been far more comfortable back in May 1979 than it was in May 2019. We were now both slightly less svelte versions of the two cadets who had been commissioned that May morning forty years earlier! We chatted with our wives while we waited for the ceremony to start.

At this point—and I'll never forget it—my aide de camp, Lt. Col. Brett "Salty" Allison, came up behind my seat, leaned down, and said in the laconic, calm voice that aviators use when giving bad news, "Sir, the chairman needs to talk to you right now." I thought quickly. The band was playing, and the lead elements of each of the battalions of the corps of cadets were coming out of their respective barracks arches. We were surrounded by thousands of people, and Bluto and I were the natural focal point for them all. As the CENTCOM commander, I always travelled with a communications team that could quickly place me in voice communication with any of my subordinate commanders, the chairman, the secretary of defense, or the president. My standard for the team was to be "in comms" within five minutes. We had set up communications back at the president's house, a lovely low country–style home a few blocks away from the reviewing stand, on The Citadel's campus.

There was nothing to do but go, and quickly. Bluto had heard Salty's message, and he knew that it had to be extremely serious for Gen. Joe Dunford, the chairman of the Joint Chiefs of Staff (JCS) and a fellow Marine four-star general, to reach out to me. Joe knew where I was and what I was doing; he would not call lightly. Thousands of eyes were drawn to us sitting there at center stage, interested in what was going on. Whispering an apology to Bluto, I got up and followed Salty out of the reviewing area, walking fast. Most of the people there that day knew who I was and that I commanded Central Command. An abrupt departure at the beginning of the most important parade of the year for The Citadel would start tongues wagging—and lots of speculation.

At Bluto's house, my communicators quickly established the call to the chairman. There were a variety of communications links available, but this time we would talk on the one with the very highest level of classification. "Chairman, this is Frank," is how I began the conversation. I knew what he was calling about. For the past few days, we had been getting intelligence indications that Iran was planning a series of attacks against our forces, and those of our friends and partners, in the Central Command region. The information was quite precise, and the intelligence community seemed to think that it was credible. I agreed with their assessments. The Iranians, pressed hard by the economic and diplomatic impact of the U.S. "maximum pressure" campaign, had apparently come to the conclusion that they needed to take some form of military action to reset the terms of the relationship. There was new information, made available in just the previous few hours.

The Joint Staff had seen and reviewed it, and that's what drove the chairman's need to talk to me. The potential Iranian attack could come in the form of a "state-on-state" operation—perhaps from some of their more than three thousand ballistic missiles—or it could come in a more deniable manner—an improvised explosive device against our forces in Iraq, or an attack on shipping in the congested, narrow waterway of the Strait of Hormuz. All of these were possibilities.

As Joe Dunford and I weighed the reports, we both agreed that a proxy attack was the most likely. It could give the Iranians reasonable deniability, make it hard for us to attribute, yet still cause pain. We also knew that the Iranians had been emboldened by a series of recent decisions to greatly reduce U.S. force presence in the theater. Most significantly, we no longer had the continuous presence of an aircraft carrier and its accompanying ships. Aircraft carriers are unique icons, powerful symbols of U.S. commitment and power, and the Iranians carefully noted when they were and were not in the theater. Perhaps most significantly, a carrier was a moveable piece of U.S. sovereignty; in a theater beset with access, basing, and overflight restrictions, nobody could impose limitations on her operations. We had not had a carrier in the theater for many months. We had also reduced our number of fighter and attack aircraft squadrons significantly, and our Patriot missile batteries, used to defend against ballistic missiles and aircraft, were at an all-time low.

He then asked me if I needed anything. This was the crux of the matter, and the heart of our conversation. I knew the question was coming, and during the flight up to Charleston from Tampa earlier in the day, armed with some of the intelligence we were now discussing, I had jotted down some ideas for when this moment came. I knew that the carrier USS *Harry S Truman* and her consorts were operating in the Mediterranean, and I also knew that there was an amphibious ready group (ARG) with more than two thousand Marines in the Med as well. Without hesitation, I said, "I want the *HST* [shorthand for *Truman*], and I want the ARG. I also want more fighter squadrons." As usual, Joe had thought this through himself, and he told me that he would work the problem. We both knew that there were good reasons why many people would disagree with any decision that brought a carrier back into CENTCOM.

My request for the carrier was based on my belief that we needed to reestablish deterrence with Iran. Since taking command in late March 2019, I had done a lot of thinking on this. Clearly, if the Iranians were in advanced attack planning, deterrence had been lost. I believed that in the CENTCOM area, deterrence with Iran was achieved when Iranian leadership recognized that the potential goal they were pursuing was not worth the potential cost we could impose. Deterrence by punishment is only one of two possible approaches; the other approach is deterrence by denial—creating cognitive doubt in the mind of the opponent that they would not be able to carry out the action contemplated. Both of these approaches are heuristic, and since they occur in the mind of the adversary, effectiveness can be very hard to observe or quantify a priori. On the other hand, it's very easy to see when deterrence has been lost—it's always clear in retrospect. We did not maintain, and I did not request, forces for deterrence by denial. The carrier and more land-based Air Force fighter squadrons were all things that could impose cost on Iran and contribute to deterrence by punishment.

Joe ended the call—we agreed to talk again the next day, Saturday, and then again on Sunday, May 19. I went back out to rejoin Bluto at the parade. Joking with Salty, I told him that "if I don't go back out there, folks are going to be looking for Russian bombers in the sky." I got back in time for the pass-in-review, where the corps of cadets passes in company sequence in front of the long gray line of seniors. I took the opportunity, as all old graduates do, to take a step forward and salute when Cadet Company N "November" of the Fourth Battalion passed by. At The Citadel, your company is the center of your military and social existence. Saluting the guidon was not only a token of respect for my classmates, but also a recognition of all that had come before and followed us in Company N.

Moments like that had a way of recharging your batteries. I also had a lot to think about. I knew that in my call with the chairman, I had just made my first decision in a new cycle of escalation with Iran. In many ways, my entire professional life had been shaped toward this moment. I was worried, because I had great respect for the Iranian ability to attack unprovoked and violently virtually anywhere across the theater, but I was also confident—in both the force I commanded and the support I knew I would receive from the Joint Staff and ultimately the secretary. I was also confident in my own training, preparation, and judgment.

Marilyn and I had a great afternoon and evening in Charleston. It was a wonderful opportunity to reconnect with many old friends and classmates. There was a large representation from the class of '79 on hand—I think we all shared in the heights our class had risen to. The next day I addressed the class of 2019 and their families and friends. Unlike my graduation, which had been under the verdant magnolias in front of Bond Hall, the college's administration building, the 2019 commencement was in McAllister Field House. While not quite as traditional a setting, it did have the significant advantage of not being affected by the weather—always a consideration in Charleston in May.

As I made my remarks, the events of Friday afternoon weighed heavily on me. I had been on the phone repeatedly throughout the night with my staff and my subordinate commanders, and I could not escape the feeling that we were on the brink of a disastrous confrontation with Iran. I told the graduates nothing new or revealing in my remarks, which were probably as much for my classmates in attendance as they were for the class of 2019. One thing I pointed out to them, which was even more poignant because of what I knew was brewing on the other side of the world, was that this would be the last time they would all be together. After I was finished, and degrees were presented, they would scatter—men and women—some to service on active duty, others to the professions or other callings. But they would never be assembled again and never wear cadet gray again. Like Cadet McKenzie in 1979, the soon-to-be graduates of 2019 politely applauded the old general at the podium and turned to face the future with hope and excitement.

For me, graduation weekend 2019 at The Citadel marked the beginning of the Iran crisis that would define my time at Central Command as much as anything. It would prove to be the primary problem that we would confront over the next three years, and it would weigh me as a commander in every way a commander could be measured. A central thesis of this book is the assertion that commanders are uniquely important. While they are only a subordinate part of the vast national security process, they exercise a profound influence with their advice for decision-makers, and then, of course, they face the sternest test of all: that of execution. Commanders alone both give policy advice to senior civilian leaders—participating in their deliberations—and then take the decisions of those leaders and transmute them into corporeal action. In the U.S. system, it is the combatant commander who exists at this melting point. Because of this, the temperament of the commander is at the center of what a command achieves or fails to achieve. Early Saturday afternoon, Marilyn and I flew back to Tampa and into the vortex.

2
CENTRAL COMMAND

Thou cam'st on earth to make the earth my hell.
A grievous burden was thy birth to me.
—The Duchess of York to her son, Richard III
Richard III, Scene 4, Act 4

My path to command of Central Command began indirectly. In April 2015 I was serving as the commander of U.S. Marine Forces in Central Command (MARCENT). I had assumed command in May 2014. The assignment marked a return to Tampa for Marilyn and me; I previously had served as the J-5, the director for strategy, plans, and policy, from 2010 to 2012, working for Gen. Jim Mattis. We had enjoyed Tampa the first time, and I had found the problems of the theater to be both challenging and rewarding. When Commandant of the Marine Corps Jim Amos had offered me the opportunity to be promoted to three-star grade and return as the Marine commander for CENTCOM, I jumped at the opportunity. We lived in a lovely home on Hillsborough Bay, among thirty or so other general and flag officers who worked at either CENTCOM or Special Operations Command (SOCOM). The Marine Corps played a relatively minor role in CENTCOM, principally because of the "functional" design of the theater, where Army, Navy, and Air Force component commanders—my three-star peers—commanded all forces within their air, land, and sea domains. As a result, Marines in the theater were almost never under my operational control. Instead, they worked for Naval Forces Central Command (NAVCENT), Army Central, or Air Force Central. Despite this, Marines had much to contribute to the theater and were heavily employed in Afghanistan, and, increasingly in Iraq in the counter–Islamic State in Iraq and Syria (ISIS) fight. I travelled quite a bit as the MARCENT commander, usually spending a week to ten days every month in the theater. I would fly commercial into

Kuwait and then move around the theater in a Marine Corps Cessna Citation, known as a C-35. Marilyn and I also enjoyed life in Tampa. We had the opportunity to make many friends out in town, where we found people in the area to be warm and welcoming. In short, life was good.

I expected to remain at MARCENT for about two years and detach in the early summer of 2016. My predecessor, Lt. Gen. Bob Neller, had gone on to command Marine Forces Command in Norfolk, and I expected a similar assignment or perhaps even a joint assignment to round out my career. Marine lieutenant generals typically did two assignments before retiring. To retire as a lieutenant general in the Marine Corps was the pinnacle of professional success. The small size of the Marine Corps meant it only had two four-star generals—the commandant and the assistant commandant. Unlike the other services, there was no web of four-star positions inside the Corps. Three stars was about as good as it got, and I was proud to retire at that grade. Marilyn and I had talked idly about eventually returning to Tampa, or going back to Charleston or even my hometown of Birmingham.

On a sunny afternoon in April 2015, I was sitting at my desk in the MARCENT headquarters, which was a modest single-story building adjacent to the CENTCOM parking lot. The CENTCOM headquarters consisted of two huge four-story steel and glass buildings that looked exactly the same— one of them housed the intelligence functions of the command, and the other the commander and the rest of the staff. They were imposing, and the small Marine headquarters, what my predecessor Bob Neller called the "doublewides," was particularly unpretentious in the shadow of the massive CENTCOM edifice. The secure phone rang, and it was the office of the commandant. "Please stand by for General Dunford," the aide told me. I quickly looked over my daybook—was I expecting this call? I also quickly looked at both my secret and unclassified computers while waiting for the connection to be finalized. Nothing there.

Joe Dunford and I had a long and deep personal history. We first met when we were captains, after company command, and we were in a summer seminar together before we went out as Naval Reserve Officer Training Corps instructors. He went to teach at Holy Cross, and I went to the Virginia Military Institute. We hit it off and stayed in touch over the years. In 1993, after

I graduated from the School of Advanced Warfighting at Quantico, Joe was instrumental in bringing me to Headquarters Marine Corps to relieve him as the senior member of the commandant's staff group, the speechwriting and support team for the commandant. He became the senior aide to the commandant. We worked closely together for two years with Gen. Carl Mundy. Following that, we both went to Camp LeJeune, where he became executive officer of the 6th Marine Regiment and I became executive officer of First Battalion, Sixth Marines, one of the battalions within the regiment. In the years that followed, we had stayed in touch, in the way that friendships developed in the Marine Corps, not limited by the frequent geographic separations. Joe's wife, Ellyn, and Marilyn also became friends, so we spent a lot of time together. I viewed Joe Dunford as one of the finest Marines I had ever known, and I felt that his selection to be the 36th commandant was a huge boon to the Corps. We talked frequently, but as commandant, he didn't call out of the blue during business hours unless there was business to be discussed.

I couldn't see anything in my notes or in recent traffic that would indicate why he'd want to talk this afternoon—but I'd know soon enough. Sure enough, after the pleasantries, he got right to business: "Frank, thanks for taking my call. You might want to clear your desk off before I tell you what I'm going to do, so you won't hurt yourself." I wracked my brains about anything I'd done, but I felt innocent—as innocent as a Marine lieutenant general could be—so I told him I wouldn't react to whatever he had to say by killing myself. "Frank, I'm going to nominate you as the Marine Corps' choice to be the Joint Staff J-5. I have reason to believe that you'll be selected by General [Martin] Dempsey, so this isn't a shot in the dark. Are you interested?" I leaned back in my chair. The Joint Staff J-5, or the "big J-5" as all the combatant command J-5s called the position, was the dream job for any planner or strategist. The Joint Staff J-5 was the senior uniformed military planner for the United States, and it called for working at the intersection of military planning and policy at the highest level. Would I take the job? In a second. "Commandant, I'd be honored."

I also had to probe: "How certain is this?" Even as I asked the question, I was reviewing in my mind who was who on the Joint Staff, centering on the "big three": the director, the J-3, and of course the J-5. This was important because the director assignments on the Joint Staff had to achieve a balance of service equities. The Marine Corps always fought hard to gain one of the big three, but it was hard to compete with the bigger services. The Army, Navy, and Air Force had bigger pools of flag officers to nominate for these jobs, and, frankly more paths to gain the qualifications necessary to compete for them. Getting one of these key positions would be a major achievement. Joe responded to my question: "Frank, I feel pretty certain about this. It's the chairman's call, as you know, but I think he's going to go with you." Joe further told me that the change would occur in the fall. I perhaps should have asked something deeper and more profound, but I could only think of one question: "Can we get on-base housing up in DC?" Chuckling as he hung up, Joe told me that he'd look into it.

After the call, I sat for a few minutes, collecting my thoughts. Some things now began to come together. In the fall of 2014, Gen. Martin Dempsey, then the chairman, had visited Tampa for a Buccaneers–Green Bay Packers football game to flip the coin. I was there as well to deliver the game ball. As we stood on the sidelines before the ceremony, making small talk, he said, "We have plans for you, Frank." It seemed a little enigmatic. At the time, I didn't think anything about it—just polite words from the chairman. Now it began to fit together a little better. I was excited about the possibility of being the Joint Staff J-5, but I was also very happy at MARCENT. It was command, and command in a theater of war. Later that afternoon, when I told Marilyn, she had the same reaction—excited about returning to northern Virginia, and sad to leave Tampa again, where she had really flourished. Her price for going was simple and direct: season tickets for the Washington Nationals baseball team. I felt we could work that out, and so we agreed.

Over the next few weeks, the nomination process ground on. I knew how the decision would be made: in a personnel meeting with Secretary of Defense Dr. Ash Carter. There would be a list of nominees, one from each service. Short biographies would be appended. The chairman would make his recommendation, and the secretary would either agree or propose an alternative. For the three-star billets on the Joint Staff, the chairman's recommendations were almost always accepted without debate. Sure enough, that's what happened, and by the early summer it looked like a done deal. It was then that things began to get complicated. General Dempsey was the "hiring official," but he would be retiring in fall 2015. If I got the job, I would work for him for only a short time. Who would relieve him?

Of course, it turned out to be Joe Dunford. As a result of that, I spent almost two years on the Joint Staff as his J-5, and then Joe asked me to be the director. The director of the Joint Staff (DJS) is perhaps the most challenging and sought-after three-star job in the U.S. military that doesn't involve operational command. That officer manages the Joint Staff for the chairman but

Map 1. CENTCOM

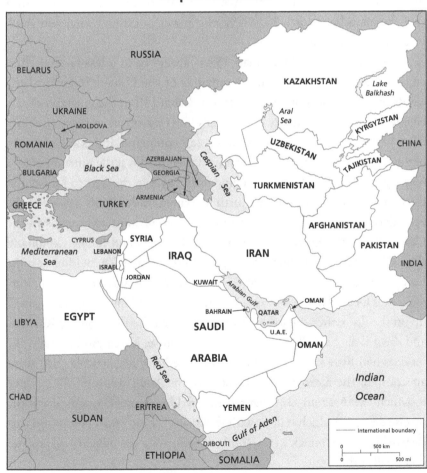

also serves as a conduit to the combatant commands, the services, Congress, and the civilian leadership of the department. Historically, the DJS position was a clear precursor for four-star command. Thirty-seven of the forty-eight officers who have been the DJS were subsequently four-star leaders.

In the summer of 2018 Secretary of Defense Jim Mattis nominated me to be the commander of Central Command. I was excited about the possibility of the assignment. Most of my colonel and general officer career had been spent in the CENTCOM region. I felt that I knew the issues and had benefitted from the opportunity of learning from then-General Mattis when he was in command. In early December, I testified before the Senate Committee on Armed Services, and then I was confirmed later in the month. I took command on March 28, 2019, relieving an old friend, Gen. Joe Votel. It felt like I was coming home.

Central Command (see map 1) has always been a less-favored child among the regional combatant commands of the United States, and the words of the Duchess of York to her son Richard III in the epigraph of this chapter are a good summary of the prevailing view of the military establishment of the United States about this upstart command. It was an old axiom of the British army that they always fought their battles at the junction of four map sheets. The Middle East, ranging from Egypt in the west to Pakistan in the east and Kazakhstan in the north to Yemen in the south, fell along the boundary between the two most important combatant commands in the U.S. military—the European Command (EUCOM) and Pacific Command (PACOM, later Indo-Pacific Command). In the mid-1970s, neither of these headquarters had time for or interest in the Middle East. European Command was focused on the Soviet threat, while Pacific Command, picking itself up off the floor after the loss of Vietnam, shared the focus on the Russians and the still-nascent Chinese threat and, of course, Korea. Additionally, the services had little interest in the region. The Navy in particular had scant affection for the narrow, shallow waters of the Arabian littoral. The degree to which the Arabian Gulf figured in any U.S. strategic calculus was the precise degree to which it dealt with the Soviet Union and a perception that they held plans to attack to the south, overrunning the oilfields of Iran and potentially other states.

By the mid-1970s U.S. policy in the region was based on maintaining relationships with two key anticommunist states: Iran and Saudi Arabia. It was a fraught time; in 1968 Prime Minister Harold Wilson withdrew British forces from the region. The United States, fully engaged in Vietnam, had little excess capacity or interest in filling the hole "east of Eden." Over time, the relationship with Iran became dominant, based on geography (Iran controlled the northern accesses to the Gulf region) and the friendliness of the Shah of Iran, Mohammad Reza Pahlavi, who had been reinstalled on the Peacock Throne by the Central Intelligence Agency (CIA) and British partners in 1953 after a twelve-year interregnum. He was an autocrat and a despot, but he was also virulently anticommunist.

After President Jimmy Carter's inauguration, his administration looked at the region through two very different and often competing lenses. Zbigniew Brzezinski, the national security advisor, argued for a greater U.S. military presence in the Gulf, based largely on the theory that oil exports from the region were critical for maintaining both the U.S. and other Western allies' industrial bases. In a conflict with the Soviet Union, there would be a fundamental requirement to maintain access to the oilfields of the Arabian Gulf. The opposing view was held by Secretary of State Cyrus Vance, who felt more harm than good would come from permanently stationing U.S. forces in the region—a region with strong and deep anticolonial memories. He did not dispute the need to maintain access to the oil but argued for a more nuanced "offshore" presence.[1]

Early in his presidency, President Carter laid the seeds of the future Central Command. On August 24, 1977, the president established a global quick-reaction force, known as Readiness Command, based in Tampa, Florida. While deployable anywhere, a major part of its mission was clearly the Middle East.[2] There was strong opposition to the concept, mainly from the Marine Corps and the Navy. The Marine Corps jealously guarded its self-imposed dictum of "first to fight" and saw any new rapid deployable capability, even a joint one, as an institutional threat. The Navy wasn't eager to give away command of its ships, particularly if it would be in the narrow waters of the Middle East.

Despite this presidential command, planning languished. In a pattern that continues to this very day, the services fought the idea of allocating

forces away from the Pacific, Europe, or even the United States for operations in the Middle East. What gave some impetus to the planning process
was the possibility that Russia would push through Iran, either coopting
the new regime or just brushing it aside, and gain the oilfields as well as
warm-water access. Finally, EUCOM developed an operations plan, which
was oriented less on Iran than on defending the oilfields farther south
in Saudi Arabia. There were problems with the plan. No work had been
done with the Saudis about bringing forces in—in fact, the forces weren't
even readily available, and there was inadequate strategic lift. All in all, it
was the type of plan that came to life when a combatant command exam-
ines a low-priority "off-axis" threat—and the Middle East was off axis and
low priority to EUCOM and its commander, Gen. Al Haig. In short, no
service or combatant command wanted anything to do with this "Middle
East business."

Even with this pushback from the joint chiefs, the Carter administration moved forward with what became the Persian Gulf security framework,
the broad contours of which remain to this day. It conceived of a string of
peripheral U.S. bases around the region, placed carefully to avoid upsetting
Arab sensibilities. Diego Garcia, Masirah Island in Oman, and bases in Egypt
and Jordan all came from this design. Saudi Arabia abstained but overbuilt
its capacity so that larger forces could operate from its bases if necessary. It
was an amorphous concept, less than perfect, built on a series of nuanced
understandings, almost all of them bilaterally executed with the United
States. What's important about this whole idea is that it was conceived and
executed by civilian leadership. In this case, the civilians in the department
were far-sighted, able to grasp future combinations and possibilities, while
senior military leadership remained mired in bureaucratic friction, unable to
see the far horizon. This episode should be a case study for civilian control
of the military.

The next step in the evolution of what would eventually be CENTCOM
was a study in military-bureaucratic ineptitude. Throughout 1979 the president pushed his secretary of defense for details on a joint rapid deployment
force, primarily oriented against the Middle East but globally deployable. In
a series of lengthy internal debates, the joint chiefs demonstrated all of their

worst characteristics, not particularly wanting the new headquarters but, if it was to be created, keenly sensitive about which service would command it, how it would be resourced, and how it would report to its chain of command. It finally came to life on March 1, 1980, as the Rapid Deployment Joint Task Force (RDJTF), based in Tampa. Marine Lt. Gen. Paul X. Kelley, a future commandant, would be its first commander.

Iran was always at the center of U.S. views on the region—first as a partner and a bulwark against Russian aggression, and then—after the fall of the shah in 1979, the seizure of the U.S. Embassy, and the rise to power of a radical theological state—as a nemesis. U.S. views on Iran ranged from the extremely shallow lens of post-1979 and the rise of the mullahs, to a slightly more sophisticated lens that accommodated the U.S. role in the installation of the shah in 1953. These views were—and are—all too superficial. Iran is a genuine, legitimate hegemon in its region and a real imperial power with a tradition of arms that stretches back to a height of influence around the 6th century BCE, incorporating the Achaemenid Empire under Cyrus the Great. Alexander the Great brought down the Persian Empire, but the locus of power and its memory have always remained. To deny or minimize the existence of this history and the concomitant imperial nature of Iran is to ignore the basic facts of the geostrategic situation. In fact, their inability to assert themselves in the region in modern times has largely been self-inflicted by the kleptocratic, theological monarchy that followed the fall of the shah that has managed to disrupt nearly every economic and diplomatic mechanism that could move Iran back to normalcy—or primacy. This has extended into its foreign policy, where the "permanent revolution" exports Shia violence against its Sunni neighbors and maintains an implacable intent to destroy the "Zionist entity," which is what the rest of the world knows as Israel. The fall of the shah was only the beginning of the latest chapter in the ancient story of Iran, and the revolution that has ensued is still running its bloody and convoluted course.

The Carter administration intended to maintain diplomatic relations with Iran, but it proved difficult to do so. The entry of the dying shah into the United States in October 1979 was probably the breaking point. The seizure of the U.S. embassy in Tehran and the taking of fifty-two hostages that followed made it very hard to find any common ground. In response, while the diplomats flailed, military plans were developed that would have blockaded Iran. These were seen as too risky and were hampered by the fact that there wasn't a dedicated headquarters available to assume primacy of planning and execution. Eventually, the Joint Staff established a small operational cell that developed the Eagle Claw plan, a high-risk raid into Iran that involved establishing an intermediate staging base deep in the Iranian desert and then a daring move into Tehran to free the embassy captives. For many reasons, the plan failed, and eight U.S. servicemembers died at the remote staging base inside Iran. After this debacle, Carter would not seriously consider any other military option, and he would leave office without resolving the Iran hostage crisis—but he did establish the intellectual framework for U.S. presence in the region that has carried us to this day.

Military options in the theater were now worked by the RDJTF, EUCOM, and PACOM. It was obvious that, given the rise of Iran as a threat, command and control in the region needed to be normalized—we were like the British army, planning to fight at the junction of four map sheets. President Ronald Reagan's secretary of defense, Caspar Weinberger, argued for the establishment of what was then known as a unified command—the precursor of today's combatant commands. Unsurprisingly, there was strong resistance—in an April 1981 meeting, not a single chief supported establishing a new command in the Middle East. Weinberger was made of stronger stuff than his chiefs, and he continued to push for it. President Reagan weighed in with his enthusiastic support. Despite guidance from the commander in chief, the process moved slowly, including an attempt by the Navy to kill the idea, working through Senate Appropriations Committee head Sen. Ted Stevens (R-AK). The Navy was even able to negotiate a paternalistic policy whereby the new command would not actually control its warships—PACOM would continue to operate these forces. The degree of friction this induced over the next few years was significant. There was also an unwritten agreement that CENTCOM commanders would rotate between Army and Marine generals. This agreement held for many years but is no longer in effect.

Central Command was established on January 1, 1983. Marine Lieutenant General Kelley relinquished command of the RDJTF. Army Gen. Robert Kingston became the first commander of CENTCOM in its new form. Since that January day in 1983, there have been five principles that can be used to understand CENTCOM.

First, the headquarters has always been focused on Iran, but the intensity of that focus has waxed and waned as other events have occurred in the theater. In the 1980s and '90s, Iran was squarely in the sight picture of commanders and their staffs. After 9/11, this focus became more diffuse, as the wars in Afghanistan and Iraq took up increasingly larger portions of staff and commander interest and energy. There were exceptions—during the era of General Mattis in 2010-12, planning against Iran reached new heights of excellence and effect. After he left, though, the rise of the ISIS caliphate created new vectors that drew thinking and planning away from Iran. A combatant command headquarters must be able to focus on several things at once, but in a matter of just a few days in command, it becomes obvious what any commander's highest area of interest is—and for most commanders after 9/11, it was the wars in Iraq and Afghanistan.

Second, CENTCOM has always had a very close relationship with special operations forces. This may well trace from General Kingston and his special operations roots, but it has endured. The fact that the SOCOM headquarters is also at MacDill Air Force Base may also be a factor, although the driving one is probably the fact that in organizing for combat in Afghanistan and Iraq, special operations forces were key components of the organizations that waged war in those countries. Thousands of raids and strikes have been carried out by special operations forces, including high-profile ones such as Osama bin Laden, Abu Bakr al-Baghdadi, and Qassem Soleimani. The headquarters developed a taste for clandestine operations, and commanders usually maintained good relationships with the CIA.

Third, with the exception of forces for the high-visibility named campaigns[3] in Afghanistan and Iraq, CENTCOM has always struggled for resources. The arguments of the late 1970s and early '80s about forces for CENTCOM are being heard today in the halls of the Pentagon. It remains an unpopular theater, away from marquee enemies such as Russia and China and the vast deep blue of the Pacific, always so beguiling to the Navy.

Fourth, CENTCOM is a combat headquarters. Kinetic events are directed from it every day, and orders are issued for organizations to conduct combat operations—not training, not exercises, not deterrence, but actual combat. This urgent connection to violence sets CENTCOM apart from every other combatant command. There is a difference in a headquarters that is in the fight—and there should be, since our forces forward depend upon us for their lives. Since 2001 the pace of life within the headquarters has been demanding. In 2022 and 2023 European Command experienced much of this tempo.

Fifth, CENTCOM has developed, over twenty years, a highly sophisticated approach to alliance and coalition management. International officers are embedded in the headquarters, but dozens more serve as senior national representatives. They are in Tampa not only to represent their nations, but also to receive messages from us. CENTCOM has refined the use of these officers to an art form, and it serves both the sending nation and CENTCOM very well. CENTCOM commanders must master the art of working with a coalition—one that isn't always aligned with the objectives of the headquarters.

I came to CENTCOM for the third time in late March 2019. I would be relieving Joe Votel, a brilliant, charismatic officer who embodied the close linkages between CENTCOM and SOCOM—he had commanded SOCOM before moving over to CENTCOM. About ten days before the change of command, he concluded the campaign against the ISIS physical caliphate. In a bloody and vicious series of fights near Baghuz, Syria, the final fighters and their families either surrendered or were killed. It was a fitting end to his time in command. Joe and Michelle were very gracious hosts, and they left the commander's quarters well in advance so that we could move in and establish ourselves before the change of command. I had a good feel for the headquarters from my time as the director of strategy, plans, and policy for Gen. Jim Mattis in 2010–12 and then as the Marine Forces commander in 2013–14. As the director of the Joint Staff for almost two years, I had plenty of time to consider the organization of Central Command. I had carefully watched Joe Votel synchronize all of the elements of power to bring maximum effect against the caliphate—it was the work of a master planner, strategist, and operator. That success also brought an end to a phase in the life of the headquarters. Marilyn and I took the Auto Train down from Washington. We liked the Auto Train and had taken it down for both prior moves to Tampa. We found it a great opportunity to prepare ourselves for the events that were about to begin.

A four-star headquarters is a sprawling enterprise. CENTCOM had two thousand active-duty military assigned in Tampa and the same number of civilians and contractors. They worked in two modern glass and steel four-story buildings that had been built while I was in Tampa in 2011. They were among the best headquarters facilities for any combatant command. My office overlooked the flight line and Tampa Bay. On a clear day, I could see St. Petersburg and the Sunshine Skyway Bridge across the bay. I could also watch the KC-135s on their ramp and see them deploy, usually to my theater, on the far side of the world.

A headquarters like this has its own internal set of routines—the B2C2WG—which, when decoded, meant the boards, bureaus, cells, centers, and working groups that allowed for the passage of information. The key for any commander was to make the system be responsive to his or her needs; this began by ensuring that we were looking at the right things. Even this is not as easy as it sounds, because CENTCOM existed within a larger intelligence community that had its own ideas about what we should be looking at, and why.

It was my intent from the beginning to return the headquarters to a relentless focus on Iran. It had never completely lost that focus, but in the conduct of the counter-ISIS campaign, responsibility for Iran had devolved from the general staff system of the headquarters to a series of highly compartmented cells that carried on planning, coordination, and even operations almost semi-autonomously. Within forty-five days of assuming command, I directed the disaggregation of these boutique organizations, and then we placed their functions firmly within the responsible staff directorates: J-2 (intelligence), J-3 (operations), and J-5 (strategy, policy, and plans). I wanted flag officer oversight of the sensitive activities we were contemplating against

Iran. Ultimately, these actions gave me what the Germans called *fingerspit-zengfuhl*, or fingertip control. This was a result of my strong belief that the general staff system is the best way to organize a headquarters that expects to fight. Special or unique organizations, while sometimes effective against small tasks, do not have the access, analytical throw weight, credibility, or ability to coordinate that a general staff section possesses.

The traditional general staff design has a danger—it can prevent rapid communication. This took some coaching with my generals and admirals. When I had been the director of strategy, plans, and policy at CENTCOM, it always irritated me when the commander—Jim Mattis—reached down into my organization to speak to a lieutenant colonel or major action officer. He usually sought a very discrete piece of information when he did this. I felt at the time that it was my responsibility to know that information and to provide it to the commander. I learned from that experience, and when I became the commander, I would often do the same thing that General Mattis did. Talking directly to the subject matter expert was a good experience for the young officer, and it gave the commander useful insight. I used the practice frequently in command. I told my generals and admirals that I did not need or want them to have total technical mastery of everything that went on inside their organizations. What I needed from them was *context*. I needed them to be able to see the patterns in the dots that the action officers were assembling. That's a very different and more demanding skill than subject matter expertise. In fact, too much focus on the infinite details can make it harder to see the derivative patterns, and the rate of change of those patterns is at the heart of the operational art. Operations is an art, informed by quantitative calculation, but ultimately based on qualitative judgment. I found that some officers could make this jump and see beyond the immediate; some could not. It was comfortable for some to stay in the land of tactics, details, and pure facts. We always had many of the former at CENTCOM.

I also had some very clear thoughts on what I wanted my commander's action group (CAG) to do. A CAG is a group of field grade officers and civilians that provide the commander with direct intellectual support. CAGs can be large or small. They are the glue or the finishing touch that completes and refines the work of the staff. For some commanders, they become small strategy shops that produce analysis and concepts separate from the main line of the general staff's thinking. My thinking on CAGs had developed from my experience as the military secretary to the commandant of the Marine Corps, where I managed the service's version of the CAG—the strategic initiatives group—and then the chairman's CAG, which I managed as the director of the Joint Staff. I did not want an alternative strategy shop. I did not want a body of thinkers who paralleled the work of the general staff. I had confidence in my principal staff officers, and I always wanted the last person to approve a document or concept that was coming to me to be the senior flag officer in that directorate. I did want my CAG to take a critical look at the inputs I received and communicate their thoughts to me. I also used them for many other important tasks around the headquarters, from writing my speeches to organizing external academic events for the staff and me.

While serving on the Joint Staff, I had been exposed to the systematic use of wargaming to explore the utility of plans and concepts. We had found it a good way to wring out alternative approaches. Like so many things, the *process* of wargaming often brought more insight than the solution that was reached by the game. I was intent on using this same approach at CENTCOM, where I found that Air Force senior executive Bob Unger, the J-8 or resources director, had already developed a powerful wargaming capability within the headquarters. He and I saw eye to eye on how to use wargaming to add rigor to plans and concepts. The work of his team materially strengthened and sharpened CENTCOM's war planning and helped in our staff engagements with the Joint Staff and Office of the Secretary of Defense (OSD).

I also wanted flatness, so the battle rhythm that we adopted by May 2019 was this: every morning from Monday through Thursday at eight o'clock I would convene an update of my staff, my commanders, and the senior defense officials, or attachés, from every country across the region. We would begin with an intelligence update, then an operations update. Following that, each staff section would rapidly provide a relevant update. We would next go around to each of the senior defense officials and then finish with my commanders. We could get through this in thirty to forty minutes, depending on what was going on in the theater. I would give any closing remarks, and we would drop the outstations. It was rapid-fire, and people learned that they did not need to say something unless it was necessary. After we dropped the outstations, we would go around the internal staff again, this time reviewing anything that had come up with commanders and any other topics of interest. We conducted this at the secret level. On Wednesday mornings we devoted the first twenty minutes to coalition topics and opened the meeting up to our international partners. On Thursdays we briefed at a higher level of classification, and at the end of the brief we went to an even higher level of classification, which allowed for a straightforward threat-based discussion between the commanders and me.

On Friday I gave the commanders a day off, and we held plans steering group meetings, where I spent ninety minutes or so with my planners, usually focused on Iran. Planners were typically field grade officers from across all the services. Many of them had graduated from their services' second-year command and staff programs—the School of Advanced Military Studies for the Army, the School of Advanced Warfighting (SAW) for the Marine Corps, and the School of Advanced Air and Space Studies for the Air Force. They were bright, inquisitive young men and women. As a SAW graduate myself, I appreciated the intellectual skills and knowledge they brought to the planning process, and I enjoyed the time I spent with them. Interaction of the commander with planners is critical. Planning will improve as a direct result of how much exposure planners have to the commander. This task cannot be delegated. Central Command held several war plans, all in various stages of development. Some were very high priority, and I looked at them every week. Others were not as important, and we kept them in maintenance, much like in medicine how a patient would be kept on life support, awaiting further developments.

During normal operations, this schedule gave me five to six face-to-face touches with my subordinate commanders every week and even more with my primary staff. When we entered combat operations, we would try to meet twice a day, based on developments in the theater. The briefing would be adjusted to what we called combat mode, which centered on operational, intelligence, and sustainment issues. These could become very precise and specific briefs, as we traced the relative changes we were seeing in an adversary's array. Finally, toward the end of most afternoons, I'd gather with my J-2, -3, -5, lawyer, chief of staff, deputy commander, and senior enlisted leader in my office to briefly review the day. A lot of meetings are described here; the key was to run them quickly. I personally ran any meeting with subordinate commanders. I had the chief of staff run staff meetings where we had no component commanders in attendance. I've found throughout my professional life that nothing is more important than the personal interface between commanders. My time with them was the centerpiece of my schedule, followed by the interactions with the planners. At CENTCOM, we did it frequently because we were in a genuine operational environment all the time. Had the pace been slower, another routine might have been sufficient.

Meetings like this also gave me a chance to continually enunciate my priorities. In a large organization, unless the commander constantly emphasizes what's important, friction and uncertainty will inevitably creep into the system. We still used emails, but I always tried to pass contentious orders face to face. I think it produced a style of command that was built on commander interaction, not staff processes. This was important, because my central vision of how the command would fight was built around a functional design—air, land, maritime, special operations, cyber, and space commanders would be my maneuver elements. Particularly when considering the possibility of war with Iran, the creation of a subordinate joint task force (JTF) headquarters was insufficient. Doing this had become a default position at various times in CENTCOM, and many of those decisions were warranted—our JTFs in Iraq/Syria and Afghanistan were appropriate in every way.

To confront a nation-state, though, the entire resources of the theater would have to be marshalled and integrated. That meant that the joint force commander would have to be me, and our theater design would be functional. This decision was one of my very first, and it drove everything else. To do this, though, required a staff in Tampa that could function rapidly and efficiently and direct combat activities instead of simply overseeing the activities of subordinate task forces. Luckily, my deputy commander, chief of staff, and J-3 fully understood my intent. By the end of 2019, when war did stare us in the face, I felt we were ready to fight as a theater staff. It's important to emphasize that none of this was created anew. Many of the techniques that we applied were derived from the very successful commanders who preceded me: Generals Austin, Mattis, and Petraeus, among others.

During this period, we were in a constant dialogue with the joint staff and the secretary about forces allocated to Central Command. Since with few exceptions CENTCOM "owns" no forces, everything that comes into the theater is rotational—they enter, perform their mission, and then return home. The allocation of these forces was worked out in a lengthy process and document that was called the global force management process. Rotational forces require at least a three-to-one ratio of units, since when an organization leaves CENTCOM, it must be replaced by a similar unit. This meant that significant force structure was taken up by maintaining the "base" for these rotational deployments. The services balked at these requirements. Much staff energy at CENTCOM was devoted to ensuring that we had the forces required to execute the tasks that we had been assigned. It was genuine and highly contentious "sausage making." I was determined that we would excel at this arcane art, and the succession of gifted officers working in the operations directorate never let me down.

3

CONFRONTING IRAN

A mistake in the original assembly
of the army can scarcely be rectified
in the entire course of the campaign.
—*Helmuth von Moltke*, On Strategy, *1871*

After concluding my business at The Citadel in Charleston on that bright May Saturday, we went immediately to the Air Force base and boarded our C-37—a Gulfstream 550 business jet with significant modifications for communications—and flew back to Tampa. That afternoon, I met with my staff, and we began to fill in the details of our request for forces and how we would employ them. I also talked to chairman Dunford about how to announce the request. There were several ways to release the information to the media. We could do it at CENTCOM, the Joint Staff or the secretary of defense could do it, or we could recommend that it come from the White House. While we were in these discussions, the CENTCOM public affairs team crafted a short message. I reviewed it standing in my office in my quarters in Tampa, modified it by no more than a word or two, and then sent it to the chairman. He and I also came to the same conclusion on who should release it: we both thought it would carry more impact if it came from the White House. Coming from that high a level in the U.S. government would send a clear signal to Iran that we were serious. The secretary of defense agreed, and this became the Department of Defense (DoD) recommendation. On Sunday evening, the White House released a message from the assistant to the president for national security affairs, John Bolton. His message was unchanged from the draft that we sent over. It read, "In response to a number of troubling and escalatory indications and warnings, the United States is deploying the USS *Abraham Lincoln* carrier strike group and a bomber task force to the U.S. Central Command region to send a clear and unmistakable message to the Iranian regime that any attack on the United States' interests or on those of our allies will be met with unrelenting force. The United States is not seeking war with the Iranian regime, but we are fully prepared to respond to any attack, whether by proxy, the Islamic Revolutionary Guard Corps, or regular Iranian forces."

In the hours and days that followed, I found it interesting that so many interpretations were made of both the fact that Bolton released the statement and the choice of words.[1] There was talk of a power grab by the National Security Council. The words were drafted in Tampa by a bright Navy captain public affairs officer, and the recommendation that John Bolton make the statement also came from the secretary's office. For me, the lesson was clear: the media was often wrong in their attribution, and they were usually fed their stories by people who were on the periphery of the action and who could only pass along parts of the truth as they knew it. It was a pattern that would be endlessly repeated in the months ahead.

Subsequently, the White House signaled within the administration that Iran had now become a higher priority for the president. This created tension both with and within DoD, which was in full embrace of a National Defense Strategy (NDS) that placed China, Russia, and North Korea above Iran as potential threats. The NDS was an internal DoD document; it carried no particular weight inside the interagency. It did carry great weight within the department. It seemed to me that in the days that followed, the emphasis on Iran conveyed by the White House would overcome the departmental emphasis on the NDS. I was wrong on this.

I also made a significant error in these early days. In the rush of meetings that followed, while it was clear that the Iran problem would require resources above those allocated for an "economy of force" theater, no longterm approach was adopted that memorialized these matters in writing. My mistake was to not push hard for an order from the secretary that would have established the relative prioritization of Iran, given its aggressive activities and the emerging "maximum pressure" campaign. Helmuth von Moltke's aphorism about the difficulty of correcting mistakes made at the beginning of a campaign proved very true in this case. We were never able to fully overcome the lack of guidance at the beginning of our interaction with Iran in May

2019, and I share a big part of the blame for not arguing for a more strategic approach. The lack of reprioritization meant that the massive machinery of the department churned onward, based on the written guidance in the NDS. This impacted not only the allocation of combat units to CENTCOM, but also the "below the line" funding for support activities that were critical to maintain an operating platform at the theater level. As a result, none of the services internalized our requirements, and every discussion about appropriate force levels for CENTCOM became an argument that pitted us against the core strategic document of the department: the NDS. While I felt that the document no longer accurately described the world that existed, that argument became harder to make as time elapsed. I missed the opportunity at the beginning, and it never came back.

To place this in perspective, it's important to know that the Iranians did have a plan for escalation in the spring of 2019. It was based on the use of force and was largely the brainchild of Qassem Soleimani, the Quds Force commander (much more on him later). For many months, the Iranians had observed the drawdown of forces in the Central Command theater. They watched the aircraft carrier depart, and they saw the drawdown of fighter squadrons as well. They also digested public pronouncements about the NDS, all of which took on a certain didactic tone in calling for a reorientation away from the Middle East to face China and other threats. Their long-term goal had not changed: to push the United States from the theater. While this must remain informed speculation, I believed then, and still believe now, that they saw an auspicious moment in the spring of 2019, when they could hit us with enough force to cause the United States to reconsider its presence in the region and accelerate the withdrawal that we were trumpeting. They would need to be careful, because too much force would prompt a significant U.S. response. The Iranians have always had a healthy respect for U.S. capabilities, once aroused and marshalled. They doubted our will. Given the combination of redeployments and pronouncements from the department, this was a reasonable position for them to hold.

Other things had changed in the region as well. By mid-2019, the Iranian ballistic missile force had grown to a size and level of competence that was unparalleled. They could field approximately three thousand missiles, mostly of short range—but able to hit their Gulf neighbors. They had perhaps fifty or so that could range Tel Aviv. These were accurate missiles, able to land within tens of meters of their targets. Iran also had a significant fleet of land attack cruise missiles and uncrewed aerial vehicles. Iran's real crown jewels were the triad of uncrewed long-range strike systems just discussed, undergirded by its rapidly improving air defense network. These weapons are available today; they are not aspirational. The relative importance of Iran's conventional arsenal vis-à-vis a potential nuclear capability was captured in 2020, when U.S. president-elect Joe Biden explained, in a discussion with columnist Thomas Friedman, that "in consultation with our allies and partners, we're going to engage in negotiations and follow-on agreements to tighten and lengthen Iran's nuclear constraints, as well as address the missile program."[2] The Iranian response was immediate and surprisingly consistent. Then-president Hassan Rouhani said, "The Americans were trying for months to add the missile issue [to the nuclear talks] and this was rejected."[3] Others, from current Iranian president Ebrahim Raisi to former foreign minister Mohammad Javad Zarif, have also been loud in their rejection of any linkage. During the years of sanctions against Iran, including the period of "maximum pressure" under the Trump administration, the Iranians sacrificed much in their economy to keep working on these weapons. They enjoyed at least as high a priority as nuclear weapons development.

All these capabilities were destabilizing and dangerous. Uncrewed aerial systems posed the most immediate threat to Middle Eastern security because of their low cost, widespread availability, and potential deniability (since their point of origin can be disguised by employing an irregular flight path). In the fall of 2022 this threat expanded into Eastern Europe, as Iran began furnishing drones and training for Russia to support its aggressive war in Ukraine. The Iranian drone threat has evolved rapidly, while regional responses have often been lethargic. As a result, the gap is widening, and the threat grows every day. It was even wider in the summer of 2019.

The significance of this exponential growth in capabilities should not be overlooked or minimized. By 2019 the dynamics of state-on-state combat in the theater had changed, and the Iranians had the clear ability to gain "overmatch" against their neighbors. Overmatch is a condition when the attacker can overwhelm the ability of the defender to protect key targets. Most of the Gulf states had air and missile defense systems, many of them provided by the United States: the ubiquitous Patriot. While impressive in size of inventory, the sum of their capabilities was less than the aggregate parts. Information was not shared between countries, and there was little emphasis on a common operational picture, which was a foundational concept in air and missile defense. The improvement of regional air defenses had been a long-term priority for CENTCOM. In 2012, as General Mattis' representative, I had attended conferences in the region that addressed the problem. Unfortunately, not much had happened beyond words.

What would a war in the region using these potent asymmetric capabilities look like? Such a conflict between Iran and its adversaries would be a "fires war," not a war of maneuver or invasion. Some of this was driven by necessity. Iran does not possess an army with expeditionary capabilities, although its proxy forces across the region do provide some form of power projection. The Iranian air force is small and indifferently maintained and trained. Iran does have some naval capabilities, but beyond sea denial operations, these would be very limited. In Western military thought, there is an aphorism: "Fire without maneuver is indecisive. Maneuver without fire is disastrous."

Some history is in order here. The Iraq-Iran War in the 1980s saw significant long-range aircraft and rocket/missile strikes against the population centers of both countries. Despite these city-busting tactics, neither population turned against the war. Even with this background, Iran has embraced a policy of using long-range fires as its primary overt method of war, probably based on an assessment that such an approach would be effective against its Gulf neighbors, which have vast and vulnerable infrastructures open to attack. This approach could also be applied against Israel, if Iran could saturate Israeli missile defenses.[4]

How would this war be fought? The triad of Iranian uncrewed systems would be employed to attack air bases, ground and naval bases, and population centers. The large numbers of Iranian systems available would mean that many strikes would overwhelm air and missile defenses and reach their targets. As previously noted, the initial phase of any Iranian attack would be devoted to reducing our indication and warning sensors and battle management and fire control radars. Of course, regional forces would fight back and attempt to strike the launchers and assembly areas for these systems, but the vastly improved Iranian air defense network would make it very difficult for manned aircraft from Saudi Arabia, the United Arab Emirates (UAE), or any other regional state to have good effect. Striking targets in Iran would require the cooperation and protection of the U.S. Air Force and U.S. Navy: only they have the organic capabilities needed to fly persistently into the Iranian air defense network and strike these targets with any chance of success—and enable partner air forces to accompany them.

Should the United States participate in a regional war against Iran, success would be based on the relative exchange rate between the ability of the Iranian military—including the Islamic Revolutionary Guard Corps (IRGC)—to generate long-range striking power against targets, and the ability of the United States and its partners to reduce that offensive capability while defending vital areas. Iran's theory of victory would rest on inflicting so much pain on neighboring states that the war would eventually end on conditions favorable to the regime. The Islamic Republic would have every incentive to employ a countervalue approach to targeting, going after the cities and population centers of their adversaries in an attempt to force a political solution. Iran would seek to maximize early strikes, then offer to de-escalate before the United States could gather, deploy, and apply its overwhelming strength. As a result, a war of this type could cause many thousands of casualties, both military and civilian—especially if initial efforts to de-escalate proved unsuccessful.

By contrast, the theory of victory for the U.S. and Gulf side would rest on two achievements: reducing the number of mobile launchers from which the Iranians could strike, while also imposing a level of pain on the Iranian regime that would drive it to negotiate. The preservation of the theocratic regime is a core Iranian strategic objective. Attacks that threaten to destabilize it, either through economic hardship or the reduction of the ability to govern, would be treated very seriously by Iranian elite leadership. Holding on to a significant reserve of mobile missiles is also key to an Iranian conception of post-hostilities, so attriting this force would contribute directly to regime insecurity. Although the Iranians are increasing the number of fixed, buried launch sites in the ballistic missile launch areas spread across the country, this may not prove wise in the long run; fixed sites, even when hardened, can be struck with good effect. The difficulty is finding the target, not "weaponeering" against it. Thus, the mobile missile launchers will pose an even tougher challenge, as the history of coalition efforts against mobile launchers is not encouraging. In the 1991 Gulf War, the coalition struggled to find and attack them in the deserts of Iraq. We are better at this than we have been in the past, and there is good reason to believe that the Iranians will not be able to tolerate a significant reduction of this capability.

The final piece of the puzzle that was operative in 2019 was the maximum pressure campaign, a series of economic sanctions enacted against the Iranian economy. The campaign began in the fall of 2018, with the reimposition of broad economic sanctions. Other sanctions followed. In the broadest sense, the campaign's intent was to compel Iran to come back to the Joint Comprehensive Plan of Action (JCPOA) under terms that were less favorable than the original agreement, including the addition of new restrictions on the Iranian nuclear program, and widening the "JCPOA-next" agreement to cover Iranian ballistic missiles and their proxy activities. The campaign had mixed results. It certainly slowed the Iranian economy and increased the level of discomfort for all Iranians. It had less effect on changing the trajectory of Iranian decision-making. The Iranian economy was so opaque and corrupt that it was hard to trace cause and effect. What was obvious, though, was that the Iranians ruthlessly prioritized their ballistic missiles and other capabilities and were willing to let their citizens go hungry to maintain these programs. The Department of Defense had no direct role in this campaign. The (accurate) designation of the IRGC as a terrorist organization by the United States in April 2019 had little practical impact, but it did further stoke Iranian anger and possibly contributed to the aggressive Iranian behavior that we saw through the rest of 2019.

Iranian proxies struck four commercial ships near the port of Fujairah in the United Arab Emirates on May 12. The damage wasn't significant, but it was a visible sign that Iran was escalating. This matched what we were seeing in our intelligence assessments. Our immediate response to these blatant attacks was to continue to flow forces into the theater as a sign of our resolve. In discussions with the chairman and the secretary of defense, I argued that Iran had been emboldened to undertake this cycle of aggression because of their assessment that we were drawing down our forces and at the same time being very visible and vocal about the shift to the Pacific. At the tactical level, we flexed our intelligence gathering platforms to "soak" the Arabian Gulf and the Strait of Hormuz and its approaches (see map 2). We knew that the Iranians feared our overhead collection platforms, so we flew our MQ-9s literally around the clock. We backed these uncrewed platforms up with our P-3s and with a variety of other crewed and uncrewed aircraft. I am confident that our obvious, visible overhead presence cooled Iranian ardor to attack during those early summer days. Despite this, we were unable to stop everything, and on June 13, two more tankers were attacked by limpet mines while operating in the Gulf of Oman.

Map 2. Arabian Gulf

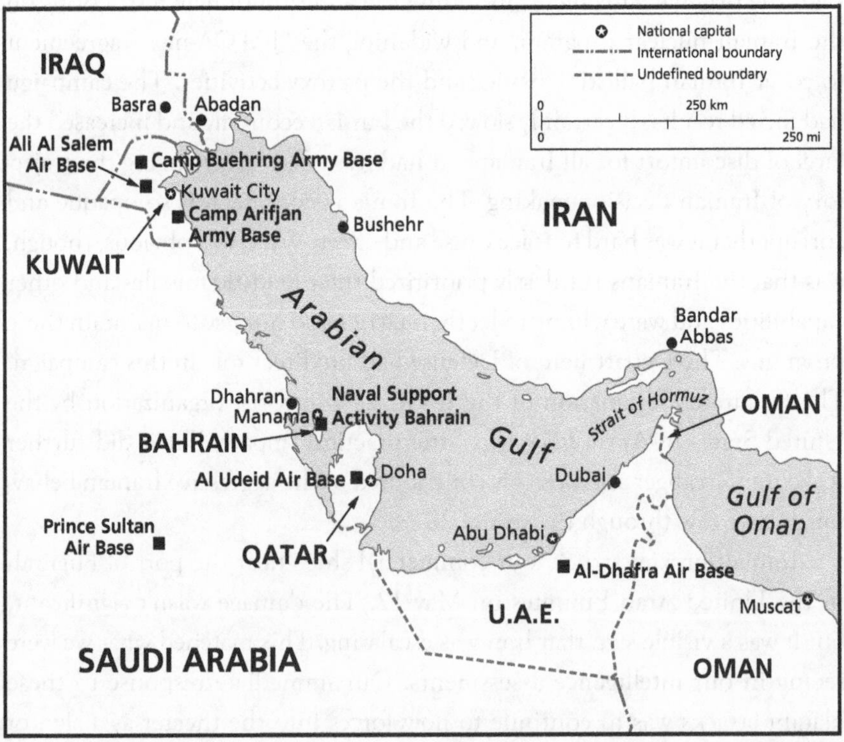

All of this came to a head on Thursday, June 20. In my home at MacDill, I kept several secure telephones beside my bed. My subordinate commanders or my staff would call only if their need to talk to me was triggered by a commander's critical information requirement, a long and clunky phrase that described a list of potential actions that merited waking the theater commander. Having been one of those subordinate commanders and a CENTCOM staff officer in the past, I knew that nobody did that lightly. To my wife's annoyance, I always set the ringtone to maximum volume on the phones. I was awakened by the shrill sound of the secure phone at about three o'clock in the morning. Knowing that it was never good to get a call at that time, I picked up the handset, looking at the visual display—it was from Vice Adm. Jim Malloy, my NAVCENT and 5th Fleet commander, calling from his headquarters in Manama, Bahrain. The classic surface warfare officer, he was cool and unflappable, and I had known him for many years. I trusted his judgment implicitly. What he had to tell me wasn't good. It looked like the Iranians had shot down one of our RQ-4A Global Hawks, a large, uncrewed jet-propelled reconnaissance drone. There was a possibility that they had also engaged a P-3C, and the mention of that sent a frisson of fear through me. The P-3s were manned aircraft, carrying ten or more servicemembers. Jim was quickly able to establish that our P-3 was safe, and he also confirmed that the RQ was operating in international airspace. After telling Jim to continue gathering more information about the attack, I woke up the chairman. As always, it was an easy and straightforward conversation. I knew that his task would be to calm the interagency and the White House and to ensure that any response would be appropriate. We were clearly aware at CENTCOM that any decision on responding would be a political, not a military, one. We were also keenly aware that a presidential decision might or might not involve using our capabilities. It was our job, though, to present the president with workable options if that was the way he decided to respond.

Within a few minutes, I had called my staff together in our headquarters. We maintained a comprehensive catalogue of response options that we could employ against Iran, should the president choose to respond to this attack. There were literally thousands of targets inside Iran, and all of them were continually updated by our intelligence and operations staffs. We quickly narrowed our proposed responses down to a set of three alternatives. We knew where the missile had been fired from that struck our drone. We also knew where other targets that the Iranians valued were located along the coast. For all these targets, we had detailed projections of possible collateral damage. We also had a variety of potential weapons to choose from to deliver the strikes. We could use manned aircraft, which would be risky, and place our aircrews over Iran. We could use manned aircraft and fire stand-off weapons, so long as the targets that we selected were near the coast. This would not require putting manned aircraft over Iran. Standoff was a relative term since we could reach hundreds of miles inland with our weapons. Last, of course, were our Tomahawk land attack cruise missiles (TLAMs). They were always a perennial favorite of civilian decision-makers when it came to targeting inside CENTCOM. They could be launched from ships, and there was no chance of us losing aircrew in the strike. They were accurate as well.

I talked to Joe Dunford frequently as the hours went by. I passed him our recommended strike options should the president elect to respond. Finally, we received word that we would strike back at Iran and that we'd hit three sites along the Arabian Gulf. TLAMs would be the weapon of choice. This was one of our preferred options, so it was easy to pass the orders to the force to prepare to launch the strikes. We had carefully selected targets that would cause a real loss for Iran if struck, but that would also minimize loss of life and other collateral damage. To this end, we recommended striking the targets at about three o'clock in the morning in the region. This would further reduce the risk of civilian or military casualties. It was my assessment that we'd possibly kill a handful of crewmen manning the missiles or, more likely, just the night security watch.

The crews on the ships worked feverishly to program the TLAMs, and I talked to my subordinate commanders about possible Iranian responses. Because of the narrow scope of our planned strike, I didn't think we would see much of a response. Additionally, we were getting indications that the decision to shoot down our drone wasn't made at the national level. As was often the case in the rickety Iranian chain of command, a subordinate commander had taken it upon himself to go after the RQ-4. Despite this, I did think it was important to push back in this case. We knew that the Iranians understood the language of force, and they would respect it. About two hours before I would need to give the order to launch the missiles, Joe Dunford called me to tell me that the president had reconsidered and would not strike. We now know that some advisors in the White House, misunderstanding how we calculate possible damage, determined that our projected casualty total for the targets was 150 Iranians. This was simply an amateurish misreading of how our complex collateral damage assessment process worked. We at CENTCOM never believed that the casualties would be that high on the targets we had selected. I would not have recommended the targets if that had been the case. Causing that many casualties would have been an overreaction and clearly disproportionate. Regardless, the president decided to call the strikes off. There was certainly no drama on our end—we were about two hours away from launch, so there wasn't any last-minute excitement. I believed then, and believe now, that cancelling the strike was a mistake. Had we executed it, it's possible that the escalatory trajectory we were on could have been suppressed. Instead, the Iranians drew a lesson from it that reinforced a belief they already had: the United States was feckless. Our friends in the region drew similar conclusions. This would shape Iranian behavior in the following months, and it's possible that our misguided restraint at this time ultimately cost Qassem Soleimani his life.

As the summer wore on, two other things happened that had great and lasting impact in the region. First, we stood up the International Maritime Security Construct (IMSC). This was a group of nations that were committed to ensure the safe passage of shipping through the Strait of Hormuz, the Gulfs of Aden and Oman, and the Bab al-Mandeb. It followed directly from our theory that visible overwatch tended to lessen Iranian aggressiveness. Put simply, they didn't like it when we saw them plan and execute their attacks. We had ample evidence that an aggressive overwatch of key chokepoints would reduce provocatory behavior. This led directly to the IMSC, which was established in September 2019. I put a lot of my personal energy and attention into this idea, but my capable NAVCENT commander, Vice Adm. Jim Malloy, was relentless and pitch-perfect in advocating for participation from like-minded nations. We gained support from Bahrain, the United Kingdom, Australia, Albania, Saudi Arabia, Lithuania, the UAE, Romania, and Estonia. A basic operating principle was that we weren't seeking conflict with anyone, only the safe passage of commerce through these key chokepoints. Nations provided ships (if able), maritime surveillance platforms, and officers to man the headquarters, which we established in Bahrain.

The IMSC proved a great success. Iran's misbehavior did not go completely away, but it became far more cautious. As with so many other international military structures, it was U.S. capabilities that provided the backbone upon which the construct worked. Since 2019 membership has adjusted—nations have left and entered, but the core work has continued, and it has reduced Iran's opportunities to create mischief at sea. This was a bright spot for collective security actions in the Middle East. It's always hard to prove a negative, but I believe the hard work of Jim Malloy and his Navy team created a collective architecture that materially reduced the Iranian propensity to attack.

The drone attacks on Abqaiq and Khurais in eastern Saudi Arabia on September 14 marked a turning point in the region. This wasn't immediately apparent, but in retrospect it is now clear that this attack of large scale and impressive design created a new reality. Saudi oil production dropped by almost 50 percent, which impacted the world petroleum market adversely. I was flying home from the theater when the attacks occurred, and I spent the entire flight home on secure calls with the chairman, the Saudis, and my staff and commanders. The attacks on these two oil processing facilities did significant damage, and while the Houthis in Yemen claimed responsibility, we soon uncovered evidence that the attacks had actually come from inside Iran. This was a shocking escalation by the Iranians. It was effectively a state-on-state attack. The Iranians had planned their routes with great precision, and the ineffectiveness and misplacement of the Saudi air defense radars contributed to the success of the attack. As a result of this attack, we brought additional air defense assets into Saudi Arabia, and we stepped up the pace and scope of our joint defense planning efforts with them as well. What we did not do—and this was the right decision—was strike back at Iran. The evidence was convincing if you could review it at a very high level of classification, but there was enough ambiguity in the releasable archived radar and sensor tracks so that nations that did not want to hold Iran accountable were able to adopt an ambivalent posture.

Setting the tactical effects of the strike aside, the long-term political impact was to drive home to the Gulf states just how vulnerable they were to Iranian attacks. It also made them painfully aware that there were finite limits on what the United States was willing to do for their defense. Actually, we were willing to do quite a bit. We deployed Patriots, fighters, and an air expeditionary wing to Prince Sultan Airbase in the Kingdom of Saudi Arabia. I sent my Marine Component commander, Lt. Gen. Sam Mundy, to Riyadh to lead a forward CENTCOM cell that oversaw defense planning. On the other hand, there was no political appetite in the United States for any offensive action. I agreed with that decision, but the Saudis continued to say that we weren't doing enough. This attack, and our response, marked the beginning of a deterioration in relations with the Kingdom at the military level that we have not yet recovered from. More generally, it became "exhibit one" whenever I visited a country in the region, and my interlocutors wanted to make a point about their lack of confidence in the United States as a security partner. The attack further emboldened Iran, and as we headed into the fall and winter of 2019, they believed that we did not have the will or appetite to push back as they continued their aggressive actions. This would prove to be a dangerous miscalculation.

4

FINISHING BAGHDADI

Anticipation is the heart of wisdom.
—*Mark Helprin*, A Soldier of the Great War

Even as we focused on Iran within the headquarters, our counterterrorist operations continued across the theater. Like so many things in the Middle East, the rise of ISIS could be attributed to the incomplete end of another war and the bad decisions that were made at that time. Theologically, ISIS rose from the wreckage of the forces led by Abu Musab al Zarqawi (killed in June 2006). The root causes of Sunni disaffection in Iraq that al Qaeda tapped were never adequately addressed by the government of Iraq or the U.S. and coalition elements. Nonetheless, relentless counterterrorism pressure greatly weakened al Qaeda. By 2010 it was a shadow of what had existed in 2006. Had constant pressure been maintained, it is possible that a resurgence could have been prevented.

Unfortunately, the Barack Obama administration's precipitous decision to withdraw from Iraq in 2011 removed both pressure on al Qaeda as well as any incentive for co-option within the national structure of Iraq. By the end of December 2011 the U.S. presence in Iraq was just over one hundred military personnel—effectively, zero. While there were many reasons to distrust the government of Iraq, the unseemly withdrawal gravely weakened Iraq's ability to respond to a new and virulent version of al Qaeda that was arising in the western desert areas. I watched this happen while serving as the J-5 at CENTCOM under General Mattis. Throughout 2011 I crafted many memoranda for his signature that argued for a robust troop presence in Iraq. We actually began by asking for a residual force of around 30,000. These arguments were rejected, and soon the proposed force levels were in the range of 5,000, and then even less. It was very hard for us to see the logic in such a significant drawdown. The intent seemed to be to simply get out, without consideration for what might happen in the vacuum that was sure to ensue. The passage of time has not been kind to the decisions made by the Obama administration. The abrupt removal of U.S. advisors, enablers, and other support mechanisms exposed the complete inability of the Iraqi army to stand alone, and it led directly to the terrors of the following years.

Meanwhile, what had been al Qaeda in Iraq was reborn as the Islamic State of Iraq, or ISI, and eventually as ISIS. Elements of al Qaeda remained, and it never recognized its next version, but the energy that had operated within al Qaeda at its height was now passed to the Islamic State. The tension between the two organizations has never been resolved, and al Qaeda to this day does not accept the Islamic State. The vision for the Islamic State came from two former U.S. detainees—graduates of Abu Ghraib—which effectively gave an advanced degree in terrorism to many Iraqis and others who passed through its gates. One was Ibrahim Awad Ibrahim al Badri al Samarra—known more widely as Abu Bakr al Baghdadi. The other was Taha Subhi Falaha, also known as Abu Mohammed al Adnani. Under their energetic and ruthless leadership, ISIS began carrying out attacks as early as 2009. By May 2010 Baghdadi ascended to lead the group.

By the spring of 2014 the Islamic State was threatening to overrun Iraq. Only a massive infusion of U.S. and coalition aid and support prevented the caliphate from claiming a military victory in Iraq. Throughout the second half of 2015 and for the three years that followed, CENTCOM oversaw a complex campaign that used partner forces on the ground to do most of the actual fighting, supported by U.S. airpower. General Lloyd Austin began this work, and he was followed by Gen. Joe Votel. In succession they crafted a well-designed campaign that inexorably squeezed the Islamic State out of Iraq, and then, with the aid of Kurdish proxy forces, into Syria.

Shortly before I took command of CENTCOM, in the early spring of 2019, we were able to declare that ISIS no longer held any ground in Syria. I know it was a gratifying moment for Joe Votel, and also for Lloyd Austin: together, and in succession, they had cobbled together disparate forces and directed a military campaign over some of the most difficult terrain in the world. They did it with minimal loss of U.S. and coalition life; the cost to our partners on the ground, the Iraqi security forces and the Kurds, had been much higher. The one thing that the Islamic State in Iraq was able to do, even as they fought their last, desperate battles at Baghuz in southern Syria, was to create a plan to disperse senior leadership. Self-protection was always a high priority for Islamic State leadership, and they had no concerns about leaving foot soldiers behind to die while they scuttled to safety.

Baghdadi's war went bad in the winter of 2018 and the spring of 2019. The caliphate, once so grandiosely proclaimed, was being reduced by constant pressure from the Kurdish Syrian Democratic Forces (SDF), enabled by our support. By 2019 the SDF had a large Arab component, which was a result of an approach that recruited local Arabs to fight beyond areas under Kurdish control. This was magnificent work by our advisors on the ground. City after city fell, and the remnants fell back south down the Euphrates River valley. As the tattered and increasingly disorganized fighters sought to make a series of final stands east of the Euphrates near the Iraqi border, Baghdadi sought to escape. There weren't a lot of good choices for him. Iraq, to the east, was no longer an uncontested safe area. The Iraqi security forces, aided by U.S. and coalition enablers, training, and occasional partnering, were proving increasingly effective at not allowing the Islamic State to shift its base of operations back into Iraq. It was probably too hard to think about getting into Turkey or some other exit route. Instead—and this could not have been appetizing to him—northwest Syria offered the best option for a place to hide while his followers died in the Euphrates pocket, and to perhaps keep the spirit of the Islamic State alive. Northwest Syria wasn't particularly salubrious, either, since it was a witch's brew of al Qaeda and Islamic State spinoffs, many of them more eager to fight among themselves over obscure theological points than to pool their efforts against the infidels (see map 3).

Nonetheless, sometime in the spring or summer of 2019, Baghdadi made his way there, settling into an isolated safehouse near the village of Barisha, west of Aleppo, and within four miles of the Turkish border. It was an indication of just how uncoordinated and disjointed the broader al Qaeda–Islamic State movement was that a nearby village actually was occupied by the Hay'at

Map 3. West Syria

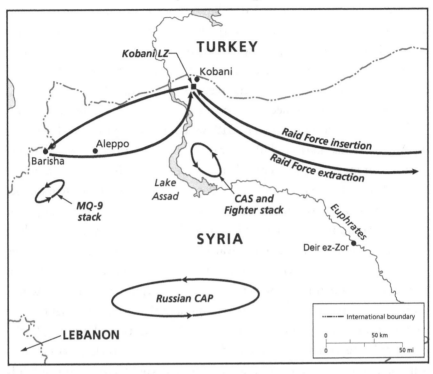

Tahrir al-Sham, a group who were no friends of Baghdadi's. In many ways, they were a proxy for al Qaeda. He settled in to live carefully, surrounding himself with a number of children and his personal bodyguard. The children were intended to make it hard for anyone to strike him with air-delivered fires—he well knew that we were loath to hit targets with noncombatants likely to be killed or wounded. The bodyguards were to be his conduit to the wider world: to be his cutouts and to take his messages far away from his location and release them in a manner that would make it extremely hard to trace anything back to him. It was a time-tested operational security approach, one practiced by generations of al Qaeda and ISIS leaders.

Both the U.S. military and the CIA were looking hard for him. After taking command, I spent a considerable amount of time with the Joint Special Operations Task Force (JSOTF) that was under my operational control at Central Command, comparing notes and being updated on how our searches were progressing. As always, his need to communicate was very helpful. On April 29, 2019, he released a "Mobilization of the Believers" video. In this he acknowledged the recent territorial losses ISIS endured, talked at some length about the need for patience, and spoke about the new Turkey Wilayat, or province. He released more messages on June 24 and September 16. In all of these cases, rigid operational security was observed; couriers spirited the messages on digital media to locations where they could be launched.

Over the course of summer 2019, we continued to look for Baghdadi. By August we had narrowed his location down to northwest Syria. Through a variety of measures, we were able to further narrow his position down to the walled safehouse near the small village of Barisha, in the Harem district of Idlib province. Over the next few weeks we examined a variety of options to go after him. In particular, we invested a lot of time in ways to strike him if we could get him on the road, away from the children and his wives. We also undertook measures to raise our confidence level that it was actually him in the compound; this was proven to a very high degree of satisfaction to me. By the beginning of October, we were confident that we had the right target, and we were also sure of his location. We remained stymied, though, by the fact that he never left the compound. We could have struck the compound with precision fires—bombs or missiles—but that would have almost certainly resulted in a number of children dying, in addition to his wives. We worked the option up just to have it available, but I wasn't comfortable with the loss of innocent life that it would have entailed. More pragmatically, it would have made it hard to definitively declare "jackpot," the word we used when we were completely certain we had either captured or killed our target. There would always be some uncertainty with an airstrike. I wanted to prevent the rise of doubt about his death; we needed to be sure, and we needed to be able to prove it.

Other planning factors now began to intrude. We were worried that Baghdadi might move, which would cause us to reset all our planning. If we were going to use a raid option, we needed a forward staging base: the Kobani landing zone, 160 kilometers east of the objective. We were in the process of withdrawing from Kobani, so we would lose access to this location in the near future. Also, the situation with the Russians in northwest Syria was getting more tense. They had been pushing against us through their Syrian proxies down at Deir ez-Zor, a key city on the lower Euphrates River in Syria. They could make a raid extremely difficult to execute if they wanted to. In short, time was no longer our friend.

In all of this, we worked closely with our CIA partners. As we refined our plans and talked over the summer and into the fall, it became obvious that a Title 10 (DoD-commanded) option was our best chance. Back in 2011 the Osama bin Laden raid had been a Title 50 (CIA-commanded) operation. It made good sense then because of the sensitivities involving the penetration of Pakistani airspace. Because of the larger tactical problems we confronted in execution, it now was more practical to keep the operation within a purely military chain of command. This was an important consideration. In 2011 CENTCOM was unaware of the bin Laden mission until hours before execution. The commander, General Mattis, had little time to prepare for repercussions or blowback. When all was said and done, he owned the risk for the operation, but he only became aware of it very late. This approach maximized operational security, but it opened the possibility of forces in the theater not being set for repercussions. This wasn't the case in 2019 regardless of who commanded the operation; CIA had been open with me and a small group of planners. Regardless, because of the essentially military complexities of the area we were operating in, it made good sense to use the military chain of command.

Events now began to accelerate. Our JSOTF gave me a comprehensive brief the afternoon of Wednesday, October 23. I took the brief in Tampa via secure conferencing. As usual, they had a good plan. It was not without risk, but I felt that we could do some things to reduce the dangers. The chairman, now Gen. Mark Milley, USA, and I discussed our options frequently during the week of October 20. We then briefed Defense Secretary Mark Esper, who was on travel in Europe. Every day brought new confirmation of Baghdadi's location. A strike on Baghdadi would not strictly require presidential permission since we already had the authorities we needed to pursue him, but this would be a large operation that would require some deconfliction with the Russians and the Turks, so it was appropriate that we brief him on the planned raid.

I flew up to DC early on the morning of Friday, October 25. The chairman and I would go to the White House, and the secretary, who was still in Europe, would join by secure phone. It was a beautiful October day, without a cloud in the sky, and almost unseasonably warm for Washington. I rode over to the White House with Mark Milley. I was armed with several "placemats," so called because they were large slides of about the size of a dinner placemat. They outlined what we proposed, embedded with maps. Our plan was to talk off the placemats, using hard copies only.

Upon arriving at the White House, we learned that the meeting would go upstairs in the residence in the room known as the Yellow Oval. I had been in the room once before. I always felt that this room had the best view of almost any room in the United States: on the second floor of the White House, it looked out over the Ellipse toward the Washington Monument. It was a view of breathtaking elegance, capturing a big slice of American history. There were three large ceiling-height windows that let in lots of light. One of the windows was also a door, and it gave access to the Truman balcony. Different presidents had used the room for many things, and President Franklin D. Roosevelt, who used it as his study, was in this room when he learned of the attack on Pearl Harbor on December 7, 1941. From my prior visit to the room, it seemed to me that President Trump used it mainly for small meetings. In late autumn, it was a particularly beautiful aspect. The room itself, while tastefully furnished, had none of the communications equipment available in the Situation Room, where briefings of this kind typically occurred. President Trump favored this room when he didn't want a wider audience to know about the meeting. This suited the chairman and me perfectly, because we remained concerned about operational security. We were ushered in, joining Director of Central Intelligence Gina Haspel and National Security Advisor Robert O'Brien. We talked quietly, taking in the view, while waiting for the president. Vice President Mike Pence joined us as well. We were to sit around a fairly small dining room table, clearly an antique. Since the room had no secure communications, we placed a portable secure cell phone in the middle of the table, and the secretary of defense joined us in this way. Unfortunately, the connection wasn't good; we dropped the link frequently. The president came in and said hello to everyone, and we began with an intelligence overview from Gina.

In short, we knew where Baghdadi was. We didn't expect him to move in the immediate future—measured in days—but he wouldn't stay there forever. We knew that there were eight ISIS members in the walled compound. Four were women, in some combination of wives and slaves. We also knew that there were at least a dozen children in the compound. Baghdadi always wore a suicide vest, and that was a matter of great concern to us—he had made it clear that he didn't intend to be taken alive.

After Gina, the chairman briefed the overall situation in Syria: it remained a complex and difficult problem. We could not expect any help from the Russians, and, in fact, we thought there was a good chance that they would oppose us if given the opportunity. Keeping eye contact with the president, I sketched out what we planned to do. He was focused and asked good questions; the vice president chimed in frequently. In short, we would fly a force in helicopters hundreds of miles to land near the compound. After landing, we would secure the ground so that no one could leave or enter the compound. We would have aircraft overhead to provide fires in support of both these actions. Once this was accomplished, we would enter the compound and carry out what is known as "actions on the objective." The team would find and capture or kill Baghdadi. We would then go back out the way we came in. It all looked very clear on our crisp maps, with their colored arrows and diagrams.

There were risks, and we talked about them. It was possible that the Russians would detect our entry and attempt to stop us. I was less worried about the raid force's helicopters, which flew low and were routed to evade detection. I was more concerned about our uncrewed support platforms. We had to place uncrewed aerial vehicles over the objective to give us intelligence, surveillance, and reconnaissance. They could be easily attacked by other aerial platforms. We had to have them over the target to go in. We agreed that we would notify the Russian high command that we were contemplating an operation and that we wanted them to avoid challenging us. The request would be complicated by the fact that we were in a standoff with the Russians around Deir ez-Zor on the Euphrates River. Near this key settlement, the Russians were pushing their proxies to build a pontoon bridge across the Euphrates. As always, they were intent on getting to the oilfields that our SDF partners protected. It wasn't an auspicious time to ask for their cooperation. Getting Russia's assent would be a heavy lift, but U.S.-Russian deconfliction of our operations in Syria had worked relatively well up to that point, and there was reason to believe it would continue.

As the meeting drew to a close, I had an opportunity to give my recommendation. Leaning across the table, looking at the president, referring to the maps laying on the table, I felt the responsibility very clearly, but I was confident in our intelligence, the plan, and the force that would execute. This was the shortest version of the chain of command—from president directly to combatant commander. I recommended that we conduct the operation. The chairman weighed in, recommending approval as well. Despite his communications difficulties, the secretary of defense concurred. The president accepted the recommendation. We were a go. We talked a little more about continuing to get an even more precise fix on Baghdadi's location, but the die was cast. I left the White House with the chairman, and we returned to the Pentagon. I planned to get back to Tampa immediately, where I would be best positioned to command the operation. The chairman and I talked for a few minutes in his office, and we reviewed how we would talk over the next few hours and days. It was Friday in Washington; we would launch the operation Saturday evening in the theater. I called the JSOTF commander and let him know that we were going to execute. The great machine, spanning half the world, began to uncoil and gather itself to strike.

A raid, as every infantryman knows, is an attack with a planned withdrawal. It is an operation that is designed to create a momentary overwhelming advantage at a time and place chosen by the attacker. Usually, a raid is executed when the attacker is unable to maintain the advantage at the point of attack because of the strength of the defender, or perhaps because of the range to the objective. In its purest, original infantry sense, raids are intended to destroy a target and then quickly withdraw. There are, however, other and more complex reasons for raids—to free hostages or to capture or kill a person. Over the past forty years, U.S. special operations forces had refined the art of the raid to an unsurpassed degree of efficiency. As a Marine second lieutenant many years before, I was taught how to patrol and how to execute raids by hard, competent instructors at the infantry officer course at Quantico, Virginia. We were good at it, and I have remembered those skills.

The relationship between what we did in that course and what JSOTF can do, though, is the relationship between a well-coached college football team and the New England Patriots. The language of the game and the concepts of play are all the same; it is in the ability to relentlessly focus on execution that there is a profound difference. They are simply the best in the world at this demanding and dangerous craft.

For a raid to capture or kill a target, there are eternal constants, whether the raid is being conducted as training at Fort Moore, Georgia, or Quantico, or anywhere else. You must have a plan to move your raid force from a base that is within range to the vicinity of the objective or directly on the objective, if the situation requires it. Once on the objective, a part of the force must be dedicated to external security: ensuring that no outside agency can interrupt the rest of the force. Part of the force then secures the objective itself, ensuring no one can leave or flee. The assault force then moves to carry out "actions on the objective." This might be a destruction mission, a hostage rescue, or a capture or kill task. Once the tasks are complete, and time is always precious in these operations, the force moves to withdraw. Of course, there's much more to it than this. A reaction force—a reserve—is positioned so that it can reinforce on the objective if needed. Medical capabilities are also staged. Plans are in place for a crashed aircraft en route. Fire support is positioned overhead. There are common procedural templates for these operations, but each raid also has unique aspects. A key to success is the opportunity to rehearse. If time permits, full-scale models will be created of the objective. All of this had been done for this operation.

Saturday, October 26 in Tampa was another lovely Florida day—or so I've been told. I spent the entire day inside my headquarters, and most of that time in the focal point operations center (FPOC), which is designed to allow me to command sensitive operations without affecting the daily operations of the headquarters. I sat at the head of a U-shaped table with several screens in front of me and several telephones, including secure instruments. On the wall at the foot of the table were two large monitors, one of which usually presented the air plot, or the overall gods-eye view of every airplane in the theater. We could shrink it down to a tighter scale if needed. For most of the day, we were looking at northern Syria and part of Iraq. The other screen was set up to be a video feed from a variety of platforms—we would be able to watch the raid in execution. Last, a monitor held the "bridge," which was a grid of all the leaders involved in the operation. Joining me around the table were my key staff officers, including my operational lawyer and public affairs officer.

During this critical period, my brain trust was composed of my deputy commander, Gen. Tom "Guns" Bergeson, USAF, a fighter pilot with extensive combat experience and a cool and collected demeanor. My chief of staff was Maj. Gen. Scott McKean, USA, a tanker with a deep reservoir of experience in CENTCOM in general and Iraq in particular. I depended upon the deputy commander and the chief of staff to ensure that I never wrote checks I couldn't cash . . . and to tell the emperor when he had no clothes on! My J-2 (intelligence) was Brig. Gen. Dimitri Henry, USMC, who had a knack for seeing patterns in complex problems. He and his deputy, Cari Gast-Mulhausen, were invaluable to me in sorting the overwhelming volume of intelligence that was flowing into the headquarters. My J-3 (operations) was Rear Adm. Sam "Pappy" Paparo, USN, a proud and outgoing fighter pilot who was probably the most experienced naval aviator on active duty. In many ways, he was my alter ego—I depended upon him to create actionable orders from concepts. He was relentless and driven but also quick-witted and a constant source of repartee, as befitted a former *Jeopardy!* contestant. My J-4 (logistics), Maj. Gen. Chris Sharpsten, USA, always thought well beyond the logistical considerations and could be depended upon to tailor support effectively as we adapted plans for ever-changing situations. My J-5 (strategy and plans) was Maj. Gen. Mike Langley, USMC, who embodied steady resolve and calmness. He was a pillar of strength. In my long career, I have been well served by communications officers, but in Brig. Gen. Jeth Ray, USA, I found perhaps the very best. He could be depended upon to listen to our plans and then to produce network-level solutions that worked in moments of stress and friction. I also leaned heavily on my lawyer, or judge advocate general (JAG), Col. Matt Grant, USAF, who had an extensive background in both the region and conventional and special operations. He had a network of lawyers—they called it the "JAGnet"—that reported information, opinions, and context in ways that were simply invaluable to me. Finally, the Joint Staff historian was on hand during this period—Col. David Crist, USMCR, was a member of the DoD senior executive service, and he was perhaps the best walking, talking compendium of knowledge on Iran and CENTCOM. His book, *The Twilight War*, was unsurpassed in its treatment of the long, tortured relationship between the United States and Iran. He and I also had a personal relationship. In the winter of 1988, 2nd Lt. Crist, then an artillery forward observer for 2nd Battalion, 10th Marines, served as the fire support team chief for Company I, 3rd Battalion, 8th Marines—commanded by Capt. Frank McKenzie. He and I once shared a two-man cave dug into four feet of snow at an elevation of nine thousand feet at Bridgeport, California. We had stayed in touch through the years, and when I returned to the Joint Staff in 2015, he was working as the Joint Staff historian. I found his insights and wealth of knowledge extremely useful on a broad variety of subjects. His first love, though, was the Iran problem. I leaned on him heavily over the next few days.

In Central Command, I had nine operational commanders who reported to me directly. Four were the service components: Army (Lt. Gen. Terry Ferrell), Marine Corps (Lt. Gen. Sam Mundy), Navy (Vice Adm. Jim Malloy), and Air Force (Lt. Gen. Gus Guastella); there were two special operations commanders: Special Operations Component CENTCOM (Navy SEAL Rear Adm. Wyman Howard) and also the JSOTF commander. I also had Cyber Command's theater component. Additionally, there were two other task force commanders: Lt. Gen. Pat White in Iraq with Combined Joint Task Force Operation Iraqi Resolve, and Gen. Scott Miller in Afghanistan, commanding Operation Resolute Support. Nine direct reporting organizations comprised a significant span of control, to use the command and control lexicon, which preferred the rule of threes. I depended upon my staff to ease the workload, but three-star commanders need guidance from four-star commanders—by personality, they aren't easily managed by a higher headquarters staff. I know that I wasn't particularly easy for the staff to manage when I had been a three-star commander in CENTCOM.

We were further organized along functional lines: Terry Ferrell was the land forces commander, Gus Guastella was the air component commander, and Jim Malloy was the naval component commander. I was extremely comfortable with this arrangement, and it was optimized for high-end warfare; since my assumption of command in March, I had been insistently pushing the headquarters to be ready for a potential war with Iran. Our obvious attention to this contingency was a key part of achieving the effect of deterrence. I talked to commanders most days, as I've already outlined.

I knew the personalities of my commanders through and through. They were seasoned professionals, many of them with years of combat experience in the region. They had their own large staffs, and they also reported through administrative channels to their service chiefs. I tried to never lose sight of the fact that these were the officers who would actually transmute my intent and battlefield opportunity into cold reality. My staff could plan, design, cajole, and coax—but it was the transmission of orders from me to my subordinate commanders that would actually make things happen. Unless you grew up with someone who was a three-star commander, it was hard to be close to them when you met in a situation like CENTCOM. I knew Sam Mundy, my Marine component commander, over many years in the Marine Corps. I didn't know the other commanders as well. Interestingly, it seemed to matter very little in the end. In the joint world, dissimilar experiences were actually a strength. What was important to me was gaining their willing buy-in and support of my decisions. Certainly, they would all do what I told them to do, when I told them to do it. They knew that, as did I. It's always much better, though, to gain willing, positive, affirmative compliance. This can only be accomplished by thoroughly explaining what the task is and what is required. It also means allowing a subordinate to ask questions and to fit the higher headquarters guidance into his or her own experiential shell. Some commanders can do this immediately; for some, it takes time. What has to be avoided, though, is a false positive—agreeing without understanding.

I have uniformly found it to be the case that commanders who understand the "why" behind higher headquarters orders will persevere when conditions change; they will adapt rapidly and aggressively. The responsibility for ensuring subordinates have this level of understanding lies squarely on the shoulders of the higher commander. I'm certain many times in my career, commanders I was working for saw that I didn't "get" what they wanted; their willingness to ensure that I saw what was desired, beyond the black and white of the field order, was a large part of my professional development. I tried very hard at CENTCOM to ensure my commanders had as much information as I did, that they understood the reasons for my decisions, and that they understood *why* I did certain things—and did not do other things. This was the team I'd fight with over the next few days.

The JSOTF that would accomplish the mission did their final conditions check at seven o'clock in the morning, and the commander then spent a few minutes with me, reviewing the plan. At 8:32 the chairman called, giving CENTCOM the "go" for mission execution. I went around my staff—intelligence, operations, communications, and my deputy commander and chief of staff. We looked good in all areas. At 8:40 I called the JSOTF commander and gave him the green light to proceed.

There were other developments, though, that threatened our plan. At about 9:45 Lt. Gen. Pat White, our commander in Iraq and Syria, called to let me know that the Russians were continuing to build a bridge across the Euphrates near Deir ez-Zor. This was several hundred kilometers from our objective, but it still could create problems for us. We had told them that we might strike the bridge if it was completed. Our worry was that they would use the bridge to push armor across the river, acting against our SDF partners. The Russians, and their Syrian proxies, had long coveted the oilfields on the eastern side of the Euphrates River. Our SDF partners held those fields. Back in February 2018, a large force of Russian operatives from the security company Wagner had tried to force their way into the oilfields. In a remarkable display of precision firepower, our tactical air controllers, paired with SDF units, directed overwhelming fire on the advancing column. Several hundred contractors were killed and many more wounded. The Russians grew wary of us after this debacle, and I knew that they remembered our capabilities even as they continued to try to find ways to insinuate themselves into the oilfields.

The Russian response this morning was to insist that they would not use the bridge for offensive purposes, but they also conveyed the usual Russian heavy-handed threat that they would strike back against us if we denied them the use of the bridge. Pat and I talked it over. None of us wanted to strike the Russian bridge. We certainly had the ability to drop it if necessary, but it would inevitably lead us to escalation, and the very real possibility of U.S. and Russian forces fighting each other in Syria. That was never a good thing, but it would be particularly ill-timed based on our raid up north. Pat recommended that we allow the Russians to complete the bridge but warn them that we would act if armor crossed. I liked his idea, and at a little after noon, I recommended to the chairman that we not strike the bridge, but that we maintain the option to do so if Russian or Syrian armor crossed. Those points would be communicated to Russia's senior military command.

Part of our plan for the raid was to reach out to key leadership of all the forces involved in Syria and tell them what we were doing—the timing was more art than science, but the intent was to let the Russians and the Turks know we were coming in on an ISIS raid, and to time the notifications so that the Russians in particular would not have the time to make a concerted effort to stop us. The Russians, of course, would tell their Syrian allies, but by notifying the Russians as late as possible, we would make it harder for them to pass anything actionable to the Syrians.

In the early afternoon in Tampa, time passed slowly. I spent most of the day sitting at the head of the table, looking at maps and following the air picture on the big monitors. I was frequently on the secure phone or talking to the bridge video conference. Time has a different quality when you're waiting for something to start. As a commander, I was balancing three things as I sat and talked to my staff and commanders. First was the operation itself. We had a good sense of the risks involved, but there is a qualitative difference in risk when the task is to fly U.S. servicemembers hundreds of miles into enemy-controlled territory, as opposed to a strike with an uncrewed platform. Second, there was the possibility of Russian, Syrian, or Turkish interference in the operation. We would try to minimize this by prior notification and also by our routing. As a last resort, we had a large and capable package of fighter aircraft that would be orbiting over western Iraq, ready to be ordered in as top cover should it be necessary. I hoped that it wouldn't, but it was always safer to be ready. Finally, the situation at Deir ez-Zor had within it the potential seed of escalation—and disaster. Underlying these essentially tactical concerns were the big-picture things that concerned me as the theater commander—what would be the impact across the region if we were successful? Would we see a paroxysm of violence from ISIS? If we did have an incident with Syrian or Russian forces, could we contain it?

At a little after two o'clock in the afternoon, we closed all of the assault force at the Kobani landing zone. At that location, they were 160 kilometers from the objective. It was already dark in Iraq and Syria by this time, and I knew that while the helicopters were refueling, the assault force would be rechecking their gear and equipment. I knew that the EUCOM commander, my good friend Air Force Gen. Tod Wolters, was calling the Turkish chief of defense about an hour later, and he reported that the call went well. I did not expect the Turks to interfere with us, but they had a lot of air defense assets on their southern border and aircraft airborne as well. We were flying very close to some of their radars. Also, at about this time, we gained final confirmation that Baghdadi was present at our objective.

At 3:30, we received some concerning news. The Russians told us that any U.S. military movement into Russian- or Syrian-controlled airspace would be a direct violation of our agreements. This was worrisome. I reached out to my air component commander, Lieutenant General Guastella, and we quickly reviewed again what we thought the Russians or Syrians could do. Nothing had changed in our assessment. The routing and operational techniques that would be employed by the raid force would make it extremely hard for anyone to see them, and it was even less likely that they would be able to take any kind of action against the helicopters. I talked to the JSOTF commander again, ensuring I knew what their minimum MQ-9 requirements were. I agreed with his minimum requirement; it was my decision now. I had taken counsel of my key commanders, but it was time to tell the chairman and the secretary what I wanted to do.

I called them back. "We should continue," I told them. "We will watch them carefully. Any action will be a clear signal of Russian intent." My thinking was that if the Russians engaged the MQ-9s, then we knew they were not bluffing. I also had a jaundiced view of the Russian and Syrian ability to quickly convey decisions from senior leadership to tactical units.

Russia's response might well be completely divorced from actual capabilities, and it could be a knee-jerk reaction to U.S. notification. We'd know soon enough. Continuing the mission was a calculated risk, but it was one we had mitigated by our actions and preparations and by understanding Russian and Syrian capabilities. Most importantly, it was a risk and not a gamble. In the language of the joint force, a risk can be contained and mitigated—there are reasonable options if things go bad. A gamble could have irrecoverable consequences. In my judgment, we weren't gambling—we were taking a calculated risk, and it was one that we had lots of alternative plans for if things didn't go as we had schemed. As part of this mitigation, I also directed Pat White to call his Russian counterpart with the same message, just to ensure that we were not depending on an idiosyncratic Russian/Syrian chain of command to process our request, and to understand what we were doing.

At 3:53 I gave the JSOTF commander the final "go." He then passed delegation for execution down to the tactical commander—the task force commander. At 4:04, the raid force began to lift from Kobani. Time now began to compress, as it always does when an operation moves from concept to execution. All of the decisions we had examined in advance and the choices we had made when we weren't under the unrelenting pressure of time were now coming into the acid test of reality.

Events were now occurring in rapid succession. We were tracking a single Russian fighter airborne at this time; there was no sense that they had gone to a higher alert level or that they were doing anything unusual with their air defense systems. I watched the MQ-9s crawl slowly across the map, heading toward the objective. In the background, the quiet verbal calls of execution checklist items being completed paced the force. Pat White reported that they were unable to get in touch with his counterpart, and the Russians promised a call-back in thirty minutes. We also called the Russian command post from our air operations center, just to backstop the notification process.

I knew that the chairman, the secretary, and the president—among others—were watching the progress of the mission from the White House. It is a simple fact that the ubiquity and excellence of our communications made it possible for the top of the chain of command to have the perception of having a perfect view of execution at the lowest tactical level. As a theater commander, I always avoided listening in to tactical communications. The lowest level I ever took my communications in operations like these was with the task force commander; I knew that he ran a communications architecture down to the tactical level—where the reporting was not always as crisp and clean as at higher levels. I always gave him some time and space to review the immediate reporting and to place it into context. At the tactical level, they're involved in a life-and-death situation, and uncertainty and confusion are always present. It's not a movie or a video game. The image of people watching the execution of the bin Laden strike from the White House had always bothered me. Now, as a commander, I had precisely the same problem. Luckily, Mark Milley was able to work the observers at his level, describing what was happening and largely keeping questions from coming below my level. I was prepared to answer questions—that was a key part of my job—but I wanted to ensure that the folks who were making second-by-second tactical decisions were not saddled with them. It worked well that night. The chairman called me at a little after four o'clock for an update, and then again at 4:50. He was feeding the beast.

About the time I ended the call with the chairman, our MQ-9s had established themselves overhead of our objective. They had not been molested in any way during their—to me—interminable flight south. We knew that the Syrians had picked them up on radar but had apparently made a decision not to engage. We'll probably never know the full story here. The Syrian air defense system was very capable of engaging the MQ-9s. We had seen a consistent pattern, though, with Syrian air defenders: if they knew that retribution was going to fall on them for shooting at something, they either didn't fire, or fired after the strike package had departed, and there was no chance of an actual shootdown. They would then report the expenditure of missiles as a victory.

We now had grainy pictures of the compound. Years of looking at these Predator feeds enabled me to rapidly gain situational awareness; our team would switch from drone to drone based on the quality of the shot, cloud coverage, and what was going on below. This directly fed the awareness of the force going in. At precisely five o'clock the CH-47s appeared in view, landed, and disgorged the force. We could see the escort helicopters scooting across the field of view overhead. Within two minutes, the 47s had lifted and moved to an offset position, where they would refuel. The force immediately took fire from the nearby town of Barisha, and the escorts returned fire immediately. At about 5:10, I spoke to the president and gave him an update: the force was in, we were moving to the objective, and things were advancing according to plan. He wanted to know why the Russians had not been cooperative. The chairman and I told him that it was probably because of the ongoing issue over the bridge down south. He seemed to accept that.

We could now watch our teams move into position on the grainy black-and-white monitors. It was easy to get an illusion of control by looking at everything from on high; the circumstances were very different down on the ground. Even with the aid of night vision goggles, global positioning systems, and good tactical comms, there was still all of the confusion and uncertainty that accompanied fighting at night, in unfamiliar terrain, hundreds of kilometers from any assistance. The individual figures moved inexorably toward their assigned positions.

In just a couple of minutes, the task force reported that they had set containment—we now had security in place to prevent anyone from getting out of the compound and also to prevent anyone from entering. We were still taking fire from the village, but our escort helicopters were working against it. There was no fire from the target compound. Even as we focused on this, the larger reality of the theater intruded: the Russian Su-35 was still airborne and was loitering over Manbij, considerably to the east. That night, alone in his cockpit, the Russian pilot had no idea how many people were watching every maneuver of his aircraft, ready to act if he turned toward the raid force. He never did. At the same time, social media began to show reports of an operation where we were—most reporting seemed to think it was the Turks. This made good sense, because of our proximity to the Turkish border.

The compound on the ground had four walls and a single building structure inside it. The walls were of mud and masonry. We had reason to expect an extensive tunnel system, and so our external perimeter was poised to be ready if anyone tried to escape in that manner. The callout then began.

This was a process that we used to ask people inside the compound to come out and surrender themselves. The intent is always to get as many people out before any assault begins. Callouts were made by colloquial Arabic speakers. At about 5:20, this bore fruit. Three adult males came outside and surrendered. At about 5:28, I updated the chairman, secretary, and president on how things were going. We were in good shape. We had overwhelming firepower on the objective, and while we were being probed by disorganized forces from the surrounding villages, we were under no real pressure. Time was on our side, but we were still concerned about the children we knew were inside the compound. The reason we had resisted simply striking this target with a standoff weapon was to preserve the lives of innocents; it was worth a few minutes' delay to try to get them out. It was at this time that we breached the compound walls, and the teams began to work their way toward the interior building. We began to take fire from this structure, which we knew as building 1. In a short, sharp engagement inside the compound, one man and four women rushed at the assault force. When they would not comply with orders to stop, they were shot and killed. At about 5:33, eleven children ran out, and they were bundled away to safety.

Listening to the reporting from the JSOTF, it was obvious that Baghdadi was somewhere inside—or under—building 1. For the next few minutes we listened and watched as the teams on the ground conducted a methodical search of the compound and prepared to gain access to building 1. At 6:16 p.m., charges were detonated against a wall of the structure, in order to blow a hole. At about this time, Baghdadi, crouching in a tunnel underneath the structure and clutching two children, blew himself up with his suicide vest. He had fallen a long way from the declaration of the caliphate back in Mosul in 2013–14. He died the death of a coward, hiding in a small tunnel, with two children. He did not even try to fight the assault force, to try to seek a genuine martyr's death. Contrary to some reports, there was no whimpering or talking from the tunnel before he triggered his vest. He died as he lived, by taking two innocent lives with him. It was an ignominious end to a harsh and evil life. My only regret was for the children that died with him. We had saved eleven, but it just wasn't possible to get to those last two.

I immediately informed the chairman of the suspected detonation. For the next half hour, the team worked to safely gain access into the tunnel underneath the building where we believed his remains to be. This was where Conan, the working dog, proved his worth. At 6:37, I could tell the chairman that the building was secure, and our operators on the ground could see Baghdadi's remains, but it was still difficult to get to them in the partially collapsed tunnel. It's easy to write these words, but it's probably worth the effort to consider just what conditions were like on the ground during this time. Dust and grit were in the air, electrical cables were sparking in the tunnel, and the sound of intermittent gunfire remanded everyone that our stay on the ground was coming to an end, and hostile elements, although unaware of why we were there, were pressing the perimeter. And everywhere, the evidence of violent, catastrophic death. At 7:10, the chairman asked when we'd be able to establish positive identification. We had some ways to do this with field kits, and they were very accurate, but we simply couldn't get into position to employ them quickly. There was also the question of the safety of the raid force. In the information space, most reports—which were now beginning to sharply spark—reported either Russian or Turkish forces on the ground. This was good enough for us as a temporary cover, but we'd want the raid force to be well away before announcing anything. Moreover, all announcements would come from the White House. I know that the pressure on the chairman and secretary was immense to announce something. It was my job to not, under any circumstances, pass this pressure on to the soldiers who were actually doing the job under the most dangerous of conditions. I'd like to think that I fulfilled that role.

In just a few minutes, the news got better. I was able to tell the president, who was now clearly audible from the Situation Room speakers, that we had high confidence of "jackpot." The president asked that we bring as much evidence out as possible—this was easily done, since it was an important part of actions on the objective. By 7:30, I was able to confirm to the president that, based on our biometric testing and visual evidence, we had Baghdadi. We would get enough to be able to further test for evidence when we returned the force to their forward operating base.

This led to my last decision of the night. The extraction went like clockwork; the CH-47s came in, the teams embarked, and within minutes silence returned to the smoky, burning ground west of Barisha. We were unable to extract all of the remains—some of the women killed had been partially buried in the rubble and could not be removed unless we took more risks than I was willing to endorse. I did not want the remains of the compound to become a shrine to Baghdadi. We had planned to finish the destruction of the compound by dropping all of the ordnance carried by the four MQ-9s that were circling overhead: a combination of Hellfire missiles and five-hundred-pound bombs. This had been the JSOTF commander's recommendation. I felt it wasn't enough. Early in the planning process, we had developed a plan to strike the compound with AGM-158A joint attack standoff missiles (JASSMs). These are precision standoff weapons with a one-thousand-pound warhead, accurate to within a few feet of their aimpoints. They could be launched from east of the Euphrates River. As the raid force cleared the objective, heading home, we first attacked the compound with the MQ-9s, and then the F-15Es launched a total of eight JASSMs. After a seventeen-minute flight, they impacted against the compound at 8:29 p.m. The explosions looked like a small nuclear weapon going off. They certainly achieved the desired effect—after they impacted, there was no trace of the compound. It looked like the surface of the moon. The mission would not be complete until we recovered the raid force, and they now extracted back to their staging bases. We tracked them carefully, as well as the slow and vulnerable movement of the MQ-9s. Nobody interfered with any of our movements out of Syria. We continued to watch the single Su-35 that the Russians had airborne; he did not choose to come north to have a look at what was going on. The mission was complete. I looked around the FPOC as we logged in the final execution checklist item that formally recovered the force.

I was very proud of our team. We had done what a theater staff was supposed to do—set the conditions for tactical commanders to execute, absorb the heat and questions from the chain of command, and do the myriad tasks of coordination, from notifying the Russians to ensuring that force protection measures were updated. I could see that Sam Paparo, my

J-3, was tired, and now that the pressure to execute was in the past, all of the feelings and concerns we had ruthlessly suppressed in the moment were now coming back. Our only celebration was to eat pizzas that were delivered to the joint operations center. I think we were all mindful of the fact that while we had ended the career of a particularly odious and evil man, nothing could bring back the lives that he had so cruelly ended. We had demonstrated to the world the long memory and unflinching long reach of U.S. power, and this was at best an unsatisfying end. Regardless, he would kill and rape no more children.

The next morning, the White House announced the results of the raid. The next week, on October 30, I accompanied the secretary and the chairman to Capitol Hill to conduct closed briefings for representatives and senators. Following that, I conducted a press briefing in the Pentagon. The briefing went well, and I was able to share some video of our force's actions on the objective. There were many questions about Conan, and eventually he made an appearance at the White House. He had been slightly injured in the raid but had fully recovered.

5

SOLEIMANI

Take your shot.
—CENTCOM commander to JSOTF commander,
4:40 p.m. EST, January 2, 2020

Qassem Soleimani was a central character in the modern history of U.S.-Iran relations. Over the course of thirty years, he became the most identifiable face of the Islamic Revolutionary Guard Corps (IRGC) and more specifically, the so-called elite Quds Force (QF). Because of his unceasing activity and affinity for the public eye, it was easy to manufacture pseudo-heroic qualities about his persona. He wasn't a character of the scale and gravitas of Adolf Hitler's brilliant general and field marshal Erwin Rommel, but he was certainly a character to be reckoned with, across the divide that separated the United States and Iran. Despite his boundless self-promotion, I always felt he was more akin to Reinhard Heydrich, the cold-blooded SS major general who engineered the mechanics of the Final Solution in Europe and who was killed by Czech patriots parachuted by their British allies into Prague in 1942 in Operation Anthropoid. From his early days to his bloody death, Heydrich was detestable, murderous, and effective. I saw many parallels to Soleimani.

To understand Soleimani, one has to understand what he did as a young man and the Iran-Iraq War. He was born in March 1957 in Kerman province, Iran, and joined the IRGC in 1979. He had little formal military training. When Saddam Hussein launched his invasion of Iran on September 22, 1980, Soleimani went to war. He rose from company commander to division commander while still under thirty years old. He saw a lot of combat and was wounded. Iranian tactics were never very advanced, so it's difficult to quantify if he came out of the war with any specific approach or even an understanding of large-scale modern ground combat. But he did emerge from the war with a belief that the U.S. support for Iraq lost the war for Iran, which only increased his disdain for the United States This period established early versions of the reputation that would cling to him until his death: fearless, controlling, charismatic, and intensely ideologically bound to the revolutionary ethos of the IRGC.

Soleimani became the commander of the Quds Force in 1997 or 1998. The force, founded in 1990, is a unique part of the Iranian order of battle, and he was the indispensable man in its development. His two decades at the helm and his natural charisma and fluent Arabic made his personal connections key in building relations with Shia Arabs and helped fulfill the larger goals of the Iranian revolution as envisioned by Ayatollah Ruhollah Khomeini. The QF "is Iran's primary means for conducting unconventional operations abroad, with connections of varying degrees to state and nonstate actors globally."[1] An elite group within the already "elite" IRGC and with a current strength of around five thousand, it has steadily absorbed responsibilities from other Iranian entities for covert operations and unconventional operations, both in the Middle East and globally.[2] Two things further distinguish the IRGC-QF. First, the commander of the QF typically has a direct line to the supreme leader, a line of communication that effectively bypasses the Supreme Council for National Security and the Armed Forces General Staff (AFGS). In many cases, even the commander of the Revolutionary Guard—the nominal officer in the chain of command immediately above the QF commander—is on the outside looking in. Second, in the chaos that is Iran's economy, the QF operates a variety of businesses with worldwide reach. While many of these have been sanctioned over the years, they still provide a significant revenue stream that supplements state funding.

These complex relationships led to endless bureaucratic maneuvering between the AFGS and the IRGC-QF, and also tension with the Ministry of Intelligence and Security (MOIS) when it came to external missions. In all of these struggles, Soleimani became increasingly effective, and he also assiduously developed the relationship he had with the supreme leader to the point where it could reasonably be called familial—a father-son relationship. He was largely unknown to the Iranian populace until 2014, when he fashioned himself as the savior of Iraq and Iran from Sunni extremists. I vividly recall his calculations early where he shifted his stance from opposing the return of U.S. forces to allowing the United States to do the heavy lifting of defeating ISIS, with him positioning Iran to benefit from our effort and then to drive us out of Iraq after the defeat of ISIS. It was a brilliant strategy, and we had no effective answer. His ego grew after 2014 and he became a hero in Iran. He made the cover of *The Economist*, and Dexter Filkins wrote a long, fawning *New Yorker* piece that made him a household name. Perhaps apocryphal, there was a recurring story about a senior official in the Barack Obama administration plaintively asking an intel briefer, "Can't you find a picture of him where he doesn't look like George Clooney?"

Soleimani became the key node for coordination of malign activities across the region. His penchant for micromanagement became more pronounced as he grew in seniority, access, and experience. This allowed him to act very quickly and decisively, without the need to coordinate with other Iranian intelligence entities (the MOIS), the conventional military (the AFGS), and even the larger IRGC when it suited his purposes. He worked steadily in Iraq, Syria, and Lebanon, but we could also see evidence of his touch in Yemen and Afghanistan. He was promoted to major general in 2011. He also grew increasingly dictatorial and relaxed about his personal security. In his mind, at least, he was untouchable. His ego grew enormously with his international fame, and he grew cocky, believing the United States would never target him. In 2019 he was quoted as disdainfully saying, "What are they going to do, kill me?"

During my first stint at U.S. Central Command in 2010–12, serving as the J-5 (director of strategy and plans), we looked hard at his activities, and on many occasions asked ourselves what the effect would be if he were out of play. During this period, General Mattis was interested in establishing a military-to-military channel with Iran. As his planner and strategist, I fully supported this initiative. It was dismissively received by the Obama administration. We often joked about using the deputy commander, Vice Adm. Bob Harward, as the U.S. interlocuter for this mission. Harward was a SEAL with a well-deserved reputation for controlled ferocity and intellectual depth. He had attended high school in Tehran in the 1970s and spoke Farsi. Sub rosa, we joked that Bob could kill Soleimani during the meeting, if certain conditions were met. This never went beyond idle speculation, but it does reflect the enduring interest CENTCOM had in Soleimani over the years. During this period, the first Obama administration, there was little appetite for pursuing him, even when it was evident that he was responsible for the deaths of hundreds of U.S. servicemembers in Iraq. Israel had at least as much reason to go after him, but they were never able to align military opportunity and political will. I never forgot our clumsy machinations and tortured debates on this subject in the interagency process, while Soleimani turned inside our deliberations and continued efficiently to kill U.S. and coalition servicemembers, as well as innocent Iraqis and Syrians.

Beginning in 2015, as the Joint Staff J-5 and later as the director of the Joint Staff, I continued my study of Soleimani. My interest in his removal from the battlefield became a running joke with the Joint Staff's Iran analysts. I was recently reminded that I asked about his activities and the effect of removing him from the fight during every Iran brief I received while on the Joint Staff. I once said, "He's a good commander who goes forward to the FEBA [forward edge of the battle area]. Things can happen in combat." I always posed the question as less focused on the act of removing him than the effect it would have on Iranian policy. No one thought we would ever do it, and therefore they never gave me a satisfactory answer to Iran's likely reaction to my hypothetical question.

One of my first acts after assuming command in March 2019 was to talk to the JSOTF commander within CENTCOM and to ask if we held any plans to strike Soleimani, should we be directed to do so. The answer was unsatisfying. Soleimani moved around the Middle East frequently, typically on civilian airlines, leaving his home in Tehran and then flying to Baghdad, Damascus, Beirut, and other locations. We could track him through human intelligence and other technical means. We were far from a "fix" solution. I directed the JSOTF commander to put additional resources against the problem and to develop some potential solutions, just in case we were asked to take action. Other organizations were interested in him as well—our CIA and other regional partners. We were guided by presidential decisions, and these regional partners had some of the same restraints, as well as a lack of operational reach into many of the areas he frequented. We saw some evidence at CENTCOM that our partners lobbied the White House very hard to take action against him. Several schemes were born, thoroughly debated, and then set aside, either because they were operationally infeasible or the political cost seemed too great. Nonetheless, the hard work eventually grew into options that *could* work—if we had the political direction to act.

I was regularly updated on these options. We refined and rehearsed workable plans to strike Soleimani if directed. As tensions rose during the Iranian proxy war on the United States and our allies in 2019, his profile continued to rise as it became obvious that he was orchestrating these attacks, which exposed his predictability. Frequently, he would fly from Tehran into Baghdad, where he would consult with Shia militants actively planning—and executing—attacks against U.S. and coalition partners in Iraq.

Some important considerations arose from the work we did on this problem in early 2019. While we worked a military track to carry out the operation if directed, our partners in the CIA worked toward their own independent solution. We shared information and ideas. I have seen the relationship between military and intelligence elements be both good and bad; for us, our relationship in 2019 in CENTCOM was the best I ever observed. The operation we executed in October 2019 against Baghdadi brought us even closer together and further strengthened the mutual trust between our two organizations. We both wanted to be able to present workable options for a presidential decision, should it need to be made.

Between May and mid-December 2019, we had received nineteen mortar and rocket attacks against our bases in Iraq. The intensity was growing, and it was obvious that Soleimani was calling the shots, principally through his Khatib Hezbollah networks. Then, during the evening of Friday, December 27, our airbase in Kirkuk, Iraq (known as K-1), received thirty Katyusha rockets. Four U.S. servicemembers were wounded, two Iraqi federal police members were injured, and a U.S. contractor was killed. While other attacks had been intended to annoy or to warn, it was clear that an attack of thirty rockets, launched into a densely populated area of the base, was intended to create mass casualties. This was a game-changer, and it was obvious to me that we would be responding.

Combined Task Force Operation Inherent Resolve, commanded by Lt. Gen. Pat White, USA, had prepared a number of responses that we could employ inside Iraq against the perpetrators of these attacks. Pat White was the commander of the U.S. Army's III Corps, based at Fort Hood, Texas. It serves as the armor reserve for the United States. He was laconic and reserved, with a dry sense of humor and a brilliant intellect. I thought very highly of him. I knew that his soldiers viewed him with great respect. Despite the fact that he came from the "heavy" side of the Army, he had spent plenty of time in Iraq and knew the ins and outs of that complex battlespace. The fact that I had attended the Armor Advanced Course at Fort Knox as a captain was a common thread that drew us together. Pat had that remarkable quality in a senior leader—the ability to see beyond the immediate and to create opportunities beyond the next battle or engagement. I trusted him unreservedly. We spoke at least every other day and sometimes more frequently.

As always, we sought to inflict precision effects while minimizing collateral damage. By early morning on Saturday, December 28, Pat's team had presented me with a range of options. These choices weren't new to us—we had been working on them for months. I preferred an option designed to balance pain for Khatib Hezbollah against the risk of killing innocent people. The strikes would all be delivered by manned aircraft. It's important to emphasize that this was all a continuous process of anticipatory contingency planning—authority to execute these strikes could only come from the president through the secretary of defense.

During this period, I worked from my quarters at MacDill Air Force Base. My office in my house was a large wood-lined study, with bookcases that ran from the floor to the ceiling. I have always liked to work surrounded by books, so my bookcases were double-stacked, and there were stacks of books in most corners and along the floor. Working from my home office proved to be a great advantage in those compressed and hectic days of late December and early January. This office provided similar secure capabilities as my office in the headquarters. Holding meetings in my home also contributed to operations security. It was always good at CENTCOM, but we were now talking about operations of exquisite sensitivity.

CENTCOM's key staff officers crowded into my home office early in the morning of December 28. We had to pull chairs from the formal dining room across the foyer to ensure that everyone had a seat. I sensed we were on the verge of momentous decisions, and these were the men and women who would craft the CENTCOM position. I had worked with many staffs over my career; the relationship between the commander and his or her staff is the basis for how any headquarters works—or doesn't. My experience as a commander and a staff officer had led me to seek a collegial relationship with my primary staff officers. They needed to feel that they could talk to me, whether they were giving good news or bad news, and have no fear that I would "shoot the messenger." The worst thing a commander could do was to be approachable and open when things were going well and then turn into a snarling, vicious screamer when things turned bad. I had seen commanders do this on occasion and had been on the receiving end of a few of these explosions.

At every level I commanded, from lieutenant colonel through lieutenant general, and now as a theater commander, I had worked hard to be consistent and steady in how I absorbed information. Over the years, I found that this wasn't something you could prescribe, dictate, or proclaim: it had to be practiced. You cannot sell yourself with words alone to bright, highly competent, experienced military officers. You actually have to demonstrate it in an unfailing manner, and any deviation, however small, will cause subordinates to withdraw. I wanted to avoid withdrawal, because I found that when subordinates are concerned about what they say to the commander, information, nuance, and trust are lost. I wanted the people in my study that morning to feel free to express opinions without concern for what my reaction would be. We had worked together for eight months and had weathered a number of coalescing events, including the raid on Baghdadi, so I had great confidence that the team was strong and had mutual trust.

Sam Paparo brought with him a three-foot-by-four-foot hardboard backed map of the CENTCOM theater, and he had outlined some options for consideration. We knew that we were going to be called upon to provide options to respond to the K-1 attacks. Sam had outlined some strikes in Iraq, which we knew Pat White was working. We focused more on broader theater options. We had a target in Yemen that we had been looking at for some time. The target was a key IRGC coordinator working with the Houthis to improve their missile systems and continue their attacks into Saudi Arabia. He had a long and bloody history of operations against U.S. and coalition forces. We also looked at options against an intelligence collection ship manned by the IRGC in the southern Red Sea, the *Saviz*. We knew that she collected against us as our ships passed in the Red Sea and in all our operations in Yemen and from Djibouti. We had a variety of ways to strike her, with a broad spectrum of damage—from disabling to sinking. We also had options against infrastructure in southern Iran, to include air defense and oil infrastructure. We debated all of these options thoroughly. None of them was new to us—these were strike packages that we had been refining for many months.

While I did not minimize the significance of the K-1 attack, I did not see the utility in broadening the conflict by a response outside of Iraq and Syria, and after I had heard all options thoroughly debated, I told my staff what my decision was: we would go forward with the options inside Iraq and Syria that Pat White was working on. There were four logistics targets and three personality targets that we felt were associated with the attack. Two of the personalities were Khatib Hezbollah facilitators; the third was Qassem Soleimani. The personality targets weren't being worked by Pat White's team; they would be addressed by our JSOTF if necessary. We would also forward but not recommend action on the Yemen, Red Sea, and metropolitan Iran options.

Even as this process played itself out on a sunny Saturday morning in Tampa, I was fielding calls from Mark Milley. He had asked about response options in the immediate aftermath of the attack on our base, and we talked frequently about developing them over the course of the day. I have an enduring memory of talking to him, leaning against the bookcases along the back wall of my office, while my staff quietly worked coordination in the small space available to us. By mid-morning on Saturday, I had sent the recommended options to the secretary through the chairman. As previously noted, all of my recommendations were against militant group targets in Iraq and Syria. Our shorthand for these disparate groups was SMG, or Shia militant groups. By late afternoon on Saturday, we received approval to execute my preferred option: striking a variety of Khatib Hezbollah targets in Iraq and Syria, all with manned aircraft, but with no execution against the personality targets. We would strike at about 11 a.m. Eastern Standard Time (EST) on Sunday, December 29. I immediately passed the word to Pat White in Iraq and also to my air component commander, Gus Guastella. We followed up with the detailed taskings.

I knew that the chairman and the secretary were going to see the president at Mar-a-Lago on Sunday to brief the results of our strikes. I had a sense—derived from talking to the chairman—that the strikes we were executing against Khatib Hezbollah targets before that meeting might not be seen as enough. I knew how those meetings would work—I'd been in a few of them. It was important that the military equities be openly discussed and the risk assessed. Then we waited. I had complete confidence in Mark Milley—I knew that he would be able, like Joe Dunford, to hold his own in the rough-and-tumble of a presidential briefing, one that could feature lots of opinions from lots of people, not all of whom were fully knowledgeable about the risks we were going to run during the operation and those that would emerge after the operation was completed. While the immediate actions we were undertaking did not include Soleimani, I knew that the president remained very interested in striking him.

Because of these concerns, on Saturday evening I sat down alone and put my final personal edits on a paper I'd asked my intelligence officer to prepare—a paper that outlined what could happen if we chose to strike Soleimani. I remained extremely concerned about what could follow a successful strike. There was no question that he was a valid target, and his loss would introduce friction into Iranian decision-making. It would also be a strong indication of U.S. will—a will that had been absent in our dealings with Iran for many years. But what would the Iranian response be? It was possible that we could achieve a deterring effect with the strike; it was also possible that we could trigger a massive Iranian response. In balance, and after careful consideration, I believed that they would respond, but probably not with outright war. This was the question I had been worrying with for several years. They still had lots of alternatives to cause us pain. I sent the paper to the secretary, routed through the chairman. I did not recommend against striking Soleimani—I merely captured the risks attendant to taking the action. When it was all said and done, in the end I supported the decision to take the strike. Today, I still think it was the right call. In the long run, lives were saved by this action.

On Sunday morning I was up early. Bringing the staff back to my house at seven o'clock, I had Pat White give a final confirmation brief to me in my study. During this session Pat mentioned firing warning shots on the two targets in Iraq. Our intelligence could not confirm who was in there, and Pat said he did not want to risk killing Iranians or Russians. I was uneasy with this decision. Pat said, "Messaging is the most important thing, it does not matter what we blow up." I took this on board, thought for a few seconds, and then said, "For the future, I'm not doing this for messaging. The best message is to kill them. But I'm not going to second-guess you."

Right after that video conference, I asked David Crist for his opinion. He said that he did not like the warning shots. I responded, "It looks feckless." I wasn't satisfied about that particular decision, but I did not want to override my field commander so close to "crossing the line of departure." To this day, I believe that when the chairman briefed the president about this later in the day, Trump became agitated: his generals were being "soft" again. This contributed to the decision to strike Soleimani, the Quds Force Yemen commander, and the *Saviz*.

At 8:30 I had a conference call with the chairman and the secretary. I updated them on the five targets. There was a lot of discussion about when to notify the Iraqi prime minister, working with the country team, and expanding the target set beyond Khatib Hezbollah to include QF in Iraq. Secretary Esper asked several questions about the surface-to-air missile sites as follow-on targets. I said that we did not expect an immediate reaction by the SMGs to the U.S. strike—but they would eventually respond. Under Secretary for Policy John Rood raised concerns about losing the coalition against ISIS by expanding the targets against the QF in Iraq. At 9:25 the chairman and I talked again, and we discussed flowing additional forces into the theater. I was now looking hard at the likely Iranian reaction to our strikes, and I argued that we were not prepared for their counterattack, should it be substantive.

Planning and final preparations proceeded smoothly for the Sunday strikes against the Khatib Hezbollah targets. It was my practice as the theater commander to stay out of detailed planning for these operations. I had complete confidence in my commanders and their teams, and frequent insertion of an eight-thousand-mile screwdriver wasn't helpful. We flew the Khatib Hezbollah strikes on Sunday afternoon with good results. We struck five sites, ranging from targets near Abu Kamal in Syria to Al Qaim, Iraq. We employed precision weapons from manned aircraft, hitting all targets within about a four-minute span. In at least one location, we struck during a Khatib Hezbollah staff meeting and garnered the unintended benefit of removing some key leaders from their positions.

The job of a theater commander during operations like these is less to manage the minute-by-minute press of tactical decisions than to look ahead. Throughout the day, I worked with my staff to refine further options and choices that we could present, taking into account the inevitable Iranian response. We had some good choices—they needed to be scoped against policy goals, which would need to come from the president and the secretary. After the strike, as the secretary and the chairman flew to Mar-a-Lago, we were kept busy in the headquarters answering questions to prepare them for the upcoming session. We provided them with damage assessments and any other atmospherics we could gather from the attacks. We put together a simple one-slide brief that the chairman used to brief the president. Our slide did note that we had used warning shots against some of the targets.

At about 6:30 p.m. on Sunday, December 29, the chairman called with the results of the presidential meeting. After a discussion of the recently completed strikes against Khatib Hezbollah, which the president thought weren't robust enough, he told me matter-of-factly that we were to strike Soleimani in Iraq if he came there. I was standing in my home office when he said this, holding the phone, and looking at CNN. It was early evening and already dark outside. Motes of dust were casually circling in the light and dark divides in the warmth of the office. It's one of those moments that you tend to remember. As usual, I was making notes of our conversation, and I froze for perhaps a second or two and asked him to repeat himself. My staff were all around me, crammed into my home office, but I didn't have the phone on speaker, so nobody else could hear. He also told me that the president had approved strikes on the Quds Force commander in Yemen and also an attack on the Motor Vessel *Saviz*, the 14,000-ton tramp freighter that the Iranians kept at anchor just off the shipping lanes in the southern Red Sea. She was manned by QF signals intelligence personnel and had been a thorn in our side for years. He also relayed that there was a sense—at least with Secretary of State Mike Pompeo and National Security Advisor Robert O'Brien—that a strike against these targets would bring them back to the bargaining table. I could tell that the chairman did not agree with this position—and neither did I.

As we ended our call, I read back to the chairman what we'd been told to do—a product of a lifetime of receiving orders under stressful conditions. He told me he would get written orders to us immediately. I didn't need to ask for him to do this: we were both professionals, and we both knew that orders needed to be in writing. At a moment like this, personal emotions aren't useful. There was much to do, and little time to accomplish it. I called the few members of my staff who weren't already on hand in for a 7 p.m. meeting. I began by telling them that, as I suspected, the strike was viewed as not robust enough. Everyone's head snapped back just a little when I said we were going to strike Soleimani, the QF commander in Yemen, and the *Saviz*. I could tell that my words had a powerful effect on my staff. We all knew what could come from these decisions, and I know that all of us were aware of our friends on the other side of the world who would now be going into the fire. We didn't dwell on it—all of us were veterans of many years at CENTCOM, and we were used to hard decisions.

I was irritated at myself for not following my instincts and changing the warning shots—I knew at the time that it would anger the president. To this day, I believe that our misguided attempt to lessen the application of force in the initial strikes on Khatib Hezbollah led us to the strike on Soleimani. I bear some responsibility for not correcting that error. This is more a criticism of the way the decision was made, though, than the basic decision itself. It was clear that Soleimani was coordinating the rising tide of attacks against us in Iraq. It was also clear that this trip to Iraq was intended to further refine and execute attacks against our forces. At the time, I supported the decision to strike him, and I have seen nothing since that time to cause me to revisit the decision.

I never saw a "smoking gun" where Soleimani was physically complicit in the execution of attacks against our embassy, but I was certainly convinced by the evidence that he was the orchestrator of these attacks. With the passage of time and the opportunity to reflect without the urgent pressure of events, I am even more convinced that Soleimani was involved in attack planning, and had he not been stopped, more U.S., coalition, and Iraqi lives would have been lost as the direct result of his leadership. I believe the attacks were very possibly going to happen in the immediate future. He wasn't going to undertake them himself, but they would inevitably follow his trip into Iraq. It was a choice between inaction and action in this case. For me, the risks of inaction were greater than the risks of action.

The orders we now had were a significant change from past practice—the Khatib Hezbollah strikes in Iraq that had just been completed—but now we would turn to Soleimani and Yemen, as well as the *Saviz*. I knew that we had good target solutions on the commander in Yemen and the *Saviz* that we could execute quickly. I needed to talk to our JSOTF commander about Soleimani to see where we were—he presented a dynamic and ever-changing target set. This was when all of the prior planning became very valuable. In the late fall, we had developed options to strike Soleimani in Syria and in Iraq. We preferred Syria, because it was evident that a strike against him in Iraq would inflame the Shia militant groups, possibly resulting in a strong military and political backlash against us. For these reasons, we had always argued against Iraq. It now looked like those objections, which I knew the chairman shared, would be overridden.

I was confident that Soleimani was a legal target. The president had authority under Article II of the Constitution; he also had authority under the 2002 Authorization for the Use of Military Force. From my extensive time on the Joint Staff, I knew that there were other interpretations of these authorities, but my advisors judged the president had the authority to order a strike on Soleimani.

A *New Yorker* article penned shortly after the strike asserted that Central Command was taken aback by the orders that we received and had to feverishly cobble plans together.[3] That assertion was incorrect. We had been working plans for all these contingencies for months and, in some cases, for years. It's hard to surprise a large military headquarters with new ideas in areas like this. I had a large, capable stable of planners who did nothing but look at and refine base plans—ideas we had in the headquarters, or ideas that we derived or inferred from higher headquarters tasking. We then looked at sequels—what happens after the plan becomes an order and things actually happen, generally in accordance with the vision of the plan. We spent most of our time, however, on branches—what happens if the plan doesn't work exactly as designed. Most plans don't work as advertised, and the ability to change to meet new circumstances is the heart of what we called the operational art. I felt that we were masters of this at CENTCOM.

There were three steps in the kind of targeting we were now pursuing. First was finding the target. This process started from broad generalities and patterns that over time became narrower and narrower. Second, fixing the target required that we translate all of the movement, pattern of life activities, and other information into a narrow window of time, space, and opportunity. Finding was a quantitative, scientific activity. Fixing was an art. Finally, finishing was the kinetic application of a weapon against the target, consistent with collateral damage concerns and the law of armed conflict. This too was an art. The Soleimani fix and finish work had come a long way since I first asked the question, back in the late spring of 2019. When he arrived in Iraq, he typically landed at Baghdad International Airport. Not unlike a visiting U.S. delegation, he would be greeted and transported quickly away. We had good visibility that lasted until he left the large airport reservation and entered the crowded streets of Baghdad. We began to lose the fix part of the equation then. This was the great virtue of the road structure at Baghdad International Airport—unlike in the city, there were few other vehicles. Generations of soldiers, airmen, and Marines serving in Baghdad knew this road as route Irish. Ironically, quite a few U.S. and coalition servicemembers had died on Irish as a direct result of the actions of Soleimani and his henchmen.

We felt that if we could strike Soleimani on the airport access road, moments after deplaning, we could both minimize collateral damage and ensure maximum effect. We had MQ-9s armed with variants of Hellfire missiles that would be used to strike his vehicle and that of his security escort as well. As always, there were significant constraints—the MQ-9s could not stay in orbit above the airport endlessly, so we had to have a good idea of when he might arrive. The weather would have to be good, so that we could get the visibility needed for a good shot. Ultimately, we had useful information that Soleimani would possibly fly from Tehran to Baghdad on Tuesday, December 31. The information looked good enough to act on. By late in the evening of December 29, we had a good idea of how we wanted to sequence the strikes. As always, our preference was to execute at night, although we knew our opportunities would be driven by his schedule. After much discussion, we decided to strike Soleimani first and then the commander in Yemen within minutes so that he could not be warned. We would save the *Saviz* for later. I wasn't eager to sink the *Saviz* unless we had to. We had a plan to warn the crew of fifty or so Iranians before attacking the ship, but I was worried that they might refuse to abandon ship, creating a new set of martyrs.

Meanwhile, other factors began to play a role. After the successful Khatib Hezbollah strikes, protests began to develop at our embassy in Baghdad. I ordered the Marines of the special purpose Marine air ground task force into Iraq to reinforce the embassy. Throughout December 30, I was on the phone frequently with the chairman. The images from the embassy were disturbing, but I had great confidence in our security force. It's my sense that these images hardened the desire in Washington to carry out the strike on Soleimani. Also, there were repeated questions about our ability to execute the strikes, maintain security, and carry out all of the other things we'd need to do. Finally, I had a direct conversation with the chairman, where I said, "I understand the president's order and we are prepared to execute."

Working with the chargé (the ambassador was out of the country), Pat and his team moved to reinforce the embassy with Marines. We also worked out various show of force options that we could employ if the situation became critical. It's important to understand that in all cases, the host country—Iraq—is solely responsible for security of all diplomats and diplomatic property in their country. We communicated this across all levels to the Iraqi government. Their response was anemic. The penetration of the Iraqi government by pro-Iranian elements was part of this, and there was also genuine anger at what the Iraqis saw as a violation of their sovereignty with the Khatib Hezbollah strikes. Finally, the inevitable and endless incompetence and lethargy of action that surrounded all Iraqi government actions were contributing factors. It was a bubbling cauldron that gave the Shia militant groups the opportunity to gather hundreds of decidedly violent protesters around the embassy.

The Iraqi government was nowhere to be seen, and Pat White could not establish communications with his contacts. The specter of a Benghazi-like episode underlined everything we did. We got the Marines in, landing MV-22 Ospreys directly in the embassy compound. We put AH-64 gunships overhead in a show of force, popping their flares in a light show that announced their presence and capabilities. As I watched these activities, I was increasingly worried about what could happen after we struck Soleimani. Would it spur the crowd to attempt to overrun the embassy? What would our relationship with the government of Iraq be like in the wake of an attack? More dangerous, what would be the reaction of Iran? I sensed that the National Security Council—the corporate body of the secretaries of state and defense, and the national security advisor—was operating under a common assumption that Iran would not retaliate against the United States. Even the chairman told me, "The Shia militant groups will go apeshit, but I don't think Iran will do anything directly against us." This view hardened the decision to strike Soleimani. I felt it was a bad assumption by Washington and one with which I did not agree. I remained convinced that Iran would overtly respond to a strike on Soleimani. Again, I didn't disagree with the decision to strike him, and in fact I supported it, but I felt that we needed to be prepared for the most dangerous course of action, not the one that was easiest for us to react to. To his great credit, the chairman understood my arguments and was a tireless advocate for increasing force posture in CENTCOM as our plan moved forward. Somehow, we got through December 30.

I was in the headquarters early on December 31 for what promised to be a very important day. The morning wore on for us while we waited for signs of Soleimani's movement. For evolutions like this, I was typically in my joint operations center (JOC). At peak operations, it would be full, with all workstations manned, and many times with observers pressed against the back wall. Unfortunately, the JOC was undergoing a major upgrade. It did not impact operations, thanks to Sam Paparo's tireless energy, but it did require creative workarounds. There were no observers in the smaller rooms. All of these spaces were equipped with secure communications. These rooms were typically quiet, broken only by the battle captain with announcements that would go something like: "Attention in the JOC: Line 107." Everyone in the JOC had either on paper or displayed electronically the execution checklist for any operations. You could see heads go down as folks looked up the entry. This checklist captured all of the key tasks that would have to be accomplished to complete the operation. Our progression though the lines of the checklist was the best indicator of how an operation was proceeding. (See map 4.)

That morning, I again worked from the focal point operations center. We had two huge monitors up on the far wall. One showed a rotating series of MQ-9 images—black and white, with digital ranges and other targeting data superimposed. The other monitor showed the air picture in the theater, scoped to cover both Iran and Iraq. Hundreds of airplanes, including civilian airliners, at all levels flowed across the screen. We could quickly select any small crawling airplane symbol and get detailed data on the type of aircraft, altitude, heading, and other pertinent information. This was fed by a combination of our sensors and publicly available airline tracking systems. Feeding much of this were our ever-vigilant airborne warning and control system aircraft, old E-3s, modified 707s with large rotating radars mounted on top of the fuselage.

As I sat at the head of the large table, which was covered with monitors, phones, and snaking comm cables, I was accompanied by the same folks who had been meeting in my home office. Always close at hand were my lawyer and my public affairs officer—monitoring the information environment was critical. A little farther away were the intelligence analysts whispering into their phones and headsets, communing with the vast intelligence enterprise that supported us. When they had something to give me, they would walk over and whisper in my ear. Sometimes, the information was so sensitive that we had to retreat into another room for the report. Every few minutes

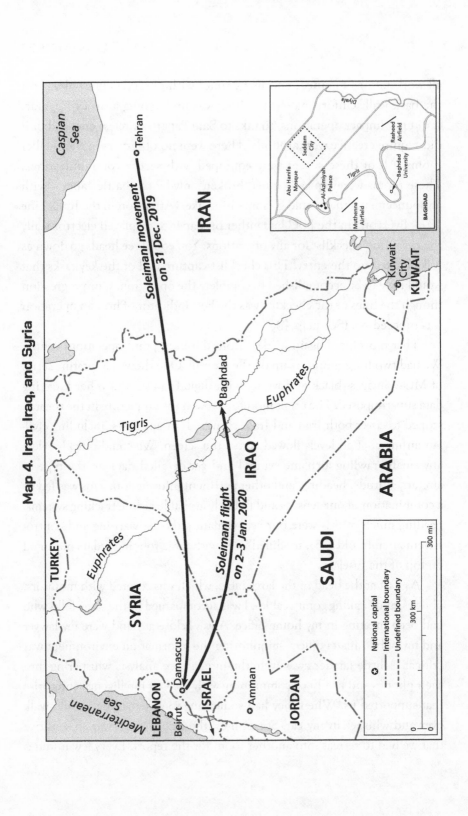

Map 4. Iran, Iraq, and Syria

or so I spoke to the chairman and the secretary, who were monitoring the situation from the National Military Command Center (NMCC) in the Pentagon. Between calls, I talked quietly with Tom Bergeson, Scott McKean, Sam Paparo, and Dave Crist.

Thinking about this gave what we were doing a very human element. Soleimani finally left home and boarded his plane in Tehran. The jet took off at about 9:45 a.m. EST for a two-hour flight to Baghdad. We were set for him there: our uncrewed aircraft were overhead and in good positions. However, his airplane wasn't beginning its descent into Baghdad. It continued to cruise west at over 30,000 feet. I was in an open conference call with the chairman and the secretary, fielding lots of questions from them as we watched the plane crawl westward, passing Baghdad. Someone in the bridge from the Pentagon asked me, "Can you shoot this fucker down?" Without deciding to actually execute this request, I called my air component commander, sitting on the other side of the world in our combined air operations center at Al Udeid Airbase in Qatar. "What have we got airborne over western Iraq right now? If I give you an order to shoot this aircraft down, can you make it work?" As always, the Air Force responded quickly and efficiently, and we moved two fighters into a trail position behind the jet. I emphasized to the Air Force that I didn't want the fighters to be seen by the jet we were tracking. We now had an option in hand to finish the mission if we were told to do so. We could use either cannon or air-to-air missiles if needed. At the same time, we worked feverishly to determine if the jet was a charter jet or a commercial flight.

While I worked these issues, conferring frequently with the chairman and, through him, with the secretary, it became increasingly apparent that the flight was headed to Damascus, not Baghdad. We also learned that the jet was a much-delayed civilian flight. There were probably at least fifty innocent people on board. Upon learning this, I told the chairman that I recommended that we not consider shooting it down. Remembering the USS *Vincennes* incident from 1988, I told the chairman that "the U.S. record of shooting down Iranian airliners is not that good." Not even Soleimani was worth that loss of life. He and I quickly agreed that we would not engage. Our fighters rolled off. The jet began its descent into Damascus. We all took a deep breath and reconsidered our options. I sat back and thought for just a moment, collecting my thoughts. Turning to the open bridge, at 10:48 EST I told the staff and commanders, "Guidance from the president remains. We are going to exercise tactical patience. We're going to take a shot when we have a shot."

At this time, we also pulled back our aircraft from the mission down in Yemen. It now seemed likely that we were looking at a twenty-four- to thirty-six-hour delay, based on Soleimani's historical travel patterns. There were indications that Soleimani would travel from Damascus back to Baghdad, so we would still have an opportunity. We felt we'd have enough warning before his next travel, so that we'd be able to get the MQ-9s back into position over Baghdad. The finish solution was still a good one. Once again, timing would be crucial.

The delay was actually helpful from a purely military point of view, since it gave us the opportunity to further reposition and harden our force posture in Iraq. Pat White and I had been talking about the inevitable Iranian response to a successful strike on Soleimani. Because of our compartmented approach to this operation, I didn't fully "read him in" until about twenty-four hours before the first strike window on Soleimani. Our five-thousand-plus people in Iraq were not there as purely combat forces. They advised and assisted the Iraqi military and security structure. To do this, they had to move around the city and expose themselves. We didn't have lots of infantry. Pat had a good plan to draw back into our bases and to assume a defensive crouch.

New Year's Day—Wednesday, January 1—came. I had an obligation in Tampa to attend and deliver the game ball for the Outback Bowl. It was a lovely, nearly cloudless day, and temperatures were in the eighties. Kickoff was at 1:00, and I took my communications team, as well as my security folks, out to the game. My family also joined Marilyn and me for the game. As always, the people of Tampa put on a great, welcoming show, and the game went well—if you were cheering for Minnesota. We were among the Auburn faithful, so it was a long afternoon. We did have the opportunity to sit in a suite, which was helpful, because right before halftime I received a call from the secretary and spent the next ninety minutes in an extended phone conference with him, his staff, and the chairman. I took the call crouched in the suite's bathroom, talking on a secure handset. My communications assistant was on the other side of the door, holding the WiFi hotspot in the air to ensure a good connection. I could hear the crowd noise rise and fall, while I tried to stay focused on the extended debate, which is hard to do on a small secure device that we call a DMCC, which stands for "DoD Mobility Classified Capability."

In the conference, I briefed the secretary that we felt that Soleimani would leave Damascus, perhaps as early as Thursday, January 2, and, if he kept to his prior pattern, he would fly to Baghdad before going back to Tehran. I told the secretary that we still had good, solid options on Soleimani and the Yemen commander. During this conversation, we agreed to hold off on sinking the *Saviz* until we knew the results of—and reaction to—the two strikes we were contemplating. We also discussed the state of protests around the U.S. embassy. They remained concerning, but I felt that we had adequate combat power to defend the compound against any possible threat. We went around the horn, and the order to strike Soleimani and the commander in Yemen was confirmed by the secretary. I got back in time to watch the end of a very disappointing Outback Bowl.

That evening in my home office, I reviewed our plans again with our JSOTF commander, looking for loose ends or things that could cause friction the next day. There were many variables outside our control, and we all knew this. We did feel, however, that we had a good, robust plan for executing the strike if Soleimani stuck to his schedule. Pat and I separately reviewed our concept for defense in Iraq. There were risks, to be sure, but we felt we had done all we could with the forces available to protect ourselves. Most of my component commanders were not aware of the pending strike. Hard practice had taught us that the more closely we limited knowledge on operations of this type, the greater chance of success. The risk, of course, was that in a theater as large as CENTCOM, leaving a key leader out might lead to a lack of coordination or a preparatory measure not taken. Compartmentalization was an imperfect solution, but the best one we had. All these things weighed on me as I went to sleep the evening of New Year's Day 2020. It was a restless night.

The next day began early with my routine commander's secure video teleconference at 7:15 a.m. in the headquarters. We started with a brief from my key staff—J-2 (intelligence), J-3 (operations), J-4 (logistics), and then through all of the other staff disciplines. The briefing took about an hour. It was a good opportunity to review our defensive set across the theater. Throughout the morning, I was on secure calls with Washington. The chairman was first, and he confirmed that we had a "go" from the president and also said that the president wanted to make a public statement immediately after the attack. Both the chairman and I felt that this was dangerous ground, because we had not consulted with any of our allies in the region. To announce something publicly would be to get out ahead of private diplomacy that we would always prefer to work in matters like this—it's always better to let your friends know something in advance, even if it's just a few minutes.

At 10:22 I spoke again with the chairman, who told me, "I spoke to the president and you've still got a green light." He also mentioned a National Security Council meeting, where the CIA director said, "It's going to be a rough ride so everyone buckle in." This was a sentiment I wholeheartedly agreed with. By mid-afternoon, I was back in the FPOC, where the JSOTF commander presented a final conditions check. We did this through the strike bridge, a large video conference that had been established some hours earlier and connected all of the key players through a visual link at the top secret–special intelligence level. From my end, it looked like a large "Hollywood Squares" grid on the far wall, with twenty or more outstations in the conference. This was a great technique for rapidly passing information and ensuring that everyone knew what was going on. The principal participants in the strike bridge were the JSOTF commander and me. By simply pressing a button in front of me, I could speak to him directly and to everyone on the bridge. If I needed a point-to-point call, I had a yellow top secret phone at hand, and when I picked it up, he would answer on the other end. This phone was also my primary means of communication with the chairman and the secretary. We finished our condition check and were "green" on everything. The only worry was building overcast in the Baghdad area, which would prevent our MQ-9s from operating directly overhead. In order to stay below the cloud deck, they would need to offset some distance away, for if they were too low directly overhead, they could be heard and seen. There were also fuel limitations on the MQ-9s. If things were delayed too long, we wouldn't be able to keep them on station.

By late afternoon, tension began to build. We believed—pretty strongly—Soleimani would be on the flight from Damascus to Baghdad, but he had not yet boarded. The flight was delayed an hour, and then again. During times like this, my habit was to sit quietly at the head of the table, talking occasionally to the JSOTF commander, my J-2 and J-3, or to Pat White in Iraq, and drinking endless amounts of coffee. All of my computers were at my station, so I could also review my emails and catch up on routine correspondence. Everyone is looking at the commander in times like these, so I was very much aware of how my calmness—or lack of it—would be transmitted to everyone. Any unease or anxiousness on my part would be felt by all. I had a great team around me, and a great team on the other end of the secure video teleconference with our special operations task force, so I felt that we had good control over those things that were within our reach. There were many things outside of our control, though, and we would need to be ready to flex. These were the branches to the plan. The countless hours that staffs and commanders had put into planning and the development of branches and sequels were now ready to pay off. It's an axiom of these kinds of operations that you have all of the time in the world for careful, thoughtful consideration of alternatives when you're planning, and then no time during execution for detailed exploration of fast-developing alternatives. Time turns against you in these moments; it becomes compressed and precious. You need to rely on the vast work done when time wasn't the most valuable commodity in the universe. I was confident that we were ready. Carl von Clausewitz's observation that "habit breeds that priceless virtue, calm," was particularly apt. At CENTCOM we had a culture—a habit—of calmness in moments of great stress.

Finally, movement! Soleimani was delivered to the airplane in Damascus, boarding from the tarmac as he typically did. The jet backed out and taxied for takeoff. The flight, a regularly scheduled commercial jet, took off from Damascus at 3:30 p.m. EST. We knew the flight time—it was about an hour.

I called the chairman and told him. He and the secretaries of defense and state would watch the action from a secure conference room in the NMCC in the Pentagon. The aircraft soon appeared on our tracking systems, and I watched it crawl east. Remembering our disappointment of a few days before, I kept a close eye on the text box under the icon, which displayed its heading and altitude. It began to lose altitude, and we were able to rapidly confirm that it was headed for Baghdad. The JSOTF commander and I conferred again—all was ready. The weather was a factor, but we could adjust. The MQ-9s had plenty of fuel.

The jet landed at Baghdad 4:35 EST, and all my attention now shifted to the big visual displays, where we were looking at the images from the MQ-9s. They were sometimes grainy, sometimes crystal-clear, in black and white contrast as they worked in and out and around the cloud deck. It was now past midnight in Iraq. The jet taxied up to an arrival area, and we watched as disembarkation stairs were pushed up to the front cabin door. At 4:40, we confirmed that it was Soleimani. At this point, the JSOTF commander called me point-to-point and said, "Sir, things will now happen very quickly. If there's any intent to stop it, we need to make that call now." I had my orders, and I knew the secretary's intent, so I simply told him, "Take your shot when you have it." That was all that passed between us, and this was the only conversation on the strike bridge, except for the calls of line numbers on the execution checklist as they were tripped. We watched Soleimani deplane, be greeted by a group of people, and then get into a car. We didn't know it at that moment in time, but the powerful Shia leader Abu Mahdi al-Muhandis got into the car with him, probably to brief him as they drove to where Soleimani would spend the night. His car and a security vehicle pulled away from the plane and began to negotiate the warren of ramps, parking areas, and streets to get to the access road—what we knew as route Irish. At 4:42 we set the strike posture—we were now simply waiting for the most opportune tactical opportunity. I had long since passed tactical engagement authority to the JSOTF commander, and he had further passed it down to the team that would release the weapons. Hard experience in countless raids and other operations of this nature had taught us that devolving this authority to the lowest possible tactical level as early as possible allowed for those with the best knowledge of the immediate tactical situation to act quickly, without referring back to higher headquarters.

Minutes passed. The loose two-vehicle convoy picked up speed as it pulled away from the airport buildings. There was no conversation on the strike bridge—everybody knew what they were doing, and there was no need for banter or cheerleading. There was no countdown—nothing but silence as the vehicles moved across our field of view. Both vehicles were marked by laser. I remember that I stood up at that time and leaned forward to get the best possible view. It was very quiet in the FPOC—everyone's eyes were glued to the big monitors. Then suddenly, a great flash of white arced across the screen. It was 4:47 p.m. on January 2 in Tampa and 12:47 a.m. on January 3 in Iraq. The car was obscured completely. Parts of the vehicle could be seen rising in the air. The second vehicle was struck a second or two later. The MQ-9s held their targets, and we reattacked a minute later, dropping a total of eight weapons, just to ensure success. There was no cheering, no fist-bumping, just silence in the FPOC and across the strike bridge as we watched the fires. The JSOTF commander and I conferred briefly, and then I called the chairman and the secretary and reported that it looked good, but we would need to assess before declaring "jackpot."

Meanwhile, we had another target to attack, so our attention shifted to Yemen, where we watched a similar strike against an isolated house, which occurred at 5:00 p.m. EST. It also looked good, but we were not as confident about the Quds Force commander's location as we had been about Soleimani's. It would take a little time to determine if we were successful. While it later turned out that we missed him, the timing of the two strikes was a remarkable achievement by our JSOTF and a testimony to their skill and ability. There was no time to try to savor or even deeply consider the significance of what we had just done. We had force protection measures to put into place. I had to tell my component commanders who were not read in about what had just happened. We had friends and partner states in the region that had to be notified. All of this needed to happen in the immediate aftermath of the strike. My staff arranged calls for me, and across the theater, my subordinate commanders worked the phones to bring our friends and partners up to speed on what had just transpired. In the course of the evening in Tampa—and in the early morning hours in the theater—it became apparent that we achieved success against Soleimani. It also became increasingly obvious that we missed our target in Yemen.

I was home by around 9:00 p.m. The first news reports were beginning to appear on CNN and other networks as I sat and talked to Marilyn. It had been a long day. Only now did I have the time to think about what had happened. For me personally, as Marine, it had been profoundly satisfying on a deep, emotional level. Qassem Soleimani had the blood of hundreds of U.S. servicemembers on his hands, and he had been actively plotting to kill more. As the theater commander, the joint force commander, it was more complex and problematical. As a young general in the CENTCOM headquarters, I had watched the Obama administration national security apparatus—and the George W. Bush administration before that—grapple ineptly with the dynamism and leadership that Soleimani brought to the fight. I had also watched the Israelis try their hand against him, with no luck. He had become a central node for Iranian policy execution in the theater. He drew so many skeins into his hands that it was hard to see how he could be effectively replaced. On the operational level, this was probably a good thing for us. It would also signal our will to the Iranians. They had always doubted our ability to take an action like this, and for good reason—we had never done so over the course of at least two administrations, despite good reasons to. Now they would have to recalculate. On the other hand, Soleimani was an iconic symbol to Iran, and there would be a significant response; of that I was sure. At the strategic level, it seemed likely that his death would create a new environment, and I was far less certain that I knew its contours.

The actual decision to strike Soleimani did not come out of a deliberate planning process. It was a decision made by the president, who was getting input from his advisors at the national level that Iran would not retaliate. No one at CENTCOM or in the intelligence community shared that view. That didn't mean it wasn't worth acting; it merely meant that we were not sanguine about the aftermath. Sometime in the days immediately before the strike, I clearly recall a session with my key staff in Tampa. Again, we were more focused on the next steps than the actual strike itself. During that conversation, we talked about the advantages of taking the strike. It would remove the most valuable leader Iran had, the nexus of the long war against us and our interests, and also act to break the rhythm of impending attacks. Underneath all of this, though, there was another significant factor, and I remember what I said word for word: "The next day, we will still be here, but Soleimani will still be dead." By this I meant that his experience, his leadership, his knowledge, and his will to action would no longer be available to Iran. Additionally, the act of striking him showed resolve that had been absent from U.S. policy on Iran for many years.

I talked to the chairman around midnight, after a conversation with the JSOTF commander, and told him that we were declaring "jackpot" against Soleimani. We did not "own the ground" on route Irish, so we couldn't approach the still-smoldering wreckage, but we had enough information through human intelligence and other means to make the call with confidence. We also confirmed the secretary's decision to not prosecute the *Saviz*. After this call, and with an ear half-cocked for updates from Iraq, where trouble seemed inevitable, I went to bed. It was a dramatically different world than the night before. I slept well.

6

AFTERMATH

Luck is the residue of design.
—*Branch Rickey*

Over the next five days, I watched and participated in actions that brought the United States and Iran closer to open state-on-state conflict than at any time in the past forty years. By the time the sun came up in Tampa on Friday, January 3, it was already afternoon in the theater, and protests were heavy in Iraq. At my morning intelligence brief, it was clear that Iran was contemplating some response. The question, of course, was what it would be. They had several choices of weapon and target. The response could be from their proxy groups, in Iraq, Syria, Lebanon, or Yemen. A response in Afghanistan even seemed possible, through Taliban connections. Potential targets could range from direct attacks on U.S. forces to deniable attacks against our partners in the region.

I wanted a little time to myself, just to think about what the most likely Iranian response would be. On Friday morning, after our morning intelligence and commander's video conference, I sat in my office and made a list of things I knew: First, they would respond. Second, I didn't think they wanted an all-out war. The history of Iranian retribution was one of careful calibration. They knew the correlation of forces and understood that in any general war, they would ultimately lose. Third, because of the importance of Soleimani, emotion might cloud their response in this case. Fourth, I was confident that they would come after a U.S. target. Since May, they had generally worked against partner and allied forces in the Gulf, seeking nonattribution and the weak spot among our friends in the region. Even though they had shot down our RQ-4 in June, there had been no loss of life, and further, it was still unclear to us at what level that had been approved in the Iranian leadership. Striking Soleimani changed all that, and the layers of proxies and deniability would fall away, leaving only the two principal antagonists confronting each other: Iran and the United States.

My fifth point was perhaps the most important one. The individual who had typically held sway above all others in these debates was now silent. Soleimani could not give advice to the supreme leader, he could not cut the Iranian high command out of policy deliberations, and he could not go off by himself to direct action without approval, secure in the knowledge that his relationship with the supreme leader would trump all else. This was a huge change in the structure of Iranian decision-making. When coupled with an emotional response to the death of Soleimani, we were in uncharted terrain.

Over the course of the day, we watched the Iranians bring their theater ballistic missile force to an increasingly higher level of readiness. We also observed them begin to bring their air defenses to a higher state of readiness. There were also other developments: on January 3, the Iranians named Esmail Ghani, Soleimani's former deputy, to be the next commander of the Quds Force. As with all Iranian senior leaders, we had a great deal of biographical and other information on him, so we began to consider how he would change their approach. In the days that followed, I stayed in constant communication with our intelligence enterprise, both my excellent J-2, Gen. Dimitri Henry, USMC, but also with the CIA and the National Security Agency. They all had part of the picture—but it was very hard to create a single integrated picture of what might happen next. Throughout all of the months of tension and provocations leading up to early January, it had always been our intention at CENTCOM to ensure that we could absorb any Iranian attack without undue—or better yet, any—U.S. or coalition casualties. If we could do this, we felt that we would maintain decision space for the president. A successful mass-casualty event as the result of an Iranian attack would set us on a course for war. Over the previous months, I had argued relentlessly for additional forces for this reason—not enough forces to fight Iran with our warplans, but enough to deflect the blow that was now coming. I had uneven results with my arguments. I had received some forces, but not enough—at least in my own mind. I was also aware that no commander ever has enough forces, and there were potential hotspots across the globe that also had claim for these forces: our forces deployed against Korea, China, and Russia. Of course, it was unlikely that those forces would shortly be on the receiving end of a theater ballistic missile attack.

In conversations with commanders in Iraq, I approved dispersing our personnel, aircraft, and other high-value equipment. In taking actions like this, there was a fine line between doing it too early, thus giving the Iranians the opportunity to revisit our dispositions and refine their targeting, or waiting too long, where we could be struck before moving anything. By the morning of Tuesday, January 7, it was clear that the Iranians were contemplating a ballistic missile attack against bases in Iraq and Kuwait. There were other possibilities, but we thought these locations were most at risk. In Iraq, we were most concerned about al Asad, Erbil, Taji, and our embassy in Baghdad. By late morning in Tampa—early evening in Iraq—we were confident enough of the potential targets to begin to move people and airplanes around. Where we could not move them away from airfields, we repositioned them far away from the ramps where they had been. We also made sure that personnel at all of these bases were refamiliarized with where the bunkers were and the warning signals for missile attack. We knew that the Iranians did not have the overhead satellite capability that we possessed, but their human intelligence on the ground was always impressive.

By late afternoon, our suspicions were hardening, based on our ability to understand how commands were passed to the Iranian ballistic missile force. We expected an attack overnight, and we thought it might be pretty large. We believed they had the capability to launch up to a hundred missiles, and that could be combined with an uncrewed aerial system or land attack cruise missile strike. A combined strike would be very difficult to defend against, but we considered that such a strike would most likely be directed against bases that were defended by our Patriots. I was sitting in my office, working the phones with Washington, when the JOC called. It was Rear Adm. Sam Paparo: "Boss, they're launching." "On my way, Pappy." I left my office and walked the two hundred paces to the JOC. Once there, I went into the FPOC. The rest of the team was either there or arriving.

In order to understand what would happen over the next few hours, it's important to recognize the space-based warning system that the United

States has for ballistic missile launches. An artifact of the Cold War with the Soviet Union, it is composed of satellites in geosynchronous orbit, thousands of miles above the Earth. They have extremely discriminating infrared detection capabilities, and the motor of a ballistic missile was exactly what they had been designed to look for. Typically, we would get notice of this seconds after ignition. Back in the Pentagon, in the National Military Command Center, a team of fifty or so servicemembers led by a one-star general manned the watch for this. I had done this myself as a brand-new Marine brigadier general. When a launch was detected, a recorded voice would come over the loudspeaker, saying "Warning, strategic missile launch, Iran," or wherever it originated. The one-star in the NMCC, the deputy director for operations, would immediately assess the launch and then convene a warning meeting, bringing in the experts from North American Air Defense Command (NORAD) to determine the nature of the threat.

I took my seat at the head of the table. "Looks like multiple launches, could be targeting al Asad and Erbil," Sam told me. I could see the projected parabolas displayed on the large screens at the end of the room. At the same time, the NMCC had convened an attack assessment conference, a large secure telephone meeting involving key players on the Joint Staff, OSD, and also other agencies. These conferences are a product of the Cold War, so the first step—always—is to determine if there is any threat to North America. Given the projections of the tracks of these missiles, launched from western Iran, it was obvious very quickly that our homeland wasn't threatened. On the other hand, they would be falling on their targets in Iraq in just minutes. The warning system is particularly good for these types of attacks; all our bases in Iraq quickly received warnings of immediate impact, and all personnel were told to seek immediate cover.

I brought Pat White up on a video call just to check in. He was in his quarters in Baghdad, wearing full battle gear and with his helmet on. He was remarkably calm and collected. The first impacts occurred at a little after 6:30 p.m. EST, or about 2:30 a.m. on Wednesday, January 8, in Iraq. We quickly characterized the attack as being most likely missiles of the Zolfaghar design. Over the next hour, others followed—more Zolfaghars, and then some Qiam Mod 2s. They attempted to launch a total of sixteen missiles, all from mobile

Map 5. Iran and Iraq

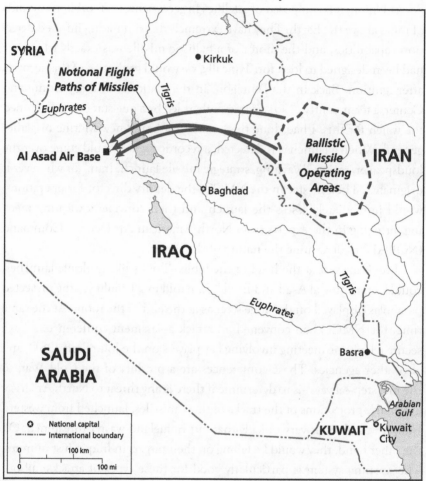

launchers. Later we were able to determine that one may have exploded upon launch. Ten hit al Asad, and one hit near Erbil. Four broke up in flight. All came from launch areas in western Iran (see map 5).

As we continued to track the attack, in the back of my mind I was thinking about what it was like at al Asad. I had spent a lot of time in and around that airbase. It's in the western high desert of Iraq, and in January it is a cold, dreary place. It rained a lot there in January, and the low, threatening skies made it a depressing place to live and work. The endless cold wind made it unpleasant to be outside. Even after our last-minute redeployments, we had hundreds of men and women inside the base. I knew that the "big voice," the early warning system, would be shrieking the alert, and our servicemembers would be hunkering down inside the elaborate bunker system. Would it be enough?

At this moment, and despite all that we had done, I expected heavy casualties and loss of life at al Asad. We knew the accuracy of these missiles—it was measured in the tens of meters. The Zolfaghar, a solid fuel missile with a seven-hundred-kilometer range, was probably the best of the Iranian medium-range systems. It carried a warhead of several hundred pounds. The Qiam 2 was a liquid fuel design with slightly longer range that also carried a warhead of several hundred pounds. We had good bunkers there, we had moved forces out and around, but the incoming missiles had large warheads and were reasonably accurate. We did not have any missile defense systems in Iraq at this time. With a limited number of these systems available, it's always a zero-sum game when you decide what to protect and what not to protect. It was a classic commander's dilemma. We thought it would be unlikely for Iran to launch an attributable state attack on Iraq; it seemed far more likely that they would go against Saudi Arabia, or even our bases in Kuwait, Bahrain, or the UAE. We had seen them posture to do just this in May 2019. In January 2020 we were not protecting Iraqi bases with Patriots, and now we would have to depend on our passive defenses and the dispersions ordered by commanders. The last missile impacted at about 7:50 p.m. EST, or 3:50 a.m. in Iraq. This wasn't clear to us immediately, and we continued to look for evidence of more launches. I remained in the conference call with the chairman and the secretary, and the president joined in. There were at least fifty people on the call. These calls were never the best way to have calm discussions. Every four or five minutes, either the deputy director for operations or NORAD interrupted with an update on the attack.

My ability to gather information and understand what was going on began to outpace NORAD's because I could talk to people on the ground, while they were limited by the capabilities of our spaceborne sensors and our radars. At about 8:10 p.m. EST, I felt we had enough information to give an update, so I briefed that we had taken multiple hits at al Asad and some, but fewer, at Erbil. We had no casualty reporting yet, because we did not know if the attacks were over. The last thing we wanted was to have people out of their bunkers assessing damage should another attack occur. It was a very tense time on the call. There was no doubt in my mind that the president was prepared to hit back, and hard, if we suffered casualties. The call was finally terminated when it became obvious that this particular attack was over, and there was no sign of more developing.

I talked to all of my subordinate commanders and brought them up to speed, warning that we could be in action within a few hours. With Dimitri Henry, I looked carefully at the totality of Iranian readiness. They had brought their missile force—the crown jewel of their arsenal—to a higher state of readiness, but it was uneven. The units in western Iran—the ones that launched the strikes—were at a high level. On the other hand, while the overall readiness of the force was elevated, we did not see the countrywide dispersions that would indicate preparations for a full-scale exchange. Not surprisingly, their air defenses were at an elevated level of readiness. At about this time, we got the first indication that a civilian airliner had gone down near Tehran. We would learn later that an IRGC air defense element shot down a Ukrainian civil airliner as it departed Khomeini International Airport in Tehran. This shocking act of incompetence both exposed significant weaknesses in Iranian command and control and added further pressure to a situation that was already stressed. This wasn't all clear to us that night, but there were indications that there were some real problems in the Tehran area.

By around 10:00 p.m. EST, there was great pressure on CENTCOM to provide an assessment of damage and, most importantly, casualties. I resisted this pressure, and the chairman was helpful in fending off the insatiable demand for information. There were several reasons why it took a little time to gain battle damage assessments. First, it wasn't worth the life of a U.S. servicemember to move around al Asad and do the assessment while the strike was in progress. Second, from the tone of the president and senior leaders in the conference call, it was obvious to me that potentially momentous decisions could proceed from what we reported. We needed to be right. I was in constant touch with Pat White during this period, and I'm sure he probably felt my need to know more was intrusive and overbearing as well! While this worked itself out, we received reporting from the Department of State that that Iranians had reached out through an intermediary and conveyed that the attack just completed was the response to the strike on Soleimani. There would be no more attacks, at least not immediately. This communication had the ring of truth about it. We added it into our calculations as we continued to look hard at the Iranian war machine.

Finally, at around midnight, I felt we had enough information to give an initial assessment. From what our teams on the ground could determine, there were no kinetic injuries to any of our people either at al Asad or Erbil. There was significant material damage at al Asad, including the loss of one helicopter. I called the chairman and passed this on. It was my report of "no casualties" that led within the next few hours to a presidential tweet on this. Of course, as time went by, the symptoms of mild traumatic brain injury (mTBI) began to emerge in some servicemembers. The signs were certainly not evident that night, and it remained our best judgment in the immediate aftermath of the attack that there were no casualties. Eventually, 110 personnel were evaluated with symptoms of mTBI. Seventy-five of them were treated and remained in theater. Thirty-five were evacuated to Landstuhl Regional Medical Center in Germany. Of those, seven returned to duty in either Iraq or Kuwait, and twenty-eight were further evacuated to the United States. Nobody ever pressed me to shade or minimize these numbers. I am confident that our troops received the best medical treatment and in a timely manner. If we appeared slow in reporting the numbers, it simply reflected the often late-emerging symptoms that are characteristic of these kinds of injuries. Moreover, this was the first exposure of the force to large ballistic missile–sized warheads, much larger than the 107mm and 240mm warheads we had been seeing. Eventually, almost eighty Purple Hearts were awarded for these injuries as the result of a formal board process led by Pat White in Iraq. There was a huge flurry in the press about the "no casualties" comment. It came from me and wasn't forced on me by anybody. It reflected our best call at the time. As the data changed, we changed our assessment.

Later that month, I had the opportunity to visit al Asad and walk over the ground where all the Iranian missiles hit. As I did so on a cool, windy late January afternoon, talking to the commanders and senior enlisted leaders there, it became clear to me that the Iranians were not trying to avoid casualties with their attack. Instead, their missiles were targeted at locations where we had aircraft positioned and where maintenance and living areas were. We escaped serious casualties because commanders repositioned aircraft, personnel, and some equipment after the Iranians took their last prestrike look, which was probably some combination of commercial overhead imagery and human intelligence on the ground. Most of their warheads exploded against nothing. Additionally, the base had good concrete bunkers and high T-walls, all of which compartmented blast effects and further minimized damage. We were also a little lucky—but commanders in theater had made that luck.

In a wise and farsighted decision, the president chose not to respond to the Iranian attack. It was the right decision. We had struck against the heart of the Iranian terror machine with the death of Soleimani. The importance of the strike against him and its aftereffects has become clearer over time. In late April 2021 Foreign Minister Mohammad Javad Zarif, in a lengthy interview that was apparently part of an oral history project, noted that "by assassinating him in Iraq, the United States delivered a major blow to Iran, more damaging than if it had wiped out an entire city in an attack."[1] The Iranian response was essentially a punch that landed on air and did not cause loss of life. I am not minimizing the injuries that our forces on the ground suffered at al Asad, but the brutal fact was that it could have been far worse. We had an opportunity to de-escalate, and the United States took it. Nothing else would change—the maximum pressure campaign would continue, and tensions would rise again, but we had dodged a major theater war.

In the days that followed, I took stock of the events of the first ten days of January. We had reestablished a form of rough deterrence with Iran by striking Soleimani. They didn't think we would take bold and aggressive action. Because we did so, they were forced to recalculate. This was a major win for us. On the other hand, for the first time in the history of warfare,

U.S. forces were subjected to ballistic missile attacks. This was a clear state-on-state attack; there was no attempt to hide its origin or attribution. You can only cross the Rubicon once. It was my judgment that the bar to these kinds of attacks was now lower, and we would see more of them in the future. We could also see evidence that decision-making in Iran was increasingly chaotic and stressed by the death of Soleimani—the person who typically "spoke last" in key meetings—and also by the embarrassment over the jetliner shootdown. We were now in a new phase in our relationship with Iran. We had both struck at each other hard; our blow had landed with telling effect, and theirs had little impact. Both sides pulled back from the brink, if only for a few days.

7
THE SUMMER OF
OUR DISCONTENT

*The test of a first-rate intelligence is the ability to hold
two opposed ideas in the mind at the same time, and
still retain the ability to function.*
—*F. Scott Fitzgerald,* The Crack-up

In the aftermath of the death of Soleimani, the Iranian approach changed. In 2019 most of their pressure had been on our partners in the region: Saudi Arabia, the UAE, and others. Using deniable attacks, they sought to destabilize the global economy while pursuing their ultimate objective of ejecting the United States—and our Western partners—from the region. After the death of Soleimani, the focus of their efforts became Iraq. If the United States could be forced out of Iraq, the geographic center of the theater, then other nations might follow suit. Additionally, the Iranians had many advantages in Iraq; a Shia majority, deep cultural connections, and an extended contiguous land border. There were disadvantages as well, including the history of the long and bloody war between Iraq and Iran that dominated the decade of the 1980s in the region.

At the same time, they drew a lesson from the Soleimani strike: that the United States could—and would—push back hard if pressed. For the first time in many years, they had seen the naked power of the United States, and it was a sobering discovery. This led to operational guidance to both Iranian forces and their proxies: avoid major attacks on U.S. forces. Deniable and small-scale attacks would still be conducted, particularly if they could not be directly attributed to Iran. This made itself felt most in Iraq, where attacks continued against our bases throughout all of 2020. In the spring of 2020

Iranian leadership felt they had a genuine political path to push the United States out of Iraq. It was a reasonable goal: on January 5, 2020, the Iraqi Council of Representatives passed a non-binding resolution calling for the withdrawal of all foreign forces from Iraq. Prime Minister Abdul Mahdi called for the withdrawal of foreign forces. The Iranians applied considerable pressure on parliamentarians, as well as the Iraqi government, trying to bring the issue to a head. This is where they felt the loss of Soleimani most acutely. In years past, he would have been an indefatigable presence in this political process, applying pressure, threatening, cajoling, rewarding. But he was gone. His successor as the Quds Force commander, Brigadier General Esmail Ghani, had none of his charisma and only a rudimentary command of Arabic. He could not go into Iraq, meet with the fragmented Shia parties, knock heads, and muster the support that Iran had been able to count on in the past as a matter of course.

Meanwhile, the Iraqis finally were able to form a government, and with a prime minister whom we felt would be a partner going forward. As with all Iraqi government formation, the path had been tortuous and slow. On April 9, Iraqi President Barham Saleh charged National Intelligence Service director Mustafa al-Kadhimi with the opportunity to form a government. He wasn't anyone's first choice: earlier attempts by other prime minister candidates to gain Council of Representatives approval had failed, in January and April respectively. We saw in Kadhimi a man we could work with, and the Iranians apparently saw something as well, because they instructed the Iran-aligned Shia parties to support him. As usual in Iraq, everybody got something they wanted—and something they didn't want.

As I sifted through intelligence reports and talked to analysts and experts from across the government and academia in the spring of 2020, it was clear to me that if Soleimani were alive, Kadhimi would not have gotten the nod. A major underlying factor in his rise to power was Iranian inability to coalesce around another candidate. While they put a brave face on it and claimed to be supportive of the new prime minister, the facts argued otherwise—the seating of Kadhimi was a major victory for a genuine political process in Iraq, not dictated by any outside element. It was also good for us.

As we continued through the summer, the question of which forces would remain in CENTCOM became more urgent. Since we had never established a comprehensive plan to quantify the military element of the maximum pressure campaign, throughout 2020 the department managed through a system of expedients whereby the secretary considered force elements individually, rather than as a cohesive, coherent whole, applied within an overarching concept. The cliff would be September 30, when our missile defense batteries, fighters, and ships—to include the aircraft carrier—would depart the theater. The chairman had tried to get a decision from the secretary on these matters through the late spring and into the summer, but without avail. Instead, we continued to deal with force elements individually rather than as a whole.

Finally, the secretary set a date of Wednesday, August 19 to consider forces for CENTCOM. It was billed as a strategy meeting—to have broad discussions on prioritization, rather than the usual detailed examination of our requests in a line-by-line manner. It would be an unusually large meeting, with not only the OSD staff but also the service secretaries in attendance. The chiefs would be present, of course, and also the European and Indo-Pacific commanders by video conference. Because of the large attendance, the meeting would have to be held in the Nunn-Lugar conference room, a very unusual venue for a strategy meeting. Policy would run the meeting, according to the invitation, and the meeting would last an hour. I was allocated five minutes near the beginning to make my case, and then the services would be able to respond, followed by the other combatant commanders. I knew that I would have only one ally in the room, and that would be the chairman. I've been to many meetings in this room and knew it well, and I also knew the people who would be in the room with me for this meeting. It was still a very lonely feeling. The night before, I'd spent some time scripting my remarks so that I would ensure my points were made and within the allotted timeline. As usual for meetings of this kind, I wrote a first draft of our position, then circulated it among my senior leaders for their review. We were staying at the Intercontinental Hotel on the Wharf in southwest Washington, so I spent the evening looking out of my window across Washington Channel to the Potomac while I made my final edits.

The problem we were confronting begged for a strategic discussion and then strategic-level decisions by the department. In short, it was my position that our department's basic strategic document, the National Defense Strategy, did not fully account for some of the decisions made at the highest level of our government: to wit, the maximum pressure campaign against Iran, and the president's fixation on denying Iran a nuclear weapon. The NDS predated the maximum pressure campaign, so the designation of the Middle East as an "economy of force" theater could not have anticipated the different direction national leadership went on Iran. The core question that now confronted us was this: do we change the relative prioritization within the NDS to accommodate the changed nature of the strategic environment, or do we continue to embrace a strict constructionist reading of the NDS? We all agreed that the long-term threat was China, and then Russia. Could we find a "middle path" that would deal with the transient nature of the Iran problem—maintaining deterrence against Iran while still continuing to focus on China and Russia?

Unfortunately, the meeting did not stay at the strategic level. I delivered my input, which was nothing new to anyone in the room. It felt this time, though, that I was speaking for the record. As we talked, I tried to make it clear that the 2018 NDS did not foresee the relative prioritization of Iran by the administration—a prioritization that had now become a fact of life.

The 2021 Global Force Management Plan (GFMP), as the direct output of a literal reading of the NDS, did not acknowledge in any way our current economic and diplomatic activities against Iran. This made the GFMP obsolete at the moment of publication, and it necessitated the endless series of force adjustments that we were now wading through. In this sense, the implementation of our guiding strategic document in the department was not aligned against the highest-level objectives of the United States. I also argued that this was a temporally bounded disconnect—it would not last forever, and there were clear conditions where we could move from the current state to a future state that would be more aligned with the aspirations of the NDS. I reiterated that the current state—and the requirements that came from it—were defined by the security conditions created by the maximum pressure campaign. The forces that I was arguing for in that room were aligned against the requirements necessary to deter Iran while this economic and diplomatic campaign continued, to defend against Iran should we be attacked, to execute response options as directed by the president, and then to defend against the inevitable Iranian counterattack. The last requirement was important, because it limited further escalation. If we had a low-level exchange with Iran, it was important to ensure that we were able to prevent significant damage or loss of life. By deflecting the Iranian riposte, we would be able to find an off-ramp. This is what had happened in the aftermath of the al Asad strike. I did not want or need forces positioned in the region for execution of a war plan against Iran. We all recognized this wasn't prudent and would be a misallocation of valuable forces that could be used elsewhere. I argued instead for forces that could limit an Iranian response—these were far fewer than what was contemplated for a war plan.

In the back and forth that followed, we discussed a theory that proposed that we could withdraw forces from CENTCOM and then rapidly reinforce should the situation dictate. I didn't believe this was a tenable proposition for two reasons: First, the withdrawal of forces would both convince our partners and friends in the region that we would not stand with them, and it would accelerate Iranian hegemonic ambition. We knew that our reduced posture in the spring of 2019 was an inducement for Iranian aggression. Withdrawing forces removed our ability to deter and to act to prevent escalation in its early stages. Second, I made the point that it's not as easy to rapidly reintroduce forces into the theater as some would like to believe, particularly if our force structure was reduced to near-zero, as the force management plan proposed.

Should the maximum pressure campaign be ended, then conditions would be very different. However, from where we stood in the summer of 2020, the maximum pressure campaign had not been ended. It appeared likely that it could even intensify to a higher and more unpredictable level in the next few months. In the meantime, though, CENTCOM requirements remained well above what was envisioned in the strategy of the NDS and its operationalization in the fiscal year 2021 Global Force Management Plan. Strategy documents are only useful if they describe the world that is, instead of the world that we might wish to inhabit. Implementation of the NDS did not fully accommodate the world as it was, given the maximum pressure campaign. I did not have a solution for the disconnect between what I saw as practical reality on the ground and the aspirational implementation of the NDS, except to observe again that strategy documents should be based on the environment they describe.

I was also speaking to an audience of one—the secretary. I knew the chairman would be supportive, and I knew that literally everyone else in the room disagreed with what I was saying. That was fine with me—we weren't going to solve this problem with a seminar approach. It would require a decision, and one at the strategic level. After me, the chiefs each spoke. It was the usual litany of complaints: too hard, too painful, not enough of this or that. I was particularly disappointed in my own service, which seemed intent on shaking the dust of CENTCOM off its boots while looking wholly toward the Pacific. To a degree, I could sympathize with their tales of woe—nobody had told them in a planning document to support CENTCOM. On the other hand, for over a year, we had sustained significant force deployments into the region. In my own mind, again, I ascribed this to our inability to give strategic guidance back in May 2019 that would have established a new relative prioritization for CENTCOM.

The secretary began to ask very specific questions about force elements. For example, you say you need X number of fighter squadrons, why is that so? This had already been answered in laborious detail in the orders book itself, but we rehashed it again for fighters and then virtually every other force element. The chairman interjected more than once, trying to steer the discussion to the big question that we needed to answer: "Is this a priority?" If it was a priority, then it would be straightforward to answer the questions about whether to allocate these forces. Instead, though, the meeting devolved into a reductionist approach. It seemed to me that instead of dealing with the issue of prioritization as a single big matter, there was a belief that the problem could be deconstructed, and by dealing with literally dozens of smaller decisions, we might somehow elicit a more palatable answer. This approach also gave the illusion of control and certainty. By asking a series of specific questions about individual force elements, answers would of necessity be quantitatively based and narrow. On the other hand, the essence of the art of military planning is the ability to knit these specific capabilities, often stove-piped when considered in isolation, into a larger concept. We were missing this in our conversation. It was intensely frustrating, because we seemed to be avoiding the core question that, once answered, would provide a clear roadmap for hierarchically subordinate decisions.

The meeting went well over an hour. It devolved into a lengthy series of questions for me on specific force elements, the complaints of the chiefs, and then the opinions of everyone on what should be done—most recommended a significant reduction in forces. This was exactly the outcome I had seen in several previous meetings on this subject. We did not have a strategic-level discussion, and we did not get a decision from the secretary that afternoon. Everybody left the meeting with various degrees of frustration and angst.

I felt this meeting perfectly summed up the inevitable result of a lack of clear strategic guidance. As the CENTCOM commander, I had an unambiguous vision of what my responsibilities were and what my tasks were under the variety of strategic documents that were ultimately authoritative. Because of my experience on the Joint Staff, I also had an appreciation for the global scale of the department's problems. The inability of the interagency process to clearly identify and state the gap between the vision of the White House and the dictates of the internal Department of Defense strategy—the NDS—led to endless short-term stop-gap measures, where we argued ceaselessly and bitterly over apportionment of forces. The fact that the secretary ultimately had to adjudicate these matters may have given the impression of great energy and industry, but we were attacking symptoms, not the core problems. I, or any other combatant commander, would have saluted smartly and followed orders that told us we were not going to get what we had asked for. Absent that clear and direct guidance, which we never received, commanders engaged in an ongoing free-for-all for forces. This process ate up staff time, disrupted focus, and prevented the establishment of clear strategic priorities in action, not just in words. I knew that Secretary Esper was a fair and dispassionate decision-maker, and I was ready to accept whatever his decision would be.

Late the next day, we did receive a decision. We would retain our current posture well into 2021, with the exception of the carrier presence. The Navy's inability to generate carriers forced us, as a simple matter of physics, to plan to go without a carrier for the period from mid-November through March.

There were some things we could do to compensate for this loss, but it would still take away an important asset during a period of heightened risk. By mid-September, it was obvious that Iran wasn't going to challenge us directly in Iraq or anywhere else in the theater. They could see the polling data from the presidential race, and they didn't want to do anything that might give President Trump the opportunity to respond to an Iranian or proxy attack with an action that could coalesce support behind him, particularly in the days leading up to the election.

As with all things in the region, though, it wasn't as simple as this. There was still a strong element in Iranian strategy that aimed to push us out of the region. The Iranians also did not have an understanding of what a redline would be for us in these attacks. I was confident that our redline would be lower than their calculations. These factors were magnified even more in Iraq, where the Shia militant groups were under imperfect control—at best—from Iranian leadership. This posed a particular problem for us, since over the past few years the Iranians had armed them with extremely capable weapons, ranging from rockets and mortars to highly accurate short-range ballistic missiles. While they acknowledged the leadership of Iran, and Iran was certainly morally responsible for any action they might undertake, the militant groups had a certain freedom of action. As summer turned to early fall in Baghdad, rocket and mortar attacks continued against our bases. These attacks were notable for their inaccuracy. Our counter-rocket capability at the embassy in downtown Baghdad was also very useful in preventing something more serious. Attacks also continued against our supply convoys, which did not have U.S. or coalition personnel protecting them. The danger of these attacks was simple—sooner or later I believed they'd get lucky and kill or injure U.S. or coalition personnel. We would then be back in an escalation spiral.

I did a great deal of thinking about how to respond to such an eventuality. I talked at length with Pat White and, after he returned to Fort Hood, his very capable replacement, Lt. Gen. Paul Calvert, USA. Paul was another in that seemingly endless line of competent and dedicated Army generals that came from the University of North Georgia, the state's military college. In short, our reaction to casualties in Iraq tended to follow a predictable pattern: not unlike Claude Rains giving the order to "arrest the usual suspects" in *Casablanca*. Operationally, in the past this had always meant air-delivered fires against militant infrastructure. We had done this in March. The Iraqis hated it when we did this, since they saw it as an infringement on their sovereignty. It wasn't terribly effective, since the likely targets knew what was coming and took measures to disperse and protect themselves. It would also put even more pressure on the prime minister. I wanted to do something different. After an attack either directly or indirectly attributable to Iran that caused casualties, I proposed that our response would not be to unilaterally strike targets with airpower inside Iraq. Instead, we would go after targets outside of Iraq. There were several of these, ranging from our old friend down in Yemen to various intelligence-gathering platforms at sea across the region, manned by IRGC and Quds Force operatives. This approach would give Prime Minister Kadhimi some maneuver space in his own country, it would punish the Iranians directly without striking metropolitan Iran, and it would be measured in scale.

Unfortunately, at this critical time, our own government became "wobbly" on our posture in Iraq. On September 22–23, I traveled to Washington for congressional outreach—an opportunity to update House and Senate committee chairs and ranking members on CENTCOM issues. It also gave me an opportunity to visit with the chairman one on one. We needed to talk. The day before I left to come up, he had called me to deliver verbal direction to rapidly develop a plan—what we called a commander's estimate in planning lingo—to assist in the withdrawal of all our diplomats from the embassy in the Green Zone in Baghdad, our support compound at the Baghdad International Airport, and our consulate in Erbil. This was a surprising order.

I reached out to Paul Calvert in Baghdad, waking him in the middle of the night, and read him into our task. I then passed the planning task to my operations, logistics, intelligence, and strategy flag officers. My approach to these unanticipated, uncoordinated, and short-sighted taskers reflected my view that whatever I thought of the appropriateness of the task, we needed to answer the purely military question first. Only then would I be able to give my advice on whether this was sound policy. I also called our first-rate ambassador in Iraq, Matt Tueller, and discussed my task with him. He had seen parallel direction from the State Department. Like me, he felt that the thinking behind this guidance was unsound. We were in a relatively good place in Iraq. The Kadhimi government was addressing many of our concerns about corruption. They were taking measures to increase security around our bases. Like everything in Iraq, it was a slow, tortuous process, and it did not move as quickly as we might have wished, but the trajectory was positive.

In talking to the chairman, I learned that the task came from a White House that was worried about the continual rocketing of our bases and the belief that U.S. or coalition casualties were inevitable. So far, so good—I too was worried about these attacks, and I also felt that despite the magnificent efforts of our commanders on the ground, sooner or later we would take casualties. The White House solution was to deliver a strong message to Prime Minister Kadhimi and President Saleh, threatening to pull out completely and striking Khatib Hezbollah targets as we left. I saw no issue with placing additional pressure on the Iraqi government, but if we withdrew as a result of the proxy pressure, we would be cravenly retreating in the face of an Iranian-directed campaign. The damage would be incalculable.

The staff generated the answers very quickly. The State Department would be responsible for its own withdrawal, but we would be prepared to step in as required to assist. There were a number of second-order matters that had not been considered. We had strong interdependencies between our military forces and our diplomatic presence. Our gateway into Iraq was through the diplomatic support compound at the Baghdad airport. If it left, we would need to scramble to find ways to support our forces in Iraq. More significantly, our presence in Iraq was coordinated by the high-level engagements and access that having an accredited ambassador gave us. If the diplomatic platform was withdrawn, it was unclear how we could maintain a military presence.

We also learned that inside the State Department, courses of action were being developed that envisioned a significant drawdown of our military presence in Iraq, beyond the new level of three thousand that we had just attained. There was no interagency coordination on these options. As with many discussions of this nature, they rapidly leaked, and soon the media was talking about it as well. I gave guidance to my public affairs folks that we would be completely silent on this and refer all questions to the secretary of defense's public affairs people. News of these developments was also landing in the national capitals of our coalition partners in Iraq. No advance coordination had been done with any of these nations, which had almost a thousand troops spread across Iraq. Just like the United States, they did not like to be surprised by developments like these.

I was confident that the chairman would be able to argue our case in interagency meetings. I also felt strongly enough about the matter to send the secretary of defense (routed through the chairman) my formal recommendation on the way ahead. In short, it encapsulated the points made in the preceding paragraphs—we were holding our own in Iraq, with some positive signs. The actions we were now contemplating would literally seize defeat from the jaws of victory. I could not promise that we would not take casualties—in fact, I believed that we would—but I considered that a risk worth taking.

By mid-October we had refined a plan to withdraw our diplomats should we be ordered to do so. We were also seeing indications that the Iranians were urging their proxies in Iraq to hold off on attacks, at least through the election. This direction, coupled with renewed Iraqi efforts to prevent attacks, seemed to be having the desired effect—attacks against the embassy and our bases drew down. We remained uncertain about what direction we would receive on drawing down our embassy. This state of affairs continued until after the U.S. election—and then everything changed.

8

DRAWING DOWN THE LONG WAR IN AFGHANISTAN

Doesn't seem so long ago
When we thought that we could change their minds
We'd stay here and fight it out
With a love that we could weaponize
—*Jason Isbell, "Overseas"*

My personal history with Afghanistan began at the Pentagon when it was attacked. It ended for me as the last commander of our forces in Afghanistan in August 2021. There is a strange and elegant symmetry in those two facts. In that twenty-year period, I fought on the ground in Afghanistan, served as a staff officer in Kabul, commanded the Marines in that country, and, finally, oversaw our final exit. During these years, my son grew up, attended the Naval Academy, and deployed twice to Afghanistan as a Marine infantry officer. At the very end, coming out was the most challenging and wrenching emotional event I experienced in my long career. I am still trying to put it in perspective, and I know that many others who served there are trying to do the same thing. I have not yet succeeded, and I often think of the many friends—U.S., coalition, and Afghan—we lost there, and, most of all, those for whom I was responsible who died while I was in command.

On September 11, 2001, I was a brand-new eager and energetic colonel working as the executive assistant for the operations deputy of the Marine Corps, Lt. Gen. Emil R. "Buck" Bedard. The Marine Corps had long resisted moving its headquarters into the Pentagon, preferring the old "shoeboxes" perched on Arlington Ridge that overlooked the building. When the Marine Corps did finally make the move, most of Headquarters Marine Corps was relegated to the least desirable office spaces. We were on the A Ring, tucked up on the fifth floor, the innermost and least accessible part of the building. The ceilings were lower, the passageways were narrower, the lights often did not work, and the restrooms had not been significantly improved since the 1950s.

That morning, we were prepping Lieutenant General Bedard for a pending trip to Mexico. Buck Bedard had a reputation as a stern and demanding leader, and that was true—but he was also warm, humorous, and totally dedicated to the Marine Corps. He had plucked me from relative obscurity three months earlier to be his executive assistant. In fact, I was so junior that while wearing the eagles of a colonel, I was still being paid as a lieutenant colonel. He had been my division commander when I commanded an infantry battalion in the 2d Marine Division. He must have seen some promise in me down at Camp LeJeune, and I genuinely enjoyed working for him. The key leaders of plans, policies, and operations, the branch of headquarters that Bedard led, were all gathered for the briefing in our small and slightly dilapidated conference room. Bedard sat at the head of the table, and everyone else took seats around it. My job was to ensure that the briefing went smoothly, orchestrating the sequential presentation of information from the different briefers. I would walk back and forth from the conference room to my office, where I would work emails, talk to other executive assistants across the headquarters, and try to stay one step ahead of my high-energy general.

I was at my desk when Col. George Flynn, the military secretary (the Marine Corps term for the commandant's executive assistant) to the commandant of the Marine Corps, called me at about nine o'clock to say that a plane had just hit the World Trade Center. Since this call was the beginning of twenty years of engagement on Afghanistan for me, I wish I had said something profound, but I clearly remember that I said, "You're shitting me." What jumped into my mind immediately was the July 1945 incident where a B-25 had flown into the side of the Empire State Building in heavy fog. The idea that it could have been a deliberate attack did not cross my mind. George told me that the commandant was at a funeral in Washington. Hanging up, I walked into the conference room and whispered the news to

Bedard. He grunted, and the briefing continued. I took my seat against the wall and listened to the briefers.

Just a few minutes later, the political advisor to Bedard threw open the conference room door and, with a wild-eyed visage, shouted that a second plane had hit another Trade Center tower. Bedard looked meaningfully at me, and I knew what that meant: Go and check it out, including the possibility that the political advisor—a Department of State officer—had gone nuts. I pulled up a television image in his inner office, and it was clear that something significant was under way. At the same time, the Marine Corps operations center, led by an old friend of mine, Col. Ron Johnson, called on our secure line to say that two big jets had impacted both towers of the World Trade Center. I pulled Bedard from the meeting, which rapidly broke up. We stood in his office for a few seconds and watched CNN. The secure phones began to ring, as Marine headquarters across the United States began to absorb what was happening. Bedard worked the phones, talking to Marine commanders. He also reached out to the director of the Joint Staff, Army Lt. Gen. John Abizaid, who, like Bedard, was trying to piece together what was going on. I went back to my small office immediately adjacent to his and exchanged what I knew—not much—with the other executive assistants. One thing was clear—there were airplanes in our airspace that we could not account for and that appeared to have malicious intent.

Shortly after ten o'clock, the red switch secure phone shrilled in Bedard's office. He was on another line and gestured for me to pick the phone up. It was Ron Johnson, from our command center. What he told me will remain with me until the day I die: "Frank, inbound jet for the Pentagon. Langley is launching fighters, but they're not going to get here in time." I quickly told him to hang on and handed the phone to Bedard. As Bedard listened intently, a large explosion shook the building. It was 10:03, and American Airlines Flight 77 had ended its tragic flight. Our eyes locked. I told him, in a statement of the obvious, "General, I believe an aircraft just hit the building." He put the phone down and we went out of our office and across the passageway to the windows that looked down across the courtyard. Directly across from us, great tongues of flame and oily black smoke were boiling into the sky. There wasn't much to say.

For the next few hours, we stayed in our office, and I observed a genuine lesson in executive leadership, as Buck Bedard reached out to everyone across the Marine Corps and calmed them down. The commandant was stuck in traffic across the river, so he wasn't able to communicate except on an open line. Bedard updated him frequently, and we stayed plugged into the National Military Command Center as situation updates were passed. I have never forgotten how calm, focused, and rock steady Buck Bedard was on that terrible morning. I've been in a few situations like that as a senior leader since then, and I've always tried to channel his preternatural calm. We maintained power and communications in our office, so we stayed, despite orders to evacuate. Finally, smoke began to infiltrate, and it was becoming difficult to breathe. We told our command center that we were going to move from the Pentagon up the hill to the headquarters annex. Had we waited any longer, we would have had to crawl out of the building, and Bedard had a bad hip—I didn't want him subjected to that. Outside, at the Mall entrance, a disorganized mess of people was trying to get away from the building. We drove up to the annex, fighting our way through bumper-to-bumper traffic, and finally got inside the compound. I noticed two things: the sky was still perfectly clear, and it was very quiet—all air traffic had been grounded. Usually, at the Pentagon you are bombarded by the noise of planes in short final approach to Reagan Washington National Airport. That was gone. I knew there were fighters overhead, but I couldn't see them. What I could see, though, were snipers on top of the old building we were going into. In the course of a few hours on a warm, cloudless September day, we had gone from peace to war. Everything changed.

The attack began a series of days, weeks, and months that ran together as I supported Buck Bedard in his role as the operations officer of the Marine Corps. We moved Headquarters Marine Corps out of the Pentagon and back to the Navy Annex. What I remember the most from those frenetic days, though, was accompanying him back to the Pentagon on the morning of September 12 for an operations deputies meeting in the JCS conference room known as the Tank. The area around the Pentagon looked like an infantry battalion fighting position; soldiers were everywhere, and the scene had a raw, powerful sense of underlying anger and urgency—dramatically different from the calm flow of commuters in and out that I had been used to. Overhead, the plume of smoke from the still-burning north side of the building could be seen. Inside, the passageways had an old, familiar smell—that of the battlefield. Jet fuel, burned plastic, scorched and melted metal—and something darker as well. I remember that smell, and I had lots of time to consider it as I sat for two hours outside the Tank with fellow executive assistants while the operations deputies met. The weeks and months that followed were a blur of activity, as the Marine Corps reset for Afghanistan. I escaped from Headquarters Marine Corps in the summer of 2002, with orders to command a Marine expeditionary unit (MEU), a combined arms task force, with aviation, infantry, and logistics elements all under the command of a colonel. It's the best unit to command in the Marine Corps.

I took command of the 22d MEU in October 2002 and deployed into Afghanistan in spring 2004 (see map 6). We flew into Afghanistan from the helicopter carrier *Wasp*, off the Makhran coast of Pakistan. Initially based at Kandahar, we soon moved about one hundred miles north into the Tarin Khowt bowl in Uruzgan province. There, for several months, we fought a surprisingly high-intensity war against Taliban forces who chose to mass and maneuver against us. With two maneuver battalions (one Army, one Marine), the MEU could fight across a wide battlespace, supported by our rotary wing aviation (based out of Forward Operating Base Ripley at Tarin Khowt) and theater air—everything from our own AV-8Bs from Kandahar to B-1s known as "bones" flown up from Diego Garcia. We named our base Ripley in honor of Col. John Ripley, a man of legendary courage in the Marine Corps. It was a profoundly rewarding and dynamic time to be in Afghanistan. My most enduring memory of that time was the soft, fine desert sand that was everywhere in the Tarin Khowt bowl. It permeated everything—sleeping bags, uniforms, and even our food. We even scraped a runway out of that harsh soil, and our C-130s made nightly runs in to resupply us, avoiding the danger of mines along the road to Kandahar. At night, in that vast bowl and with no ambient light, it was possible to see the stars and even the Milky Way with an unwinking, uncaring cold beauty that I will always associate with Afghanistan.

Map 6. Afghanistan

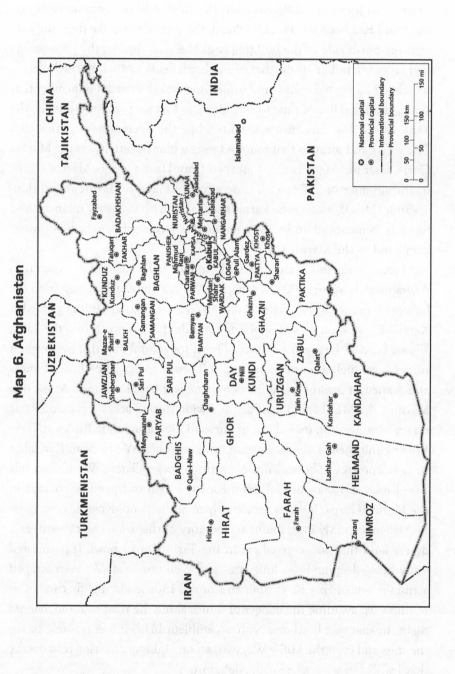

We were on our own down south, registering people to vote for the upcoming presidential election, and the fighting was good. I left Afghanistan in 2004 with a colonel's perspective that we had opportunities in Afghanistan, but we seemed to be perennially underresourced. The big war in Iraq got everyone's attention—and resources. In fact, had we arrived just a little later in the theater, the MEU would have been diverted into Iraq, where things were beginning to heat up. I found the Taliban to be resourceful and determined fighters who made very effective use of every fold of ground and cover. Because they were so lightly equipped, their tactical mobility was superb. We always maneuvered slowly, compared to their fleeting movements. When we could fix them, which was seldom, our use of artillery and airpower could yield significant casualties.

I went back to Afghanistan as a brigadier general in June 2009 to join the International Security Assistance Force (ISAF) staff in Kabul. I was coming off the Joint Staff, where I had served as the chairman's special assistant for presidential transition. I was assigned as the deputy to the deputy chief of staff for stability. It was a very challenging year, but it provided good exposure to a genuine international headquarters.

During my year in Afghanistan, I learned a lot about how the State Department worked on the ground, both inside the embassy and out in the Afghan hinterlands. It was a great learning experience in interagency relations. I came away with a strong respect for the career foreign service officers who manned our far-flung diplomatic outposts. I was particularly impressed with Phil Kosnett, a foreign service officer who worked political-military affairs at the embassy in Kabul. We had a shared interest in collecting and playing paper-based wargames of the 1970s and 1980s, and it gave us a strong mutual bond. One of the stability shop's responsibilities inside ISAF was outreach to the embassy, so Phil and I met regularly to compare notes and to try to find ways to make our relationship more effective. It also gave me the opportunity to see the strengths and weakness of coalition warfare.

I took three observations away from that year in Kabul, and they colored everything else that happened there for me. First, we were as much a part of the problem in Afghanistan as the Taliban. We were smothering an essentially medieval country with billions of dollars of aid and projects and trying to work them all at a frenetic pace. Afghanistan—both the society and the government we had created—was incapable of digesting what we were giving them. Corruption was endemic, and despite the establishment of several well-intentioned anticorruption task forces, we made little actual progress in rooting it out. Second, I watched as the civilian-military team broke down in Afghanistan. It was possible that it would never have worked, given the personalities of the ambassador, retired Lt. Gen. Karl Eikenberry, USA, and the new commander, Gen. Stan McChrystal, but it was irretrievably beyond repair by the spring of 2010. Third, I was able to see first-hand the importance of Pakistan to the Taliban. Across the permeable border, they could refit, rest, and plan without any viable threat from us. The core of the Taliban's command and control was in the mountainous town of Quetta in southern Pakistan, and the most violent branch of the movement, the Haqqanis, were safely ensconced farther north, also in Pakistan. All were off limits to our forces. Occasionally, Pakistan would apply some pressure, but it was never enough to reduce their ability to operate. I came to see this as the absolutely critical failure of all our plans, and I grew to believe that there weren't enough U.S. forces in all the world to establish order in Afghanistan, so long as Pakistan was open to the Taliban. It was a logical error in our approach to counterinsurgency that could not be papered over or compensated for.

I had an opportunity to spend time in Afghanistan again in the fall of 2010 as Gen. James Mattis's representative. He had just taken command of Central Command, and he gave me the task of assembling a team of experts and then going into Afghanistan to look at the progress of the campaign. My report would be to him alone, with no other copies distributed to anyone. General David Petraeus commanded in Afghanistan during this period, and he was very welcoming and accommodating. Over several weeks, my team and I travelled over most of the country, talking to not only U.S. military and diplomatic leaders but also Afghan leaders. This study gave me the opportunity to gain a fresh perspective on the war and our chances for success. In October 2010 I gave my report to General Mattis. The key takeaway for me as a result of this study was the importance of Pakistan as a base for the Taliban, and a recognition that unless we were able to choke off this haven for them, we were doomed to failure. Our plans, our money, and our nation-building efforts would come to naught unless we could correct this fundamental problem. Nothing since then has occurred to make me change that judgment.

When I left Afghanistan in June 2010, I spent the next nine years watching and participating in the conduct of the campaign. First, I was at Tampa in 2010–12 as the CENTCOM J-5. I then served as the Marine Forces Central Command commander, with responsibility for all Marines in Afghanistan. I did not have operational responsibility for these forces, but I visited them often and kept current with their situation. After that, I served as the Joint Staff J-5 and director of the Joint Staff from 2015 to 2019.

Time passed. The McChrystal surge, time-limited by the president, proved self-defeating. By 2015 we had begun the process of drawing down our forces, and the ability to mentor and actually advise the Afghans declined significantly. President Trump entered office with a clear intention to end our participation in the war in Afghanistan, but he found it hard to do so when confronted with the realities of the war itself. As the Joint Staff J-5 I accompanied my boss, Gen. Joe Dunford, and Secretary Mattis to meetings in the White House, where we argued for stability in our posture in Afghanistan, not dramatic reductions. It was obvious to me that President Trump was torn as he confronted the reality of the situation. He could have ordered us out at that time, but he did not. His anger was simmering, though.

In late March 2019, when I assumed command of CENTCOM, Afghanistan was not my highest priority. Iran occupied that spot, but Afghanistan was always at the top of my mind. I knew and trusted our commander in Afghanistan, Gen. Scott Miller, USA, and we talked frequently. Scott and I had known each other for many years. Our paths first crossed in Afghanistan, and we had stayed in touch in the intervening years. I considered him one of the finest soldiers and commanders the U.S. Army had ever produced. He was calm and steady in a crisis, and his oft-demonstrated personal courage was legendary in both special operations and conventional forces. Our staffs worked closely when tasked to prepare options to present to the secretary. There was never any daylight between Scott and me, and I tried to give him great latitude not only in his operations, but also with his outreach to the interagency. At all times, I kept in the back of my mind the difficult situation Stan McChrystal had been placed in while in command. He was effectively on an island without anyone to talk to, a situation that was ultimately untenable when stressed. I promised myself that I would never allow that to occur with Scott Miller.

I did not immerse myself in the negotiations with the Taliban, but Scott and I would often compare notes on what we were hearing. The beginning of the endgame for us in Afghanistan can be traced to the U.S.-Taliban agreement, signed in Doha, Qatar, on February 29, 2020. This agreement was the culmination of many months of negotiation between representatives of the Taliban overseen by Mullah Abdul Ghani Barader, smart and media savvy, who was able to position a patina of reasonableness over the essential starkness of the Taliban belief structure and view of the world. The lead U.S. representative was the special representative for Afghanistan, Ambassador Zalmay Khalilzad, a long-serving U.S. diplomat with deep ties to the region. It had been a long, painful, and often opaque negotiating process. Ambassador Khalilzad did not share much within the U.S. government, and what he did share was always aligned with his negotiating objectives of the moment. For Scott Miller and me, it seemed as though he was intent on solving a three-body problem, where the Taliban, the government of Afghanistan, and the United States were all simply pieces that he could maneuver on a chessboard in his mind. We were all, to some degree, in the dark about the exact nature of his outreach.

The military equity was straightforward. We wanted to prevent attacks against the homelands of the United States and our allies being generated from Afghanistan. The Taliban wasn't threatening these attacks—they had no external ambitions. Their goal was to reimpose their medieval version of sharia law across Afghanistan. The threats came from our old nemesis al Qaeda and the newer threat of the Islamic State that, in Afghanistan, was known as ISIS-Khorasan (ISIS-K). Both of these groups maintained a clear, unambiguous intent to execute these "external operations," and, of course, they had both demonstrated a strong ability to do so. Our working theory was that the continuous pressure that had been applied against these groups over the years by our forces in Afghanistan had prevented them from initiating these attacks. If the pressure was removed, they would be free to renew the connective tissue that would allow attacks to occur again. Because of this view, we were keenly interested in what any agreement had to say about preventing these potential attacks.

There were four key components to the U.S.-Taliban agreement. The first element asserted that the Taliban would commit to ensuring that al Qaeda and other terrorist groups would not use the territory of Afghanistan to threaten the security of the United States or its allies. The second element was an agreement by the United States to withdraw all foreign forces from Afghanistan in a two-stage process. The first stage called for a reduction to a U.S. troop level of 8,600, and a commensurate reduction by our allies, within a 135-day window (this worked out to be mid-July). At the time the agreement was signed, our force level was about 14,000, so this would be a significant drawdown. We also agreed to withdraw from five bases and transition them to Afghan security force control. The second stage, which was to be conditions-based, called for the withdrawal of all forces, U.S. and coalition, within nine and a half months—which was May 2021. Setting a date was an enormous strategic mistake that gave renewed life to the Taliban, even as it deflated the government of Afghanistan. We also agreed to stop airstrikes against the Taliban. In the full view of hindsight, this was probably the single tactical decision that contributed most to the collapse of the Afghan military, but it wasn't evident at the time. We gave this critical enabler away without any recompense from the Taliban except airy promises of future behavior. Taken together, these two decisions represent some of the worst negotiating mistakes ever made by the United States. They were both purely a reflection of our desire to have an agreement at any cost.

The third element of the agreement called for intra-Afghan negotiations between the government of Afghanistan and the Taliban. As a precursor, the government of Afghanistan would release five thousand Taliban prisoners, and the Taliban would release one thousand prisoners they held. This requirement was also problematic. It reinforced the Taliban with a group of people ready and able to fight, and many of them figured prominently in the ensuing campaign that destroyed the country. This exchange was forced on the government of Afghanistan by our negotiators, and in addition to the aid it gave the enemy, it also widened—perhaps to an unbridgeable degree—the trust deficit between President Ashraf Ghani and Ambassador Khalilzad. Fourth, and finally, the government of Afghanistan and the Taliban would negotiate a permanent and comprehensive ceasefire.

There were many problems with this agreement. Most significantly, the government of Afghanistan had been largely excluded from the negotiations— through a combination of Taliban refusal to meet with the seated government and Khalilzad's secretive, compartmented style. There were also fractures within the Taliban, which was hardly a monolithic organization. They deeply held the belief, though, that they were on the cusp of a military victory, and we were negotiating just to get out—whatever the consequences for our Afghan partners. With the passage of time, it appears that was exactly the case. And our Afghan partners, represented by the government in Kabul, felt that we had been less than honest and open with them in the negotiations. To sum it up: by the late spring of 2020, the government of Afghanistan worried that we were negotiating to establish a "decent interval" for our departure and would consign them to battle it out with the Taliban without enabling assistance. On the other side of the hill, the Taliban sensed our strong desire to end the war, and that encouraged them to develop maximalist positions in the negotiations. Both the Kabul government and the Taliban were exactly right. We sought a decent interval, and our desire to end the war dominated everything else in the room.

At the same time, I thought that the key—and potentially redeeming— part of the document was the emphasis on conditions. We were very clear that reductions in U.S. forces would be based on parallel actions by the Taliban that demonstrated their ability to keep their part of the bargain. I always questioned this, but I also felt that the conditions language was strong enough to recommend signing the agreement, and that was the advice I gave. That was also Scott Miller's recommendation and the chairman's as well. It is now painfully clear to me that we were wrong to give this advice. I do not think our opposition would have changed any decision, but I was wrong to believe that our government would actually require conditions to be met. Shame on me for that. Additionally, in retrospect, we undervalued the pernicious effect that this agreement would have on the Afghans—both morally and operationally.

On May 14, 2020, I flew up to Washington to discuss the results of the planning order CENTCOM had been given by the chairman. We had received the order on April 10 and had agreed that we would take thirty days to work a response. A planning order is a directive from a higher headquarters to a subordinate unit to prepare a concept plan to carry out whatever tasks were assigned. In this case, the task was to present a plan to completely exit Afghanistan by May 2021. This date was consistent with the date negotiated by Ambassador Khalilzad and the Taliban in negotiations at Doha. The order was to me, as the combatant commander, but our four-star commander in Afghanistan, who worked for me, was the senior leader closest to the problem.

Wednesday, June 3 was a big day for Central Command and our Afghan plan. I flew up from Tampa early that morning. I was scheduled to brief the president at 11:30 on our recommended way ahead on Afghanistan. We had boiled down the presentation to two slides, one of which was a combination of pictures and facts—intended to communicate the unique challenges that Afghanistan presented. The second slide represented our recommended way ahead. This short presentation was the culmination of hundreds of hours of work by my staff at CENTCOM and Scott Miller's team in Afghanistan. It was the distillation of the response to the Joint Staff planning order that we had been issued on April 10 and that had resulted in my commander's level two base plan, which was the technical description of the document that we produced that took U.S. presence in Afghanistan to zero by May 2021.

Upon reaching the Pentagon, I was able to sit in my liaison office and watch the secretary's televised statement about the June 1 Lafayette Park incident, where he and the chairman had walked with the president to visit St. John's Episcopal Church, across from the White House. I thought the secretary said all of the right things to the joint force, and it was obvious that he felt the burden of those images. I knew then that the White House session would be very dynamic. The chairman was good enough to offer me a ride over in his vehicle, which was a great kindness.

Mark Milley was very concerned about the Lafayette Park incident. Like the secretary, he felt keenly the signal that he had sent by appearing with the president and by wearing battle dress. We talked about it at length in his office and then again in the vehicle during the drive over. He was already mulling over what he needed to say to the joint force by way of explanation, and it would culminate with his very effective and well-received remarks at the National Defense University graduation on June 11. When we arrived at the White House, we went into the Old Executive Office Building to get our COVID-19 tests done, which were mandatory for meeting with the president. Attorney General Bill Barr was getting his test done at the same time, and it was then that I learned that our Afghanistan meeting had been pushed back about an hour. Another meeting with the president would occur first with the attorney general, the secretary of defense, and the chairman about further troop deployments inside the United States. We walked to the White House and then up the narrow staircase to the first floor. As we gathered in the small waiting area outside the Oval Office, we were ushered into the Cabinet Room. The secretary, chairman, and I sat at the large table for a few minutes, making desultory conversation, and then they were called in to see the president. I was left alone in the Cabinet Room for what ended up being almost an hour.

I had been in the Cabinet Room several times before, but always with a group of other four-star generals and admirals, typically for a round-table discussion with the president, a photo op, and usually a short question and answer session between the president and media poolees. Today, I was completely alone. It was, and remains, one of the most remarkable experiences of my professional life. Sitting at the center of the table, directly across from where the president sits, placed the famous paintings of George Washington and Harry Truman to my right. To my left, at the other end of the room, were the busts of Washington and Benjamin Franklin. The bust of Washington had always struck me as incongruous, since he was in a toga, but it was representative of him being called the "American Cincinnatus," after the famous Roman general who, as Washington did, stepped down and returned to life as a private citizen after his presidency. Directly behind me were paintings of Presidents James Monroe and John Tyler. In the middle of the bustling business of the White House, the room was cool and absolutely quiet. Like any good Marine, I reviewed and then rereviewed the brief I was going to give in a few minutes. After that, I sat quietly, enjoying the solitude and taking in the room. I didn't expect to ever be back in the Cabinet Room alone for so long a period of time. Given the circumstances of the day, the topic of my briefing, and the centrality of this room to modern U.S. political and military history, it was a powerful and moving experience.

The Marine Corps does not produce four-star generals who are acutely sensitive to mood or who are overly emotional or spend a lot of time in self-examination. Senior leader introspection is not a hallmark of the Marine Corps—introversion, yes, introspection, no. I believe I was squarely in that mold. I never agreed with Plato's observation that "the unexamined life is not worth living." In my business, if you're given to frequent overt self-examination, you're probably missing something else that you should be doing. Being there alone did give me an opportunity to renew my appreciation for the sweep of American history. For me, the room was a time machine that left me recharged in a way that is difficult to describe. The history of our Republic, measured in decades, was palpable. It was easy to imagine President John F. Kennedy across the table dealing with the exigencies of the Cuban missile crisis, or President Lyndon Johnson grappling with Vietnam—the war he did not want, and the war he could not get rid of. The Johnson image and his Vietnam problem resonated with me. That hour alone in the Cabinet Room, in the presence of American history, will be one of the most significant memories I've had in uniform. When an aide opened the door and told me that we were moving to the Situation Room for my brief, I was ready to go.

The term Situation Room is a little bit of a misnomer. It is actually a set of several conference rooms under the West Wing of the White House. It is adjacent to the presidential mess, and often the smell of cooking food drifts over. This time, we were to meet in the largest of the conference rooms, the John F. Kennedy Room. I had been in this room—and the other conference rooms—literally scores of times as the Joint Staff J-5, so this was old and comfortable ground for me. I was a little surprised that the president was taking the briefing in the Situation Room; when I had briefed him on the Baghdadi strike in October 2019, we did it in the "little oval" room in the residence. The Kennedy Room is a long, low-ceilinged conference room, with a large table that dominates it. It's something of an oppressive, closed space. Video monitors are on two sides of the room, and a global digital clock gives times around the world with one unique thing that I've only seen in the White House—there is a separate block for "POTUS location," giving the time wherever the president is. Today, it matched East Coast time. Seating is dictated by the Situation Room staff, and seating cards were laid out for us. At the table for the brief was a seat for the president at the head of the table, and then to his right, a seat for the vice president, then the secretary of defense, and the chairman, and last on that side was the director of national intelligence. On the other side of the table was the secretary of state, the White House chief of staff, the director of the Central Intelligence Agency, and the national security advisor. I was a briefer, not a principal, so I sat against the wall behind the defense secretary. My two hardback charts were sitting on an easel at the front of the room next to the president's seat. I had brought hard copies of the brief over for everyone in the room, and my efficient and capable aide, Army Lt. Col. Jibrael Means, quickly set a numbered copy out for everyone. We had oversize copies for the president, vice president, and secretaries of state and defense. The room filled up quickly, with everyone standing and talking quietly, waiting for the president and vice president to arrive. I knew that the session in the Oval with the president and the secretary of defense must have been stormy, and the secretary and chairman were subdued.

The president entered, and we began. I had briefed the president before, and I knew that it was important to engage his interest at the beginning and to stay on point—working relentlessly to get the core message across. Over the previous weeks, we had ruthlessly pared down the scale and scope of the brief to the essential decisions we needed; I knew that there would be Sturm und Drang in the brief, but I was prepared to try to hold him to the narrative and get a decision.

I began the briefing by assuring the president that we were here to talk about "going to zero" and that nobody challenged that direction—all we were doing today was talking about how to best carry out his direction. He was engaged and interactive from the beginning. His attention went between the slides in front of him and where I was standing, a few feet to his right, with my briefing easel and hardback slides. We had the usual preface of general-bashing that always began these sessions, and I left it to the chairman and the secretary to respond. As I always found, the secretary and chairman were energetic and forceful in defense of those leaders who had gone before in Afghanistan. Everybody else in the room studied their notes. We also had a diatribe on leaks, and this time I found myself in complete agreement with the president. Too many times, sensitive matters were discussed in meetings like this, and by the next day they were on the front page of the *New York Times* or the *Washington Post*. Finally, the president talked for a short while about all of the money that had been poured into Afghanistan—and with so little effect. Again, it was difficult to disagree with him.

My first chart featured pictures of the harsh terrain of Afghanistan. I shared with him my observation that while much of Iraq could be mistaken for the high desert of California or another Western state, Afghanistan was unique, particularly in the north and east. The terrain there was almost surreal in its sharp-edged, haunting beauty. He asked me if I'd spent much time there, and I told him that I had, and my son had also deployed there twice. I did tell him that at first light in the morning, and as the sun went down in the evening, Afghanistan was one of the most bewitching places in the world. We had a good back and forth about infrastructure, most of it about the Ring Road, or Highway 1, which is the only road that was intended to link the entire country together in a big circle. It's never been finished, and the security situation makes it hard to use. I was able to make my key points without much digression. While there were 8,200 U.S. military personnel in Afghanistan, there were also 7,500 coalition military personnel and 19,000 contractors. All of these people would have to be extracted. We calculated that it would require four hundred C-17 sorties to just bring out the U.S. personnel and the 2,900 or so coalition personnel that we were obligated to withdraw (coalition nations would extract their own personnel above that number). We had 224 total C-17s in our inventory—this task would eat them all up. Contractors were the responsibility of their companies, but in a contested environment, it would probably devolve upon us.

The personnel numbers were actually the easiest part of the problem. We had more than $4 billion worth of equipment in Afghanistan. This was composed of over 400,000 short tons of equipment, with over 5,400 pieces of rolling stock, including 876 mine-resistant ambush-protected vehicles, valued at $1.9 billion. We estimated that it would require a staggering 8,860 C-17 sorties, plus 125 C-5 sorties, to get this equipment out by air. We didn't want to bring it out by air, but the surface movement challenges were significant. We estimated that we would require 15,000 truckload equivalents to remove the equipment. The total Afghan line-haul fleet was 1,250 vehicles, indifferently maintained. Two routes were available—the northern route, through the Salang tunnel and under the Hindu Kush, into Tajikistan, Uzbekistan, Kazakhstan, and on into Russia and beyond. This route was impassable between October and March. The southern route, through Pakistan to the port of Karachi, was shorter but fraught with security concerns, and it required dependence upon Pakistan—they frequently closed the route to signal their displeasure over some real or imagined slight. In short, getting out was a daunting problem. The president asked a number of pointed questions, as did his advisors. At the end of this part of the presentation, I felt that we had established a clear view of what we called the "facts bearing on the problem."

We now turned to the heart of the brief—going to zero. I showed the president a simple slide that recommended only one way ahead—first, by reducing the U.S. force presence to 4,500 by the end of October. We would begin to withdraw equipment as rapidly as possible while in execution of this drawdown. Both Scott Miller and I agreed that with a force presence of 4,500 U.S. troops, we would be able to keep the North Atlantic Treaty Organization (NATO) and the coalition aboard, continue to support the government of Afghanistan, and execute the counterterrorism missions that were the very reason that we were there. We would also be able to support our CIA partners in their counterterrorism missions. We could do this regardless of whether we had a reduction in violence agreement in place with the Taliban. This first part of the brief had been modified from earlier versions. We had been directed to prepare a "zero by November" plan as well as less draconian options. The White House chief of staff, meeting with the secretary and the chairman, had recommended that we not show this option. He was worried that the president might choose it. It had been my best advice that going to zero in this manner would cause the collapse of the government of Afghanistan and the loss of most of our equipment and would fracture the NATO and coalition partnership; we would end up with a situation not unlike May 1975 in Saigon. I was happy to not brief a course of action that I believed would prove disastrous.

At this time, I had no idea of how all of this would play out in little over a year. It was a key objective of everyone in the Situation Room to paint a picture that would enable the president to choose the 4,500 option. We all recognized the disaster that would ensue with a precipitous departure. To my surprise, the president was very measured as he asked questions about what this force level would mean. He seemed to be very comfortable with the 4,500 number.

The next part of the brief turned to the first decision. After attaining the 4,500 force level, how would we get to zero by May 2021? Here there were two paths—the first was an option to go to zero by January 2021. The second was to further reduce to 2,800 by January 2021 and attain zero by May of that year. We could execute either of these options. We felt that the zero by January option was only marginally better than the zero by November alternative. We would still leave behind vast amounts of equipment, we would alienate the government of Afghanistan, and our partners would run for the exits. While we strongly preferred the May 2021 option, the secretary, chairman, and I felt that it was most important to gain agreement on the October numbers. The president approved this approach. We would examine the slope of the line for further reductions in future briefings.

We also discussed how we would be able to continue counterterror pressure against al Qaeda and the Islamic State in Afghanistan after we removed all our forces. This was a very important point to me, and I had been emphasizing it for some time both within the department, principally with Secretary Esper, but also with National Security Advisor O'Brien and retired Lt. Gen. Keith Kellogg, one of his assistants. My point was simple: at zero, it would be extremely hard to effectively operate inside Afghanistan with any counterterror force. The idea of "offshore basing," either from a naval platform or an adjacent country, presented enormous difficulties. The potential risks to our force would be very high. There was surprising attachment to this fantasy by some senior leaders. My arguments were informed by years of practical experience, and most significantly by the Osama bin Laden raid and by Eagle Claw, the attempt to rescue our hostages in Iran in 1980. The point I always made when referring to the bin Laden raid was that we crashed a helicopter on the objective. We were able to compensate for this because we had intermediate staging bases quite close by and we were able to quickly generate a "spinning backup" as well as a quick reaction force. In an extreme long-range raid, we would not have these luxuries of scale. Everything would be far more tightly coupled.

There remained a fascination with using long-range precision strikes, the old weapon of choice of the Clinton administration—the uncrewed long-range cruise missile, embodied in the TLAM. The arguments against this approach were embedded in history—none of the strikes were effective. They were always late, and they actually contributed to a perception of weakness on our part in the region. In fact, a reasonable argument can be made that given the culture of the region in general and of Afghanistan in particular, we were held in contempt when these stand-off strikes were used, however tactically effective they promised to be. We often overlooked the messaging component of actions like these. The point I made was this: operations from a distance were certainly possible, but they would be very difficult to execute.

As we began to wrap up on Afghanistan, the president made a reference to Iran, and I told him that I was also responsible for that country. I mentioned that we were working on options for him regarding Iran and that after the secretary had approved them, they would be presented to him. His interest was piqued, and he began to ask a series of questions about our Iran war plans. This was a topic far removed from Afghanistan, and I had no map or briefing materials with me, but I did have strong command of the subject, and we talked for some time about the state of our planning. I was confident that if we had to fight Iran, we would prevail. The costs would be high. We had done significant work at Central Command, attempting to understand just what it would mean to fight such a war. It was a grim picture, and I didn't hide the human and material losses that would certainly occur. The description of this encounter in Secretary Esper's book is accurate.[1] When we finished, it was clear to me that the president wasn't interested in the war with Iran that I had described.

I walked out of that meeting with what CENTCOM needed to begin the next step in Afghanistan. We would draw down to 4,500 U.S. military personnel by the October/November timeline. As always, there were many matters associated with the decision that needed to be resolved. First, we had to have a plan to tell our coalition partners; this meant NATO engagement at the highest level. Second, we had to communicate this to the government of Afghanistan; Scott had been prepping them for this decision for some time, so it would not be unexpected. Third, we had to develop a plan—what we called a "Tic-Toc" (a term of art derived from the sound of a clock ticking against a timeline)—for public rollout. A key part of this, and thankfully not a CENTCOM worry, was the notification of congressional leadership.

I called Scott Miller that afternoon and passed him a verbal order. He recommended that we keep the direction "soft" until he had a chance to reach out to our partners—particularly NATO. As usual, this was good counsel, and that was the approach we adopted, working with Gen. Tod Wolters, the EUCOM commander and the Supreme Allied Commander Europe. We also agreed that my headquarters would task him to produce a plan for execution, and he would submit it within ten days. This was largely memorialization of decisions and guidance that had already been given, but getting it all in writing helped focus the staffs.

We now had a plan, one that would take us through the end of October and establish a platform in Afghanistan from which we could either sustain a long-term presence or, if directed, continue the drawdown. I felt the meeting had been a very important inflection point. As I flew back to Tampa late that day after talking to Scott, I made a mental list of risks and potential friction points that we were going to have to overcome. More than anything else, I was concerned about possible divergence between CENTCOM's assessment of conditions for further withdrawal and potential presidential decisions that might not take those factors into account. For Scott Miller and me, acceptable conditions meant everything from a reduction in violence and attendant intra-Afghan dialogue to the most important thing of all: a clear and verifiable decision by the Taliban to not harbor al Qaeda and ISIS. The bottom line, from a military perspective, only accounted for the future composition of the government of Afghanistan and conditions there to the direct degree that those factors influenced the ability of al Qaeda and ISIS to generate attacks against our homeland.

I was then, and am now, relatively less interested in other factors—except as they impacted our core national security interests. This perspective may appear cold-hearted, but there was no other way to approach the problem from a military perspective. Many of our problems in Afghanistan could be traced to a very expansive view of social and other actions that were seen as necessary to establish a lasting favorable security environment. They had all failed. I was also concerned that Ambassador Khalilzad, who was not present for any of the White House meetings, was so committed to his negotiated peace process that he would not be able to force the Taliban to be accountable for their actions. I believe that concern was well borne out by subsequent events.

My final thoughts on the June 3 meeting centered around the intersection of politics, military strategy, and personalities. Everyone in the meeting knew that getting out of Afghanistan was a core political tenet of the president's. He had run on that pledge and had been elected to execute it. As the Joint Staff J-5 and later as the director of the Joint Staff, I had been in meetings with the president where we had recommended either holding the line on troop strength or, in some cases, slightly increasing our posture. I had seen his almost incandescent rage as we laid out the arguments. He had acquiesced to our recommendations in those sessions, but those meetings had been ugly, and it had been clear to me then that we were arguing against a fundamental and closely held belief. We were now at the end of that long and painful road.

I think the president bitterly regretted not following his political instincts in early 2017 and ordering a withdrawal at that time. We also knew that November 4, 2020, was the date of the presidential election, and fulfilling a major campaign promise before the vote was very important to him. Anyone who thinks that there is a clear divide between political calculation and strategic considerations at the highest levels of national decision-making is being naïve. It isn't possible to separate the two. Winston Churchill summed it up very well when he wrote that "the distinction between politics and strategy diminishes as the point of view is raised. At the summit, true politics and strategy are one."[2] We were at the summit.

In the weeks following our White House meeting, Scott Miller worked with Tod Wolters at NATO to brief our partners. This culminated in a briefing he conducted at the North Atlantic Council in early July. Due to the strong leadership of Secretary General Jens Stoltenberg, NATO was firmly on board with our plan. This entire process drove home again the importance of consulting early with allies and coalition partners so they could work within their own political systems to generate support. Scott and Tod were magnificent in this effort.

Events on the ground in Afghanistan were not as promising. By the end of June, Taliban attacks remained at high levels, although they scrupulously avoided attacking U.S. and coalition forces; instead, they were all directed against our Afghan partners. Part of the problem was the Afghan dependency upon security checkpoints, which distributed forces across the country in non-mutually supporting positions. These small outposts were vulnerable to being overrun and were also candidates for insider attacks. The government of Afghanistan was also feeling the pressure of these attacks, and they were beginning to hit back at the Taliban. The Afghan air force flew many missions during this period. On several occasions, we provided limited air support for Afghan forces as well, but because of our adherence to the Doha accords, these fires were defensive in nature.

Intelligence reports indicated that the Taliban believed they could achieve a military victory if they could hold us to a withdrawal and a cessation or reduction of aid to the government of Afghanistan. It was a reasonable thesis, and, of course, it was proved valid. In order to do this, though, they would have to avoid substantively participating in genuine intra-Afghan talks, which were a core element of the peace deal. If they did participate, they would seek to control the agenda and drive hard to their position. It had been envisioned by Ambassador Khalilzad that these talks would be linked to a reduction in violence and eventually a ceasefire. Unfortunately, the Afghan government wasn't helping. Bitter internecine political fighting between President Ghani and former chief executive officer Abdullah Abdullah made it hard for them to create a coherent position. Had they been able to do this in May and June of 2020, they could have held the upper hand in these talks. Their inability to rise above the moment and take the long view—a hallmark of Afghan politics—was a crippling factor.

Even with these negative developments, from what I read and saw in operational reporting, it was clear to me that the only pathway for the Taliban to seize control of Afghanistan was the military route. They weren't actually a popular force in the country, polling consistently with approval levels of 15 percent or less. In a genuinely fair political dialogue, they would not prevail. The Bolshevik solution was their best path—seizure of the state by a determined minority group. This could only happen if we cut off support for the Afghan government.

It was during these dark days of late June that the reporting on Russian efforts to pay bounties for the deaths of U.S. servicemembers at Taliban hands broke. I was aware of this reporting. In January 2020, while on battle-field circulation at Bagram, I had taken a detailed brief on these reports. I found them disturbing—and they made my blood boil. I also did not see corroboration. There was no smoking gun that provided definite proof. I sent the intelligence analysts back to their cubicles, with many questions and guidance to search even harder for linkages. This would be a significant event if it could be proved. We were never able to prove it. Not proving the case in a legal sense, though, was very different from what a commander does with conflicting intelligence on the battlefield. I was used to weighing compet-ing streams of intelligence and making hard choices. I had seen enough to make this threat appear very possible. Scott Miller and I talked about what else we could practically do. In Afghanistan, we were already at the highest level of force protection. Whether the Russians paid the Taliban or not, the methods of their attack would not be different: rockets, mortars, improvised explosive devices, complex attacks. We did not expect Russian bombers to attack us from Tajikistan. We had done as much as human ingenuity would allow to prepare for these attacks. At significant costs to our global readiness, we had positioned elite commando forces in Afghanistan to respond quickly to emergent threats.

For a commander, assessments like these were very personal, because we were talking about young men and women entrusted to our care. I felt it as a mortal responsibility. Scott and I agreed that we would watch the situation closely, press our analysts hard, wring out the intelligence sources, and be ready to respond quickly. I also had the opportunity to pass some recommendations up the chain of command, through the secretary. I recommended to him that we consider a demarche to the Russians—tell them what we suspected, without compromising sensitive sources and methods—and tell them to "knock it off." The problem at the end of the day remained: we did not have the evidence to make a compelling case.

In July, I went back into Afghanistan to see President Ghani. I spent two hours with the Resolute Support Mission staff in the gardens across from the headquarters, so we could maintain appropriate social distance. It was a small island of green loveliness in the heart of Kabul. When I had been there in 2009–10, it was called the Destille Gardens. It functioned as a beer garden for our NATO allies until General McChrystal shut down the alcohol service. That had been a minor crisis back in 2009. That seemed like an event from a different universe to me now. It was a good opportunity to get back into the situation at the tactical level. As always with a staff created by Scott Miller, the principals knew their business. It was about a one-mile drive from the Resolute Support Mission compound to the presidential palace. As we left the compound main gate, I was struck by the fact that it had been almost eleven years ago to the day when we had a massive suicide attack on the access control point. I had been with General McChrystal and the rest of the staff in the morning briefing, in a bunker behind the headquarters building. The massive explosion knocked tile from the ceiling and created a huge cloud of dust. The force of it could be felt as a whole-body experience. Going in and out of the entry control point always brought back memories of that day in July 2009.

Arriving at the palace, we met in the central courtyard. It was a lovely scene—the grass was as green and lush as a putting green, and the vegetation was in full bloom. In the Kabul bowl, most of the colors were shades of grey and ochre, all covered in a fine layer of ever-present dust. The contrast with the greenery in the palace's courtyard was almost sybaritic. We sat in chairs on the grass, about ten feet apart. Scott Miller was back in the United States on Army business, so he couldn't accompany me for the visit. President Ghani had his ministers of defense and interior with him, as well as his national security advisor. We were all masked. Because of the distance between us, we used a handheld microphone and a portable public address system to talk. While effective, it did share our conversation with anyone in the central area of the palace. There didn't seem to be many people on hand to hear us, though, except for the ever-present security details.

I always enjoyed my meetings with President Ghani. This time was no exception; I found him to be conversational and direct, with just a hint of his academic training in his delivery. He was never overly didactic, but he presented full and complete thoughts and concepts in his conversation. My task was to assure him of our continued support and to ascertain where he and his government were on the prisoner release issue. When we met, his team had released almost 4,200 Taliban prisoners. The Taliban was demanding a by-name release of an additional 592. Ghani's position was clear, and he laid it out in some detail, occasionally reinforced by injects from his ministers: he would not comply with this demand, and he didn't think the agreement required him to respond to a Taliban list. Some of the names on their list were Afghans who had committed significant crimes, and some couldn't even be located. I could not disagree with his position.

We also talked about the continued high level of Taliban violence that was directed against his forces. He made it clear that he was going to have to respond to these attacks. He felt, and stated several times in different ways, that the Taliban was "fighting to win," not just fighting to negotiate. This view corresponded to what I was reading in my intelligence reports. As we reached the end of our exchange, I expressed a thought that had been building in my mind through our meeting. "Mr. President, it seems to me that all of the Taliban's activities can be explained by the fact that their central hypothesis is that the U.S. will ultimately choose to leave Afghanistan, without conditionality. Therefore, their attacks can proceed, and they will continue to go after your forces, because they don't see a linkage between not honoring the agreement and us staying to fight." He did not disagree with me. As we ended our meeting, I stressed to him that my advice on what we did would be based on the conditions that I observed. Clearly, what the Taliban was doing now was incompatible with a recommendation to significantly reduce our posture in Afghanistan.

On the way out of Afghanistan, I wrote up my summary of the meeting and sent it to the chairman and through him to the secretary of defense and other key officials. It wasn't a cheerful report. I had always felt that the path of negotiations offered the only way to get to a peaceful solution in Afghanistan, and that the path would be narrow and difficult. Now, the difficulties were accumulating. I knew that the United States had met its obligations under the agreement. After my meeting with President Ghani, I felt that his government was moving to meet its obligations, although in an unsteady and halting manner. It wasn't obvious to me that they would be able to coalesce around a unified way forward. It did not seem to me that the Taliban was interested in meeting its obligations. In fact, it was becoming increasingly evident to me that they were, in the words of President Ghani, "fighting to win" and committed to a military and not a political solution. We were not in a good place. In retrospect, initially I probably overestimated the ability of the Afghan government to move collectively toward all of their obligations under the agreement.

Through the rest of the summer, we plodded along in Afghanistan, as both the government and the Taliban danced around the process of entering direct negotiations. In July and August, we were hung up on the release of six Taliban prisoners held by the Afghans who were guilty of "insider attacks" against either U.S. or coalition forces. The Taliban demanded the return of these six in particular. Inside the U.S. government there was concern about releasing them because of potential political ramifications inside the country if we were seen to accede to returning Taliban fighters who demonstrably had blood on their hands.

This issue was very personal for me. One of the six detainees had killed a Marine, Sgt. Kevin Balduf, on May 12, 2012, in Helmand province. Another Marine, Lt. Col. Ben Palmer, had died with him in this cowardly murder. Sergeant Balduf had worked for me in Afghanistan in 2004 as a radio operator. I knew him well. He had a young family back home in Tennessee. I signed his Bronze Star with Combat "V" award for heroism while we were in Afghanistan. To me, he represented all that was good with the Marine Corps. In my office in Tampa, I had a number of pictures, all of family members—with one exception. Directly across from my desk I kept a small montage of pictures of Kevin Balduf, including my favorite—a shot of him and me standing together at Camp LeJeune the day we returned from Afghanistan in 2004.

It hurt me to my very soul to allow his killer to go free. Despite this, when the chairman and I talked about it, the path seemed very clear. All wars end. Not all injustices can be resolved when that happens. Sometimes it is necessary to swallow hard and accept that an imperfect solution is better than no solution. The chairman, Scott Miller, and I were all of the same mind: while repugnant to us, we needed to support this deal. Eventually, a compromise was worked out where the six Taliban prisoners would go to Doha to be kept in fairly luxurious confinement until after the U.S. presidential election. Whether Qatar held them for a while for internal U.S. political purposes was immaterial to me; it was clear that they would need to be released to allow the negotiations to go ahead. It was one of the most distasteful decisions I made while in command, but it was also a clear and straightforward one. War is inherently unfair.

Finally, on September 12, all of the parties gathered in Doha for the beginning of the direct dialogue. Secretary of State Pompeo led the U.S. team, and Mullah Barader led the Taliban. Scott Miller flew down from Kabul to attend, along with Ambassador Khalilzad. In a bit of irony, I was in the theater during this time and flew into Kabul to see President Ghani the same day. September is one of the nicest months in Afghanistan, at least up north. After spending time with the Resolute Support staff, I moved to the presidential palace, this time accompanied by an old friend of mine, British Lieutenant General Giles Hill, the deputy commander of the Resolute Support Mission. Our meeting with President Ghani was again outside, and it was as lush and green as always. Accompanying President Ghani was Vice President Amrullah Saleh, his hand bandaged from the recent attack on his vehicle in Kabul that had killed at least a dozen people. I knew that the Afghans would all be on edge because of the beginning of negotiations in Doha, so my aim was to offer reassurances and let President Ghani do most of the talking. As always, Ghani was gravely courteous and soft-spoken. Saleh delivered the edged messages—their concern about violence, the return of released Taliban prisoners to the battlefield, and a general sense that the Taliban were not negotiating in good faith. I did not try to refute their message—largely because much of it was correct—but I did emphasize to President Ghani the opportunities that were now open because of the negotiations. We both agreed that the next few days would be critical. It was a good meeting, and as Giles and I drove back to Resolute Support headquarters, we felt that the government seemed to be in a good place, given the highly dynamic situation that was evolving.

As my jet took off from Kabul and headed south, I tried to review where we were in the campaign. We were fast approaching the 4,500 U.S. troop level that we had agreed to with the president. In fact, very soon U.S. forces would be outnumbered by NATO and coalition troops, who would number about 6,100. This was actually an important point: we were no longer the largest force on the ground, even though our enablers—fires, medical evacuation, intelligence, and logistical support—remained critical for all others. Even though negotiations were under way in Doha, I did not believe, in my heart of hearts, that the Taliban were serious about pursuing a negotiated path to integration and peace. The Afghans I had just met with knew that as well. The central question then became: What would we do when it became apparent that the Taliban were not negotiating in good faith? Would we stick it out at 4,500 troops? Both Scott and I felt that number, with our partners, was adequate to continue our counterterrorism and limited advise/assist missions, even in the face of renewed and wider Taliban attacks. The alternative would be to continue a drawdown that would not be based on conditions. In effect it would be the implementation of a "decent interval" approach to our withdrawal. This possibility concerned me greatly.

As my aircraft pushed south, heading back on the three-hour trip to the CENTCOM forward headquarters at Al Udeid, day turned into night. I sat and thought about Sergeant Balduf; he had sacrificed everything for this fight, as had so many other Americans, coalition servicemembers, and, perhaps most of all, Afghans. We were coming into the endgame, and I had no sense of where all of this would lead. Certainly, I knew from our planning what the various trajectories were, given likely Taliban actions and our responses. What I lacked was any genuine understanding of what our overarching national policy was. A strong and clearly articulated policy objective can provide the stability and resilience to weather tempestuous events in the field. When there is no clear objective, or when there are competing objectives, tactical events can drive the strategic direction. The last thing I had told the Resolute Support staff officers before leaving was that "something is going to happen, some event, and it is going to define our way ahead. It might be a kinetic event, a mass casualty event, or it might be a political event back home—or here—but the trajectory we think we're on is going to change. Count on it." With these unsettling thoughts in my mind, we pushed out of Afghanistan. When I got back to Tampa, I sat down and wrote a formal letter to the secretary, telling him that it was my judgment that a complete withdrawal would likely lead to a rapid collapse of the Afghan security forces and the government. I recommended that we stay at 4,500.

Meanwhile, political event friction continued back in the United States. On October 7, National Security Advisor O'Brien gave a speech at the University of Nevada and said that "when President Trump took office, there were over 10,000 American troops in Afghanistan. . . . As of today, there are under 5,000 and that will go to 2,500 by early next year." He went on to say that "ultimately, the Afghans themselves are going to have to work out an accord, a peace agreement. . . . It's going to be slow progress, it's going to be hard progress, but we think it's a necessary step—we think Americans need to come home." Shortly after this, President Trump tweeted from the White House that troops "should" be home by Christmas. The president's tweet was released ninety minutes before the start of the vice presidential debate. At the moment of these conflicting messages, we were on a firm and fully coordinated trajectory toward a troop level of 4,500 in Afghanistan by the end of November, with an agreed-upon decision point at that time to consider further reductions, based on conditions. No decision had been reached about more reductions. The speech and the tweet threatened to upend all of our planning, and they also negatively influenced our relationships with the Afghan government and our coalition partners. Building a coalition to fight a war is a very difficult task; it requires political leadership, compromise, and constant nurturing. This also applies at the military level, where constant interaction at all levels of the chain of command is necessary to keep partners aligned. Nothing damages these relationships more than surprise. With the speech and, more significantly, the tweet, we had just blindsided our coalition partners—who now outnumbered us on the ground in Afghanistan. Finally, the exchange gave aid and comfort to the enemy—the Taliban wasted no time in tweeting their own warm approval of the president's comments.

The chairman, in an interview on National Public Radio on October 11, tried to do some damage control, saying, "We're on a plan to do a responsible, deliberate drawdown to about 4,500 here very shortly. And then future drawdowns will be determined by the president." Administration disclaimers threw a further element of discord in the interagency process. The effects of these contradictions on our allies, partners, the Afghan government, and the Taliban worked against us in every way.

All of this was worsened by the actions of some administration officials, who, eager to show that they had inside information, often reached out to our allies to peddle their opinions. This was driven home to me forcefully on Saturday, October 24. I had just returned from a trip to Uzbekistan, Kazakhstan, and Tajikistan on Friday. On Saturday and Sunday, we were holding a virtual commander's conference, an important opportunity for my senior commanders in the theater to compare notes. For this conference, we had asked our "framework" chief joint officers, the senior operational planners of their respective nations, to join us. There were fifteen framework nations, ranging from NATO stalwarts such as the United Kingdom, France, Germany, Italy, Belgium, Norway, the Netherlands, and Canada, and important non-NATO partners such as Australia and New Zealand. We didn't include them in every conference, but I had found that it was a great opportunity to expose them to our planning, and it allowed them to then brief their chiefs of defense, thus helping them in the constant struggle to ensure we all had the same picture.

Since we were conducting a virtual rather than a physical event, and mindful that our audience was literally scattered across the globe, we started at six o'clock in the morning in Tampa and expected to go for six or seven hours. The timing wasn't great for anybody, but I felt it was important to not make it too easy on us in Tampa. As I came in the headquarters, I learned that our senior British military advisor needed to pass on some information before we started. The day before, on October 23, a National Security Council official and a Defense Department policy official visited the British embassy in Washington. While there, they had made explicit comments that the day after the election, the president would announce that the United States was withdrawing from Afghanistan by the end of the year. They made similar comments about Iraq, saying that we would leave there as well. Of course, these comments were immediately reported through British channels back to the foreign office and the ministry of defense. Nobody likes a surprise in matters like this, and to our British partners, it must have seemed that we were being duplicitous, given our strong messaging that we had no orders to carry out these actions. The inability to coordinate messaging across the U.S. government was irresponsible at best and catered to a narrative that we were not concerned with our partners—who now outnumbered us in Afghanistan. It was rank amateurism, uninformed by facts or operational capabilities, and did not comport to the reality of the situation.

I broke away from my conference later that morning and talked to the chairman. As I already knew, he was in the dark about this outreach. As the conference wrapped up later that day, I took the time to restate that we had no guidance to go below the programmed force level of 4,500. The chairman and I talked again on Sunday afternoon. He had talked to Secretary Esper and also to National Security Advisor O'Brien. I didn't draw any particular confidence from his recounting of their conversations. As we approached the election, it seemed likely to me that we could receive orders to get out of both Afghanistan and Iraq in the immediate aftermath, whether the president won or lost. It was a disquieting thought. Scott Miller and I talked about it, but I didn't share anything else with my staff. We had contingency plans for this eventuality, and I didn't want to risk leaks to the media—or to place even greater pressure on our commanders in Iraq and Afghanistan.

Of course, all of this came to a head with the presidential decision to draw down to the level of 2,500 transmitted to the department in mid-November. This decision was the culmination of a process that had been played out over several months. I had been given the opportunity to give advice on this, and I had done so in memoranda to the secretary on September 25 and October 13. My advice, which incorporated the best military judgment of myself and Scott Miller as well, argued that reductions below the level of 4,500 should be undertaken only if conditions warranted. In my mind, those conditions included a genuine Taliban commitment to not allow al Qaeda and ISIS-K to flourish in Afghanistan, a reduction in violence countrywide, and a renewed—and visible—decision to remain a full partner in peace talks with the government of Afghanistan. As of late November, none of those conditions had been met. The chairman's memo, dated October 23, made the same points. Our joint recommendations—the considered and coordinated opinions of the key military leaders involved in the campaign—informed the secretary of defense's memorandum of November 9, 2020, in which he made essentially the same recommendation. The secretary's memorandum was a courageous thing, directly challenging the president. I don't know if the memorandum was the immediate reason, but the president fired him the same day. Secretary Esper took a clear and unambiguous position. I believe it cost him his job, and I certainly appreciated the courageous way he stated his position.

I thought this was Secretary Esper's best moment in the department. Over the past year, I had watched him attempt to navigate between a defense strategy that did not comport with the facts on the ground in the Middle East, and the reality of deterring Iran while choking that nation through economic and diplomatic means. He had been unable to force a genuine strategic decision about prioritization from the president. Instead, we had been forced to manage through the orders book process, sending units and pulling them out in a staff drill that overrode the exhaustive and detailed planning accomplished by the Joint Staff to manage the force, given the existing guidance and prioritization of the National Defense Strategy. Guidance at this level could only have come from the president—and it didn't come. We missed Secretary Esper immediately.

Into the frantic, hurly-burly world of the late-stage Trump national security apparatus crept a bit player, Doug Macgregor, a retired Army colonel, whom the president had appointed to a special advisor post in the Department of Defense. While he was at best "an attendant lord, one that will do to swell a progress, start a scene or two . . . full of high sentence, but a bit obtuse,"[3] he seized his moment with alacrity and prepared without any consultation with anyone a letter from the president directing a full withdrawal from Afghanistan no later than January 15, 2021. He also got the president to sign it on November 11 and then caused it to be delivered to the Department of Defense directly, without engaging the national security advisor or anyone else. The letter landed with a thud on the E Ring (the outer executive portion) of the Pentagon. The chairman quickly engaged, as did the acting secretary, Chris Miller, and the letter was retracted.[4] The damage lingered. It was surprising that someone could get so close to the president, have him sign a letter, and then get it delivered without any consultation with the national security staff. With that, Doug MacGregor exited the play. It shook me up enough to talk to my subordinate commanders on November 12 and to review with them the chain of command and how orders were passed within Central Command.

If there was any good news, it was this: an affirmation that we would go to 2,500 in mid-January, not zero in late December. In the largest sense, it meant that the president was punting on Afghanistan. The long-term decisions about what we did in that country would now be made by the next administration, although we were committed to exit by May under the terms of the Doha agreement. We would avoid a sudden retreat in winter. A force level of 2,500, if properly employed, would enable us to work with our NATO and other allied partners, and with the Afghans, to continue to pursue our core objectives. They are worth restating: ultimately, to safeguard the homeland from inspired, directed, and enabled terror attacks launched by al Qaeda and ISIS-K from within Afghanistan.

I immediately reached out to our framework nation partners to ensure they weren't surprised by this decision. As always, they appreciated the heads up, even if it was only hours ahead of a public announcement. At the same time, my planners and logisticians in Tampa began the hard work of coordinating with Scott's staff for the movement of personnel out—which was easy— and the associated movement out of equipment and other material—which was extremely difficult. Scott and I had been talking for some time about the possibility of 2,800 in January—it had been a waypoint in the master plan

I gave the president in June—so we had some ideas in mind. I don't know why 2,500 instead of 2,800 was chosen by the White House as a force level. Regardless, we could live with it, albeit with slightly higher risk. As was always the case with Scott Miller, his team already had some very good and sound ideas about how to reduce our footprint while still retaining capabilities in three core areas: force protection, counterterror operations, and focused advise and assist. "Focused" was a euphemism for not being everywhere all the time. We would be forced to leave some units and provinces uncovered at various times. We would also retain the ability to manage the disbursements of payments to the Afghan security forces. NATO proved surprisingly resilient, and I was heartened to hear that they would likely keep a significant posture in Afghanistan, larger even than ours, subject to a February 2021 ministerial conference in Europe.

Of course, this process wouldn't be complete without the internecine bickering and finger-pointing that seemed to follow the Trump political appointees who filled the Pentagon in the wake of the Esper firing. It began by insinuations that Scott Miller wasn't moving quickly enough and that "the generals" were slow-rolling the president on his Afghan decision. Since I was one of "the generals," I knew this simply wasn't true. We had all been given the opportunity to give advice, and we had given that advice. It wasn't taken, but that is a prerogative of civilian leadership. Once we had a decision, everyone moved out to execute, and I knew of no officer who consciously attempted to subvert the directive of the president.

By early January we had reached our mandated 2,500 troops on the ground in Afghanistan. This was the result of a herculean effort by Scott Miller and his team and good support by U.S. Transportation Command, which had to juggle the stream of aircraft—and ground transport—out of Afghanistan. We waited to see what the next administration would do.

Meeting with Abdullah Abdullah in his office in Kabul. An exceptionally intelligent and insightful person, Abdullah functioned as the chief executive officer
of the Afghan government after narrowly losing a hotly contested presidential
election to Ashraf Ghani. The indeterminate nature of his position was emblem-
atic of the dysfunction of the Afghan government.
Dr. Abdullah Abdullah @DrabdullahCE/Twitter

Early in my tenure, meeting with King Salman of the Kingdom of Saudi Arabia. I
found him engaging. We spent some time talking about the U.S. ambassador to the
Kingdom, former CENTCOM commander Gen. John Abizaid, USA (Ret.).
Department of Defense

Welcoming King Abdullah II of Jordan to Tampa. I always found His Majesty to be a keen observer of regional and global affairs. He had a superb mind for strategy. *Department of Defense*

On a dry lake bed that served as the runway at one of our remote garrisons in Syria. It was important to get around to these small outposts so that the men and women at these bases could understand that we were aware of their sacrifices and the risks that they bore every day.
Department of Defense

Talking to Sailors while embarked on a carrier. I often requested the deployment extension of carriers in the CENTCOM region, and it was important that the Sailors and Marines who were on the receiving end of these changes had an opportunity to see the responsible officer: me.
Department of Defense

Walking with Gen. Scott Miller, our commander in Afghanistan, inside his compound in Kabul. A big priority for me was keeping an open channel of communication with this brilliant, selfless officer.
Department of Defense

Meeting with Lieutenant General Aviv Kochavi, the Israel Defense Force chief of staff, at CENTCOM headquarters in Tampa.
Department of Defense

Meeting with the Saudi chief of the general staff, General Fayyadh Al Ruwaili. We met many times and talked on the phone even more frequently. I considered him a friend.
Department of Defense

This is how it looked on the other end on August 15, 2021. President Biden is at Camp David, and I'm in the middle square in the left column on the screen. I was participating from my forward headquarters in Qatar and had just met with the Taliban. Most of my interactions with the president and his team were in this format. *Official White House photo*

On the ground in Kabul on August 17 at Rear Adm. Pete Vasely's headquarters at Hamid Karzai International Airport. Pete (in the foreground) and I are reviewing the tactical situation on a map. Between us in the background is Elizabeth Packard, the director of my action group. Her insight and strategic sense were very important during these hard days.
Department of Defense

Midafternoon in Doha on Sunday, August 15. This picture has never been released before. I'm in the center, with my back to the camera. To my immediate right, across the table, is Mullah Berader. We're in a small room, high in the Ritz Carlton. I am delivering a message to the Taliban that we are going to conduct an evacuation, and that we'll hurt them badly if they interfere. *Author collection*

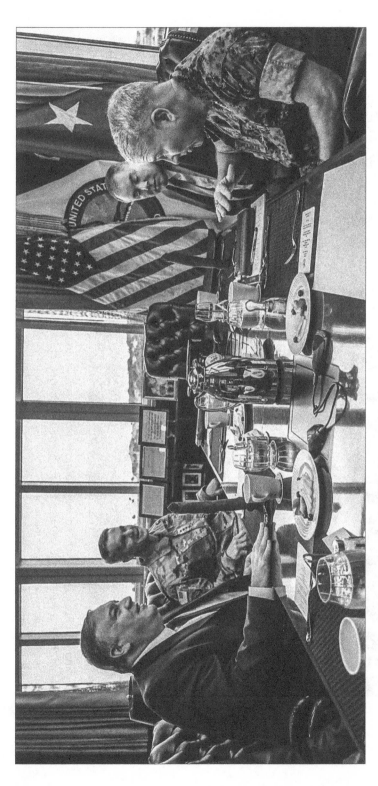

Meeting in my office in Tampa in 2019 with Secretary of State Mike Pompeo, my good friend fellow commander Gen. Richard Clarke, and Under Secretary of Defense John Rood. I always enjoyed the opportunity to be in meetings with John Rood. He had a first-rate mind and a quick grasp of essential issues. Secretary Pompeo had visited CENTCOM to receive a briefing on our family of Iran plans.

Department of Defense

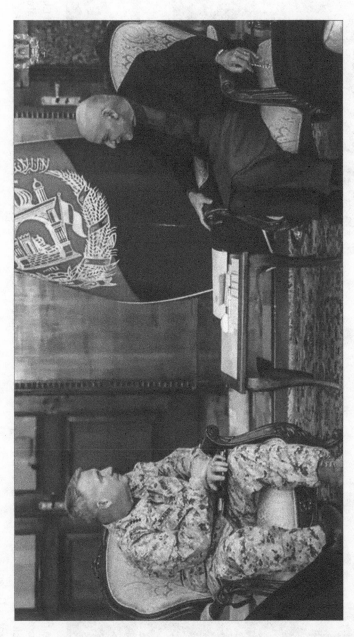

Meeting with President Ghani. I always found him to be courteous, professional, and sharply intelligent. As we neared the end, he increasingly used his subordinates to deliver bad news or protests about our actions. *Courtesy Afghanistan government [Arg]*

This was a particularly meaningful moment for me. This is the memorial at our embassy in Beirut. It honors those who lost their lives at the 1983 airport bombing and also the bombing of our embassy. Earlier that day, I had taken the opportunity to visit the site of the airport bombing.

Department of Defense

C-17s being loaded at Hamid Karzai International Airport. The work of U.S. Transportation Command and the U.S. Air Force was simply magnificent in establishing and maintaining the bridge of airlift that got so many people out of Afghanistan. *U.S. Marine Corps (Sergeant Samuel Ruiz)*

Talking to Brig. Gen. Farrell Sullivan, USMC, in Kabul, August 17, 2021. He had an incredibly tough job: running the evacuation. He was forced to constantly juggle competing imperatives, and he performed magnificently.
Department of Defense

Getting off my airplane in Kabul on August 17. It was important to be on the ground, to see the situation firsthand.
Department of Defense

On the ground at the airport in Kabul on August 17, 2021. We had weathered the storm the day before, when the southern airfield perimeter had been breached. I wanted to visit my commanders and see how the processing of evacuees was going. To my immediate left is Col. Shawn Leonard, USA, my executive officer. He was with me for all three years of my command, and I came to treasure his advice and counsel. He was one of the finest Army officers I ever served with. *U.S. Marine Corps (1st Lt. Mark Andries)*

Where national policy meets humanity. Marines processing Afghans for evacuation at an airport gate on August 20.
U.S. Marine Corps (Staff Sgt. Victor Mancilla)

The aftermath. Testifying before Congress in late September 2021. Secretary of Defense Lloyd Austin, Gen. Mark Milley, USA, and I addressed both the Senate and House armed services committees in marathon sessions.
Department of Defense

9

A LONG DECEMBER

A long December and there's reason to believe
Maybe this year will be better than the last.
—The Counting Crows, *"A Long December"*

In the 1984 movie *Ghostbusters*, scientist Egon Spengler warns his teammates to not "cross the streams," saying that to do so "would be bad." In the weeks following the election, this is exactly what we did in the CENT-COM theater—where the fates of Iraq, Iran, and the Department of Defense itself finally all overlapped and came to a decisive point, made more volatile by the end-stage activities of the Trump administration. While the result wasn't "total protonic reversal," the concatenation of internal U.S. political developments and events in the Middle East and China created one of the most tense, dangerous times I ever experienced in all my years of service.

It all began with the results of election night. There had been long-circulating rumors that Secretary Esper would be fired by the president regardless of the results. In the immediate aftermath of the election, some stories that were leaked indicated that he might remain. In an environment where the White House used leaks as "temperature tests" before making policy announcements, there was much to chew on. I was in my office in Tampa when the tweet from the president broke. My first reaction, and I'm sure it was shared by many other combatant commanders, was the hope that Secretary Esper's firing would mean that the Monday afternoon two-hour-long—and soporific—NDS review would be cancelled. This lengthy and highly detailed series of meetings, held weekly, were a core part of Secretary Esper's management style. Objectively they were useful, but they were also painful for the combatant commanders who attended by video conference. The meeting was in fact cancelled, and it was probably small of me to be happy at getting two hours of my time back. In fact, I would miss Secretary Esper.

He was a good, honorable man in a difficult situation, and I always felt he would support me in a tough spot. I don't believe he ever deserted his core ethical beliefs, and ultimately that cost him his job.

His replacement would be Chris Miller, coming over from the National Counterterrorism Center. Miller had served as an Army officer in the Special Forces. There was nothing in his career that would indicate he would be a future secretary of defense; he was a capable Army officer who served with honor and then entered the bureaucracy, where he served effectively. There would be no time or opportunity to confirm him, so he would be an acting secretary. For a combatant commander, there was little difference between an acting secretary and a confirmed one. It was important in the internal management of the department but less so in chain of command matters. Of more practical importance, though, were the other personalities who came with him. The chief of staff to the acting secretary would be Kash Patel. He rapidly proved to be the center of gravity in the department, with deep connections back to the White House. If there was an éminence grise in the department during this period, it was Patel. Other people came over from across the river and fell in on jobs within the department, including Ezra Cohen as both the acting assistant secretary for special operations and low-intensity conflict and the acting undersecretary for intelligence. Anthony Tata came in as acting undersecretary of defense for policy. They were all acting—none of them were confirmed (or confirmable). Patel did not need to be since the chief of staff position did not require it. On the other hand, policy and intelligence were two of the most important civilian positions within the department. All came with a strong ideological bias, and they were committed Trump loyalists, with deep political ties to the president.

Acting Secretary Miller issued guidance to the department on November 13 and again on November 16. He held a joint chiefs/combatant commander secure video conference during this period. This first session was an important opportunity for him to define himself and transmit his priorities to his commanders. I'm sure it's a little unnerving to sit in front of the eleven combatant commanders as well as the joint chiefs. His performance did not inspire confidence. He was very self-deprecating, which is a useful technique for lightening the mood, but he continued to lean heavily on it throughout the conference. In front of his commanders, it began to look like he actually felt inadequate in some way—not an auspicious start, particularly when addressing a group of people who have absolutely no internal monologue of inadequacy or lack of confidence.

I found Miller to be approachable and conversational any time I dealt with him. He also continued to be diffident in his new role, and I thought he leaned heavily—perhaps too heavily—on the coterie of advisors who came in with him. Those advisors seemed intent on settling old scores and implementing their own separate agendas in the handful of days before January 20. Thankfully, most of their interest was fixed on intelligence "reform" and reordering the command and control of special operations forces. The acting secretary was absorbed in the relationship between the assistant secretary for special operations and low-intensity conflict and the Special Operations Command. Meanwhile, Cohen pursued an old vendetta against the Central Intelligence Agency, attempting to cut off most support for the agency's field activities. The turbulence that all of these competing initiatives created at the top of the department was not conducive to calm, steady decision-making and leadership.

The one area in which they dabbled that could have been very dangerous was senior officer management: the four-star commanders and a select few three-star jobs. Recognizing that they had little time before leaving office, Acting Secretary Miller and those around him sought to bring in officers they approved of, which would have meant retiring combatant commanders early, all in a press to get "their" officers in command. This was overt politicization of the officer corps, and no single thing could have been more dangerous to the future of the U.S. military than a scheme like this. Luckily, the simple inertia in the system, the need for congressional consultation and concurrence, as well as the steady hand of the chairman delayed these actions until it became obvious that nothing could be done before January 20. In selecting officers for high command, the long-term interests of the nation must be at the fore: with Acting Secretary Miller and his team, choices were based on simple political expedience—and settling scores. This was a profound diminution of the office, and had it been carried through, it would have greatly damaged the officer corps for years to come.

With the political leadership of the department in a state of solipsistic disorganization, I don't think any combatant commander felt secure that there was a steady hand on the tiller. The focus—and that's probably too kind a word—was inward. From my perspective, this was particularly dangerous in the Middle East, where the Iranians could be counted upon to take advantage of any weakness they saw in our approach to the theater. Several things came together in November that added risk. The first was completely self-inflicted.

I had known Ambassador Jim Jeffrey for many years. I always found him to be an engaged, personally courageous diplomat, willing to live and work under conditions of extreme personal hardship to accomplish the mission. Part of this was probably his early background as an Army infantry officer—we had much in common. Jim had served as our ambassador to Iraq, Turkey, and Albania and then as the secretary's special envoy for Syria—and after the December 2018 decision by the president to withdraw most of our forces from Syria, he served as the special representative for Syria engagement and special envoy to the global coalition to defeat ISIS. He stepped down in November 2020. On his way out the door, he gave an interview to Defense One, which was published on November 12, 2020.[1]

Most of what he said was insightful and useful, and I found little to disagree with. In one area, though, he was damaging. He told Katie Bo Williams: "We were always playing shell games to not make clear to our leadership how many troops we had there. . . . The actual number of troops in northeast Syria 'is a lot more than' the two hundred troops Trump agreed to leave there in 2019." This was an unfortunate statement. First, it was wrong—the numbers of troops on the ground in Syria had always been reported completely, although the total numbers were not always public. The guidelines for reporting were secretary of defense-approved and were embodied in formal orders from the Joint Staff. The numbers we reported publicly did not include "temporary enabling forces," units and personnel that were brought in for short periods of time or for specific counterterrorist tasks. We drew a distinction between these two "pots" of units, but there had never been an intent to withhold these numbers. Unfortunately, this clear and approved distinction was lost on many both inside DoD and in the White House who chose to read the ambassador's comments at face value, creating the impression that the Joint Staff, CENTCOM, and our theater components were slow-rolling or trying to find ways to avoid acting on guidance to reduce forces on the ground.

In this case, the facts were easily established and were very defensible, but doing so could not fully address the second-order effect of chipping away at trust in the accuracy and honesty of the reporting chain. It had a malignant effect that would add to friction and mistrust inside the government in the critical months of December and January. There were other equally frustrating episodes. During this period, rumors circulated that senior members of the Trump administration, in both the Pentagon and the White House, were unhappy with Gen. Scott Miller, our commander in Afghanistan, and consideration was being given to replacing him. This was based on a belief that he wasn't wholly behind the administration's actions in Afghanistan. I knew from direct personal observation that Scott Miller carried out every order he was given with enthusiasm and with the skill and nuance that only a long career in tough assignments could bring. I know that the chairman felt the same way, but the rumors persisted, and of course, they reached Scott's ears. It was an unnecessary and cruel burden to add to a commander in a close fight, doing his level best to carry out an extremely difficult and often contradictory set of orders. Eventually, the rumors died out. I would like to think it was because truth overcame innuendo, but that may be an overly optimistic view.

Other things contributed to a rise in tensions in the region. The deaths of al Qaeda leaders and the daughter of Hamza bin Laden in Tehran further stoked Iranian fears. The unexplained explosion at Natanz in July 2020 had further reinforced this narrative. Whatever the objective truth behind these actions, the Iranians laid the blame at the feet of Israel, and when they did so, they also held the United States responsible. More strategically, the signing of the Abraham Accords between Israel and the United Arab Emirates on September 15, 2020, while good for the region overall, also further isolated Iran. Bahrain followed suit with a similar agreement with Israel on the same day. The Iranian response was to issue broad threats to all parties involved in this agreement.

On November 12 the president met with the new acting secretary of defense, the chairman, the secretary of state, and the vice president, among others. I was not at the meeting, but I received a thorough debrief from the chairman by phone after he returned to the Pentagon. In short, intelligence indicated that while Iran wasn't taking irreversible steps toward a nuclear weapon, they were doing things that would enable them to return to production of nuclear material should they choose to do so. The discussion turned to military options that would set their program back. As always, in meetings like this with President Trump, the intent of participants from the Department of Defense was to avoid a hasty, sudden decision—perhaps a strike—that would be irrevocable. The chairman could readily recite the many plans that CENTCOM held for a wide variety of strike options. I had talked at length with the president about these options during our June 3, 2020, meeting. All of them entailed significant risk. There were, however, other things that could be done that would slow their program without entailing the risk of war.

Eventually, the president accepted a proposal that the Defense Department would come back in a few weeks with potential options against Iran. This would include briefing him on things that were in the works and that needed either his decision or further authorities to go forward. When the chairman called me, we both knew exactly what was required. We needed to convince the president that we weren't sitting on our hands with the Iran problem—which was true. If we could convince him of this, then we would be able to minimize the chance of a sudden decision by him to strike Iran. The MacGregor example of someone short-circuiting the decision-making process was at the forefront of our minds. It had always been clear to me that the president did not seek war with Iran; it was equally clear that he would not allow them to pursue a nuclear weapon. Convincing him that planning was in motion to prevent Iranian attainment of a nuclear weapon was key to avoiding a war. The key was convincing *him*; others were more aggressive and not as risk-averse on this matter.

I called the planners together down in Tampa. We reached out to our interagency partners and got to work. The chairman and I agreed that I would prebrief the acting secretary before we finalized the briefing. When working a presentation like this for national leadership, it's absolutely critical to decide what the object of the brief is—and then narrow it to that topic. Clearly, in this case, our object was to convince the president that things were in train that would interfere with Iranian nuclear ambition. He was being listened to—we were not slow-rolling him. This was a second objective of the brief—to parry the persistent narrative that "the generals" were not carrying out his intent. The final and overriding objective of the brief would be to restate the high cost and risk of direct military action: action that, at least from where I sat, would be preemptive in nature. An underlying objective—unstated but shared between the chairman and me—was to prevent a hasty or spur-of-the-moment decision that could bring us to war.

Even as we worked on this brief, events occurred in the theater that raised the stakes. On November 23 Mohsen Fakhrizadeh, a key Iranian nuclear scientist, was killed in the Tehran suburb of Absard.[2] It was a shockingly violent and precise strike. Regardless of who actually carried out the strike, the Iranians believed it was an Israeli-sponsored action. We watched carefully over the next few days as the Iranians went through their usual investigatory processes. At the same time, we knew that they would be looking for ways to retaliate. They took no immediate action, but we all felt that some response would be inevitable.

In this pressurized environment, I flew to Washington on Friday, December 4, to brief the president on our Iran options. As usual, the day began with a one-on-one meeting with the chairman in his office. We reviewed the simple slide deck that I would present. Everything was a hard copy; we had transmitted nothing electronically. I had one hardback mounted slide that covered my major points. Our intention with the brief was to reinforce to the president that we were actively pursuing a number of options across the U.S. government, both in and out of the Department of Defense, as well as with international partners, all designed to slow the development of the Iranian nuclear program. We knew there were voices that argued for a more direct and kinetic approach to the Iran problem. Interestingly, it was the president who resisted these more aggressive approaches. My objective, then, was to reinforce the idea that there were things we could do that were short of open warfare that would slow Iran's nuclear work. We were also trying to put to rest the idea that "the generals" were delaying the initiatives of the president. This theme was a persistent drumbeat of the newly installed appointees inside the Pentagon, although neither the chairman nor I believed the acting secretary held this view. Unfortunately, it was hard for us to discern where the actual locus of power was in this confusing and ever-changing new constellation.

I rode to the White House with the chairman, and we gathered in the Cabinet Room for the briefing. The briefing itself would go in the Oval Office. Present at the meeting were the chairman, the acting secretary of defense, the assistant to the president for national security, the White House general counsel, the director of national intelligence, the White House chief of staff, the national security advisor to the vice president, and the chief of staff to the secretary of defense. Mark Milley and I were the only uniformed officers present. The director of the CIA was not present.

Except for photo sessions with my fellow combatant commanders, the last time I had been in the Oval Office for a substantive meeting was in August 2018, when Rich Clarke and I had interviewed with the president for our combatant commander jobs. That meeting had been very small—the president, John Kelly, then the White House chief of staff, and Rich and me. The office was a little more crowded this time. Everyone took seats across the Resolute desk from the president. While I had a seat, I spent most of my time standing, positioned to the immediate right of the president, in front of my small easel and my one hardboard slide.

Everything I briefed was strained through the filter of the president's guidance that told us to prevent Iran from developing a nuclear weapon, to avoid activities that would lead to a war, to ensure our actions were legal and appropriate, and to minimize risk to U.S. forces. I was confident that the plans we were sharing met all of these criteria. We had been working on these ideas for years in many cases. Nobody in the room knew these plans better than me. Taken together, they represented a genuine campaign approach to the problem of Iranian nuclearization. They were not independent actions, but rather a comprehensive, fully integrated series of actions that aimed for specific effects.

I knew it was important to engage the president's attention immediately and to keep the momentum of the brief moving. We rapidly went through the history of how we got to our current situation. The president was engaged, focused, and quite interested in both the large concepts and the small details. I outlined the various options and decisions we would need from him in order to move forward. The chairman and I tag-teamed much of this, with occasional interjections from the other people in the room. To make some points, I passed out pictures of specific systems and capabilities, knowing that the president reacted well to images and visual references.

At the end of the brief the president seemed to accept our underlying premise: while we had a number of high-end kinetic options against Iran, we were better served by not choosing to employ them at this time. It was preferable to continue to work on options, planning, and messaging capacities of the United States and our friends and partners. When we walked out of the Oval Office, I felt pretty good about where we were. Most significantly, I believed that we had shown the president that we weren't sitting on our hands against Iran and that we did not need to resort to high-risk kinetic activities to have an effect on the country's nuclear ambitions.

I collected all of my charts and the hardback graphic. The chairman and I had a few moments for a quiet discussion downstairs, reviewing the meeting outside the Situation Room. We were both pleased. We felt that we had a good way ahead to avoid a war with Iran, while still carrying out the direction of the president. This time, we left in separate vehicles; I was headed back to Joint Base Andrews and my Gulfstream for the flight home to Tampa. I debriefed my staff in a secure call from the airplane, speaking indirectly even over a top-secret connection. I felt we had done some good work and that we had achieved our major objective. The president now knew and understood the universe of actions that was in existence against Iran. I felt confident that we would not be tasked to strike Iran, unless something unforeseen came up.

There have been anonymous leaks about this White House meeting that attempted to portray a very different picture of what happened. This narrative wrongly implies that the president was looking aggressively for ways to attack Iran and that the CIA could or would not help him, so he turned to the Department of Defense. The chairman is portrayed as slow-rolling the responses. This is simply untrue. The chairman and I were completely linked on our approach to the campaign and on our approach to the president.

Further, I found the president to be rational and very reasonable in the briefing. Nobody at CENTCOM was frustrated with or angry at the way the briefing worked out or what followed from it.[3]

Only time would tell if the presentation would do anything to quiet the persistent narrative of the resistant, uncooperative generals. With the president, I felt we had accomplished the task. With his subordinates within the Defense Department below the level of the acting secretary, I was less certain. In fact, I felt that it probably would not accomplish that objective, because the concerns had never actually been based on the actual situation but rather on the need for continual scapegoating that seemed to envelop the end days of the administration.

As we entered the middle of December, we began to see ominous signs that Iranian proxy groups in Iraq were preparing to ramp up violence again. It had always been clear that the fragile reduction in violence in Iraq would be susceptible to breakdown, but a confluence of factors made it even more likely. First was the burning desire to gain some form of revenge for the deaths of Soleimani and Muhandis. The death of Mohsen Fakhrizadeh was also a factor. Second was the recognition that the disparate Shia groups in Iraq were not going to be able to eject the United States and our partners from that country through political means. Third was a belief that kinetic action would force us to withdraw and that their earlier attacks in the spring and summer had led to our base consolidation and drawdown. Fourth was a desire to "settle accounts" before the presidential transition on January 20, 2021. Balanced against these views, of course, was another perspective inside Iran: the argument that all friction with the United States should be minimized until the transition of administrations. These ideas competed inside the Iranian decision-making process, and a further complication was the fact that the view from Tehran was not necessarily the view of Shia groups in Iraq. Put another way, Iran did not have perfect command and control over the various competing groups inside Iraq.

On November 21 we received a nine-rocket attack against the Baghdad embassy. One round landed inside the embassy compound; the others missed, and an Iraqi child was killed. This was a clear sign that things were changing. Through a variety of intelligence sources as well as imagery, we could clearly see renewed Iranian interest in hitting us in Iraq. My normal routine was to take several intelligence briefs a day: I'd get a formal one from my J-2 at the morning commanders conference, then I'd get a more highly classified one from a small team of briefers a little later in the day. Finally, I'd get a briefing from my CIA representative. Many of the things that I heard weren't known to the headquarters as a whole, and some of them were so sensitive that I was the only officer at CENTCOM who could receive the material. On the weekends and on holidays, a briefing team would visit me in my quarters, usually at seven o'clock in the morning, and we would go through the sensitive traffic face to face. My practice was then to filter the points of view of the different agencies, often talking to my magnificent intelligence officer, Dmitri Henry, who had a gift for sifting through data and finding underlying structure and patterns. He could see through the noise and smoke and find the two or three key factors. I found his work invaluable to everything I did at CENTCOM. By around December 15 I had formed a commander's estimate that took the view that attacks in Iraq by Iranian proxy groups were increasingly likely. I also felt that the Iranians had a misunderstanding of what our tolerances were. It was abundantly clear to me that the loss or injury of even a single American would provoke a violent response. Even destruction of high-value equipment, such as Patriot systems, that did not include loss of life might cross that redline. It was also clear to me that the Iranians did not appreciate this fact and felt that they could kill small numbers of U.S. troops without provoking a response. This was a dangerous misapprehension, and I talked often to my staff about how we could message them on this matter.

The threat streams continued to grow as we drew nearer to Christmas. I had a trip scheduled into the theater for the third week of December. I wanted to visit Iraq, Syria, and Afghanistan. I did not plan a trip like this lightly, because I knew the burden it placed on commanders and their staffs in the theater. Senior officials would often try to get into these areas around Christmas, on the "drumstick" tour, where they sought photo ops while working—at least for a few minutes—in the chow line. It was a massive drain on resources and time. I had prevailed on the chairman and the secretary to drastically reduce these visits in the fall of 2020, citing the threat environment as well as the COVID risk. They were very supportive of my request, and we were able to greatly reduce visits to Iraq and Afghanistan.

I went into Iraq on the morning of December 20. In the aftermath of the Soleimani strike, I was a marked man in Iraq, and my travel in and out of the country was designed to reduce vulnerability to attack. After very good meetings at the U.S. Embassy with Ambassador Matthew Tueller and Lt. Gen. Paul Calvert, I paid a call on the Iraqi chief of the general staff, General Abdel Emir Yarallah. I had two key points that I wanted to communicate to him. The first was that the future strength of U.S. forces in Iraq would be arrived at as the result of a consultative process between our two nations. Second, I wanted to impress upon him the importance of the Iranians knowing that even a "small" attack on U.S. forces could unleash a significant response. I was confident that any message I gave him in that regard would get to the Iranians quickly. As usual, the meeting had somewhat of an anodyne cast, but I was satisfied that the chief of staff understood my message.

I flew out of Iraq that afternoon, headed to my forward headquarters at Al Udeid Airbase in Qatar. I was just settling in when the Dataminer application on my iPhone began to prompt me with reports of a rocket attack against the embassy in Baghdad. Within a few minutes I was talking to Paul Calvert, who confirmed that multiple rockets had been launched against the embassy. We were still in the middle of our accountability process, but there appeared to be no casualties. The chairman called, hungry for information. I knew the environment he was in, so I tried to give him as much as possible without guessing. Over the next few hours, we began to get a good picture of the attack. It involved twenty-one 107mm rockets launched from Rasheed Airbase, about seven kilometers away from the embassy. Of the twenty-one that were fired, it looked as if nine had impacted inside the embassy compound. Our counter-rocket systems had fired more than 1,200 rounds in defense of the embassy. The gym had been hit, but there were—miraculously—no casualties.

An attack of this scale represented a significant escalation. We had not taken this many rockets at the embassy since 2011. Also, given the time of day (early evening) and the concentrated target area of the missiles, it was clear that this wasn't a harassing attack. It was an attack designed to inflict significant casualties. We were able to recover three rockets, and they had Farsi language inscriptions. The Iraqis were good partners in trying to locate and exploit the point of origin site. While the militant groups in Iraq had gone to great lengths to rename themselves and create an obfuscatory tissue of false front organizations, we were able to narrow it down to a single group—Asaib Ahl al-Haqq—and to also see a link to Khatib Hezbollah and, less clearly, to the IRGC-QF, which was Iran.

The next day, I had to fly into Kabul to see Gen. Scott Miller and President Ghani, so I didn't have the luxury of giving this disturbing development my entire attention. The time zone difference between the theater and Washington was also a factor—Iraq is eight hours ahead of Washington, so the working days barely overlap. As always, though, I considered what the CENTCOM position would be. Our first requirement would be to ensure we had scrupulously accurate reporting going up the chain of command. The lessons of the January attack on al Asad weighed on me—a misreport there could have led to war. We were back on that treacherous ground again. Second, I would need to have recommendations for the acting secretary: what should our response be? On the three-and-a-half-hour flight back from Kabul to my forward headquarters on December 21, I gave it some thought. The next day I had planned to visit northeast Syria—I had gotten into southern Syria on December 20 after my Baghdad visits. Reluctantly, I made the decision to cancel my travel back into Syria. This was based on an old axiom, timeworn and hackneyed but still useful, that a commander should place himself or herself at the point of maximum friction—as Sir William Slim said, "the right place at the vital time."[4] It was my belief that the attacks in Iraq signaled a new and very dangerous phase in our campaign. I was also concerned that there might be a push from "across the river" to make this a casus belli. That wasn't a military decision—but I wanted to ensure that accurate reporting was provided and that my advice was given. It did not need to be taken, but it needed to be given.

The chairman and I talked throughout the day. We agreed that he and I would both provide written, signed recommendations. I sat down and gathered my thoughts in my office inside the forward headquarters, which was conducive to work. Built as a protected bunker, it was quiet and free of many of the distractions that always seemed to emerge in Tampa. At CENTCOM, we had a broad variety of plans at our disposal ranging from nonkinetic messaging to large and violent options. It seemed clear to me that our response should do two things: first, we needed to be proportional—our response should match the attack, which had not killed anyone. Second, and more important, this was an opportunity to send a clear message to Iran that this behavior would lead to direct conflict. Here was our opportunity to unambiguously message the fact that even a single U.S. casualty would provoke a far greater response than they had considered. The underlying assumption here, of course, was a dual one—that Iran was ultimately behind the attack, to some degree, and that the IRGC could control the actions of the proxies in Iraq. I was comfortable with that logic, based on what I was reading in the intelligence reports that were being walked in to me frequently throughout the course of the day.

I called my operations officer and sketched out to him what I wanted in my advice letter. Maj. Gen. Alexus "Grynch" Grynkewich , USAF, had proved a worthy successor to Sam Paparo. I had fought to have him assigned as my J-3, knowing him from earlier service on the Joint Staff and then as the J-3 in Iraq, where his cool demeanor, penetrating intelligence, and steadiness under pressure had been major sources of strength for Pat White. I told Grynch that I wanted my advice to capture the range of options available to us and then give specific recommendations. He was a quick study and prepared the letter for me to review and sign within four hours. By then, I was airborne headed back to Tampa. The letter would be top secret and further compartmented. We had more trouble on the airplane downloading it, printing it, and setting it up for my signature than probably went into its preparation back in Tampa. I made a few changes, but Grynch and his team had done superb work. It went back up to the secretary from the airplane, through the chairman. In essence, I proposed that we message Iran very hard, through some quiet back-channel paths, and that we also reach out to all of our interlocutors in the region and convey a consistent message: "Knock it off." If the attacks persisted, we would respond, and our response would be significant. It was a fool's errand to parse the number of U.S. deaths that would provoke a response. One was enough. I also catalogued some kinetic options that we could employ—but I was clear that I did not recommend we use them in response to this attack.

I landed in Tampa on Wednesday, December 23, at about 6:30 a.m. and went straight into my headquarters. I knew that a principals small group (PSG) would be held at noon that day in the White House to determine the way ahead. The secretary, the chairman, the vice chairman, the secretary of state, the directors of CIA and the National Security Agency, the director of national intelligence, and others would be in the meeting. It would be chaired by National Security Advisor O'Brien. While I waited for feedback from this meeting, I held my own commander's meeting. By now, I had moved beyond the December 20 attack; my focus was on the next attack—one that was very close, if the intelligence was accurate. The parallels to a year before were not lost on me. In many ways, we seemed to be drifting into another exchange with Iran. We had enjoyed a measure of luck in January 2020, when the Iranian attack on al Asad did not cause any U.S. or allied deaths. A portion of that luck had been due to actions to disperse the force that commanders had taken in the hours before the attack. We could not count on that luck continuing if we entered hostilities again with Iran. That weighed on me heavily as I talked to my leaders.

In meetings of this kind, where all commanders are on line and the staff is also available, I believe it is critical that the combatant commander clearly outline what he or she thinks is going to happen and then walk through the most likely situations that could arise. This includes sequels—the next step if things go the way we think they will, or branches, when things don't go according to plan. It is in the interchange of ideas that trust is established. It's also very important to allow every subordinate commander an opportunity to review whatever concerns they have. While some of my commanders had changed from a year ago, I was quite happy with those who looked back at me from the large monitor at the end of my conference table. Vice Admiral Sam Paparo was now my Naval Forces Central Command commander, and Jim Malloy was my deputy commander. I was lucky to have both of them. My new air component commander was Lt. Gen. Greg "Gooey" Guillot, USAF, and he had gotten off to a running start.

My bias has always been to overshare information with subordinate commanders. If subordinates understand the concept behind why I want to do something, they are far more likely to willingly and cheerfully execute their assignments. It also allows them to share insights with their subordinates, thus empowering the entire chain of command. Sometimes, a commander can be burned by oversharing, but I've felt that the positives of sharing information far outweigh the negatives.

Late on Wednesday, I learned the results of the PSG. Largely, CENTCOM's recommendations had been accepted, and some additional actions were set forth. Most significantly, the president would tweet on the attack, warning the Iranians. This was done at 4:47 p.m. on December 23: "Our embassy in Baghdad got hit Sunday by several rockets. Three rockets failed to launch. Guess where they were from: IRAN. Now we hear chatter of additional attacks against Americans in Iraq. . . . Some friendly health advice to Iran. If one American is killed, I will hold Iran responsible. Think it over."[5] Embedded in the tweet was a picture of the three 107mm warheads, with Farsi lettering. This was a clear and straightforward warning. Whatever anyone's opinion was of the president's proclivity to tweet about anything and everything, in this case it was very helpful.

We released a statement from CENTCOM later that afternoon on the same subject that concluded, "The United States will hold Iran accountable for the deaths of any Americans that result from the work of these Iranian-backed Rogue Militia Groups."[6] Concurrently, we reached out through a variety of channels to decision-makers and thought leaders across the region. By the next day, I saw that someone had leaked the PSG agenda and attendees to the media—I could only suspect that this was part of the messaging plan as well.

We also used some channels to communicate with Iranian leadership directly. All of these were above CENTCOM's level. We never knew if they had any effect, but we were certain that the messages were received and seen by senior Iranian leadership. One thing did concern us: we continued to see reporting about the health of the supreme leader. Despite his bone-deep hatred of the United States, he had proven to be a force for relative moderation when it came to launching attacks. His practice had typically been to allow planning and preparations to proceed to an advanced stage, and then to call the operation off. If he was unable to be a participant in high-level deliberations, a potential brake might be lost. As always, the reporting wasn't completely clear on this, but there was enough to convince me that his health was a factor we should consider.

As Christmas Day passed, we settled into an uneasy routine in the theater and in Tampa. In Iraq, our forces were locked down, focusing on their own force protection. I talked to Paul Calvert every morning, just to get his sense of what was developing. Over the long Christmas weekend, the intelligence briefers dutifully delivered the "book" to me at seven o'clock every morning. I would pore over the reporting and then review other material in my sensitive compartmented information facility, the small closet off my home office where I worked with top-secret material.

On December 26 I learned that the Iranians had responded to the chairman's direct messaging to Major General Mohammad Bagheri, which had been delivered on December 24. Calling in the Swiss chargé in Tehran, Kim Sitzler, on December 25, the director general of the ministry of foreign affairs for the Americas, Reza Nazar-Ahari, delivered a response. It was largely boilerplate, with the usual accusations of "warmongering" added for good measure. The note did aver, though, that Iran "does not seek escalation or war, and has no intention of initiating any direct or indirect hostile measure against the United States." I read it thoroughly and then reread it. Taken at face value, it was reassuring. If they did hold to what they said in the note, then we could see a way through this crisis. The risk that was apparent to me, though, was that as always, there were inevitable disconnects within the Iranian government. The ministry of foreign affairs did not always have insight into what the IRGC-QF was planning. In fact, the rapidity of the response—within twenty-four hours—made it seem likely that the answer did not reflect a coordinated Iranian government position.

After Christmas Day, we continued a rhythm that was disturbingly similar to that of a year before. Every morning, I took a detailed intelligence brief with my commanders. Often during the night, I would be awakened by my J-2 or J-3 regarding a message that I needed to see. Sometimes we could discuss it, and sometimes a courier had to deliver it to my quarters. I talked one-on-one with Paul Calvert frequently and came to admire his steady, calm presence. As I've noted before, the University of North Georgia has produced its share of superb Army leaders, and Paul stood among the first rank of them. Our forces on the ground in Iraq were locked down at our highest level of force protection, while we "flooded the zone" overhead with intelligence, surveillance, and reconnaissance (ISR) of all types, designed to both detect and deter activity. As far back as May 2019, we had learned that obvious and heavy overhead ISR tended to cool the ardor of the militant groups and even the Iranians. We also kept a wary eye on Iranian activity in Syria, Yemen, and Afghanistan.

We also fought yet another bureaucratic battle over forces for the theater. I had long viewed the presence of a carrier strike group as fundamental to deterring Iran, providing a ready part of any immediate response, then defending against the inevitable Iranian riposte, and, if necessary, being a basic building block for any larger response. *Nimitz*'s time was growing short in the theater. She was not in the best of shape; we struggled to keep her four catapults working. They were critical to her ability to launch her air wing into action. In December, I agreed to push her south so she could help our adjacent combat command, Africa Command, in the withdrawal of U.S. forces from Somalia, the third of the trifecta of withdrawals ordered by the president.

I felt that the carrier and her consorts sent a powerful signal to Iran. Significant intelligence supported my position. There were also other and contrary views, and any official seeking to force a preferred decision could window-shop across the intelligence community until he or she found something they could assert was revealed truth. The other tried-and-true technique in Washington was to leak it to the media, in anticipation that the coverage of a possible future event might impact decision-makers. This had often proved to be an effective technique. The choice was simple—retain *Nimitz* in the theater into January, until she could be relieved by another deploying carrier, or send her home and leave CENTCOM without a carrier during a very high risk period.

My reading of the risk in the theater was based on an evaluation of four broad threat streams, three oriented at us and the fourth at Israel. The first threat stream was what we referred to as the "Iranian state" stream. This was embodied by the personality of Esmail Ghani, the IRGC-QF commander. Through his interaction with the supreme leader and the Supreme Council for National Security back in Tehran, we judged that they held a series of strong attacks in immediate readiness but had not yet been green-lighted by the supreme leader. Further, and with moderate confidence, we believed that our force array in the theater—including *Nimitz*—acted as a deterrent. In short, this was a more or less conventional threat, and we were having an effect by keeping powerful combat forces in the theater.

The second threat stream was once removed from the IRGC, and it centered around the Iran-backed rogue militant groups in Iraq. They had been provided with lots of high-end weaponry by Iran over the years, including 122mm rockets and even close-range ballistic missiles. They still burned for vengeance over the death of Muhandis, and the exact degree of Iranian command and control—the ability of IRGC leadership to impose direction and guidance—was unknown. Third, local and uncoordinated Shia groups in Iraq, some of them far away from centralized control, still held large stocks of less advanced but still potentially lethal weapons. They certainly held enough capability to launch local, and potentially lethal, attacks. Finally, there was an enduring threat stream that focused on Israel, emanating primarily from Yemen. Iran was also still seeking revenge over the death of its nuclear scientist. By using the Houthis in Yemen as a catspaw, the Iranians could plausibly argue that they were not responsible. We thought the weapon of choice for such an attack would probably be a long-range drone, and during the latter part of 2020, the Iranians had built up a pool of these long-range platforms in Yemen.

This was a dizzying array of potential threats. Another question was timing: there were several anniversary days that might appeal to Iran. The first, of course, was the day of the strike on Soleimani: January 2 in the United States, which was January 3 in the theater. In late December, during discussions with my senior staff, we began to consider the possibility that Iran might instead choose to wait until closer to the presidential inauguration. There was precedent for this. In 1980 the Iranians chose to release the hostages they had illegally held for 444 days as President Jimmy Carter left office, embarrassing him and his administration. We began to think that a similar strategy that might appeal to them would be to launch a calibrated strike immediately before January 20—one designed to inflict pain but that would stay below the threat of a major U.S. response. Then, by careful messaging of the new administration, they might be able to both embarrass President Trump and appeal to the new president for a reset. We all agreed that it was a lot to read into the situation, where our ability to sense Iranian decision-making was obscured at best, but I kept my intelligence teams on the problem.

In the middle of this, the secretary's December 30 decision to send the *Nimitz* strike group home came as a surprise. I could certainly see the rationale for doing it, and from CENTCOM our concern was less the decision itself than the way it was—or wasn't—conveyed to our partners in the region. The flurry of contradictory leaks from the third deck of the Pentagon (the location of the offices of the secretary) that accompanied the decision seemed to paint a picture of a team in above their heads, and through this self-referential posturing we lost much in messaging that could have otherwise been gained with this decision. I knew it was the secretary's intent to signal the move as a de-escalatory step. I didn't agree with it, but my opinion was irrelevant once he made a decision. We were ready to support it. Unfortunately, the leaks by high-level defense officials, imputing positions either in support of or opposed to the secretary's decision, created murkiness and damaged us in the information environment. During this period—from mid-December until the end of the administration—it was hard to know who was really calling the shots inside the department. From where I sat as a combatant commander, all power and decisions seemed to emanate from the department's chief of staff, Kash Patel. In my long experience with chiefs of staff in the department up until this time, he was clearly the most powerful relative to the acting secretary, and taskings that came down, even from policy, would often add the observation that "Kash is really pushing this." It wasn't a good state of affairs. The most effective chiefs were not necessarily the most openly assertive and directive: genuine and long-lasting power came from the ability to work behind the scenes without upstaging the secretary. While this small group of aides has been described by some as Machiavellian, their ad hominem attacks on anyone they thought held differing views, constant self-promotion, and uncoordinated, hasty actions made them seem far more Lilliputian.

A National Security Council meeting was scheduled for late in the afternoon of Sunday, January 3, at the White House. The chairman asked me for updates on all CENTCOM operations and readiness conditions. We talked several times throughout the day; the last time was right before he went into the White House. By definition, a National Security Council meeting includes the president, so we knew that we could potentially get guidance on a broad range of issues. My input to the chairman centered around keeping adequate forces in the theater to deter, defend, and respond, without being needlessly provocative. He called me from his vehicle after the meeting; it was around seven o'clock in the evening in Tampa. Most significantly, we would keep *Nimitz*; we would order her to turn around and return to her operating area in the Gulf of Oman.

CENTCOM tended to not read too much into pronouncements by the Iranians; they made them frequently, and often they were contradictory, but I was certainly pleased that the president extended *Nimitz*. She had not actually left the CENTCOM area of responsibility, and she was still under my operational control, so this was a very easy task to carry out. We would continue to maintain a high level of readiness without provoking the Iranians. Messaging would continue. At 8:08 that evening, the secretary issued a tweet that confirmed the status of *Nimitz*. I felt badly for the Sailors aboard her. Being extended or being ordered home were easy conditions to adapt to. Being whipsawed back and forth was another matter. As a colonel and a MEU commander in 2006, I had seen the same thing, when our ships were ordered back and forth in CENTCOM in a manner that seemed to convey an inability to make a decision. Nonetheless, the decision to retain *Nimitz* was right, although it did further pressurize the situation by calling attention to the fact that she was remaining. Had we simply kept her without all of the attendant cross-messaging, it would not have been such an event in the blogosphere. Telling the world that she was headed home and then abruptly reversing the decision harvested the negative aspects of each course of action, while minimizing the potential good. It was amateur hour.

By early January, we crossed the anniversary day for the Soleimani strike. I knew that the United States had reached out with de-escalatory messages for Iran through various intermediaries, and even made a demonstration of de-escalatory intent, albeit bungled in delivery—the *Nimitz* redeployment and subsequent return. We began to see indications that the Iranians were cooling to the idea of a large, complex attack in Iraq against our forces. This became clearer over the first week of January. We still were very concerned about small-scale attacks by groups that were resistant to Iranian control, but overall the crisis seemed to be easing just a little. We could not determine if it was based on a desire to get to January 20 and a new president without sparking a war, or if they were planning a "January surprise," perhaps an attack in the waning hours of the Trump administration that would preclude the ability of the outgoing president to respond while hurling an opportunity for negotiation—or escalation—into the lap of the incoming president. The events of January 6, when the Capitol was attacked, redounded across the Middle East and gave great aid and comfort to all who opposed us. I was very concerned about what effect it might have on the Iranian decision-making calculus—would they see us as weakened? Would they think that the current president might do something egregiously offensive in the theater?

The chairman and I consulted frequently during these days; I knew that his burdens were particularly heavy, as he dealt with the situation in Washington and all of the ramifications of those terrible images. During this turbulent period, Mark Milley was magnificent. In a joint chiefs and combatant commander meeting on January 8, which most of us attended by secure video conference, he thoroughly explained what had happened on January 6, and his words had a calming effect. I know I left the Tank with renewed confidence about the role of the military in the crisis we were facing, and that boost was due directly to his leadership. In many ways, I believe this was his finest moment.

During these trying times in early January we reached our presidentially mandated force level of 2,500 in Iraq, and I formally notified the acting secretary. The reduction in Iraq, which received little of the media attention that our drawdown in Afghanistan did, was a good example of how to work with a partner nation. Through constant engagement with the government of Iraq at all levels, we were able to make joint decisions about reducing our forces, rebasing, recharacterizing their activities, and establishing a clear path to the future that included a U.S. and NATO presence. This process, while complex and incremental, gave political capital to the government of Iraq while preserving both our long-term bilateral relationship and our own policy objectives in Iraq.

By January 9 my read of the situation had evolved to encompass the following key points:

- At the pinnacle of national leadership—the supreme leader— Iran did not want to seek a confrontation with us before the transition of power.

- As always, there were competing ideas in play in Iran, and this wasn't the only line of action being debated within their system.

- The health of the supreme leader would be important for the next two weeks: if he were unable to assert himself in a crisis, then the path would be open for the hardliners.

- We needed to maintain our posture while not doing anything provocative that could light the fuse.

- I did not believe that President Trump sought a confrontation either, but I was frankly shaken by the events of January 6, and after that day I remained very concerned about what our own national leadership—or those purporting to speak for our national leadership—might direct.

In summary, I believed our actions, military and diplomatic, had convinced the Iranians that now was not a good time to go to war. The chances of a rogue group attacking us in Iraq was still very much a possibility, but I thought Iranian state-level action was less likely. I was less sanguine about what could potentially happen in the upper levels of our own government. Try as I might, I could not get the images of the mob loose in the Capitol out of my mind and the irresponsibility that had stoked those dark passions.

In a meeting with my subordinate commanders on Saturday, January 9, I reviewed these points with them. I also took a few minutes to reemphasize the importance of the chain of command—not because these battle-tested and senior leaders needed a review, but because the times were so trying and unusual that I wanted everybody to know who would be talking for CENTCOM, and how I'd talk to them if necessary.

We were pushed to the brink once more in January. Throughout my time in command and even before, when I was on the Joint Staff, Israel had been striking targets inside Syria with both crewed and uncrewed aircraft. Their targets were usually Iranian or Lebanese Hezbollah and were typically associated with the transfer of advanced weaponry from Iran to Lebanon. Israeli strikes most often occurred in western Syria, but occasionally they struck in the east. With good reason, Israel remained very worried about ballistic missiles being moved piece by piece into Lebanon and then assembled. The specter of the 2006 war was ever-present. Most of their strikes were against this line of communication. Occasionally, they would target Syrian infrastructure, most often air defense missile sites. Responses had been muted from both Iran and Syria. The simple fact of the matter was this: Israel was a hard target to hit, by any measure, and even a successful response would bring inevitable Israeli retribution.

The Israelis had great regard for Russian air defenses, which were positioned in the west and around their airbase at Hmeimim. They routed their strikes assiduously to avoid Russian radar and also Syrian radar when possible. Syrian air defenders were generally incompetent to operate the equipment that had been provided by their Russian patrons. Batteries tended to fire after the threat had passed to avoid taking an Israeli antiradar missile in the face. They also lied baldly about their effectiveness. Sometimes the Israeli strike packages would enter through our position at At Tanf, an outpost near the juncture of the borders of Syria, Iraq, and Jordan. It was manned by about two hundred U.S. soldiers. We typically had prenotification of strikes, and they would ask permission to overfly At Tanf. They did not ask permission if the routing did not take them over At Tanf. When we received these overflight requests, at CENTCOM we would evaluate the proposed target against a checklist of criteria that Secretary Mattis had issued and that Secretary

Esper had refined. Based on this, I would then make a recommendation to the secretary about whether to allow overflight.

It's important to understand that we were not approving—or assisting—in targeting. All we were doing was recommending whether or not Israeli aircraft would be allowed to overfly the At Tanf garrison. These requests were made in groups, and the proposed window of execution would be between fifteen and forty-five days into the future. Most, not all, were approved. I recommended disapproval of some at my level, and the secretary disapproved some at his level. There was no approval process for strikes that did not transit At Tanf.

In September 2018 Syrian incompetence in the wake of an Israeli strike was responsible for the downing of an An-32 Coot over western Syria, killing fifteen Russian signals intelligence analysts and aircrew. The Russians didn't like the Israelis flying into Syria, but Israeli routes were carefully chosen with an eye to avoiding the Russians, and we also knew that they deconflicted their flights with them to some degree—not unlike what they were doing with us.

This process worried me. The Israelis were striking legitimate targets that posed a danger to Israel. In doing so, though, they were on occasion killing Iranians, members of Lebanese Hezbollah, and Syrian soldiers. The Syrian response was largely limited to ineffectual barrage firings of unguided surface-to-air missiles. Occasionally, Lebanese Hezbollah would fire mortars or even direct-fire weapons into Israel, but even these operations were more like scripted *condottiere* battles of fifteenth-century Italy, where shedding blood was to be scrupulously avoided. On the other hand, the Iranians seethed. The IRGC was under pressure from the supreme leader to do something—anything—to respond to the endless attacks.

We came close to the breaking point on January 12, when the Israelis notified us they were striking targets in eastern Syria in the general vicinity of Dar az Zayr, not too far from our positions east of the Euphrates at Conoco and Green Village. These were two forward operating bases that occupied old oilfield infrastructure. I had spent some time at each base, and they were austere. The Israeli strike was a secretary-approved concept of operations, and it would transit At Tanf. It consisted of nine targets, and the Israelis successfully struck seven of them. As always, it was hard to know what was at the target, but there were significant second-order explosions and reports of significant casualties. Within six hours, a number of 122mm rockets were launched at Green Village from west of the Euphrates. We tracked eight rockets in flight, fired from a launch site about fourteen kilometers west of our positions. The 122mm rocket is a heavy weapon, and it has significant lethality. The rockets overflew our forces, landing just to the east. It was early evening in Tampa. I was on the phone within minutes with Paul Calvert, trying to gain awareness of what was going on. The number of rockets fired and the fact that they were 122mm in size were sobering.

Very quickly, we were able to understand what was going on—this was the Iranian response to the Israeli action. This was new country. For the past several years, the Iranians had responded against Israel for their attacks, often in comic opera style. Israel was a hard target for them, and even harder if the desire was to keep a fig leaf of deniability about the attack. Now, a new policy seemed to be in place—they would strike at U.S. forces in Syria. We were much easier to get at than Israel; for one thing, the ranges were much shorter, and the IRGC had a variety of weapons it could select from for such an attack. Our response on the ground to this new threat was to button up our bases and fill the sky with crewed and uncrewed intelligence-gathering and strike platforms. We also messaged Iran through the various channels available to us that we would not sit idly by while our bases were attacked. We also needed to talk to the Israelis, and I arranged for a call with the Israeli chief of defense, Lieutenant General Aviv Kochavi. He was a no-nonsense paratrooper with a keen intelligence and a good sense of humor. When we talked, I made my concerns clear—my forces were accepting the risk for his actions. With a new administration coming to power within a week, it was possible that they would not view the continuation of strikes into Syria by Israel with the same laissez-faire attitude that the current team had.

The result of this attack was to place CENTCOM at a very high level of alert across the entire theater. Even at this time, I remained convinced that Iranian leadership did not want war. It was hard to know if this was because of our visible posture adjustments, which included significant overhead intelligence platforms, or if it was driven by other reasons. In the final analysis, it didn't matter, so long as deterrence held. While we could not rule out a "January surprise" from Iran in the form of a last-minute attack designed to embarrass the exiting president while not affording him enough time to respond, every day that passed without indications of preparations for such an attack gave me hope that we would be able to avoid it.

One final event occurred in January that went almost unnoticed in the frantic and overheated information environment that characterized the run-up to the inauguration. In early January, President Trump signed the 2020 Unified Command Plan (UCP). It's a recondite document, referred to by many people but read by few. Among other things, the UCP sets forth the basic responsibilities for all of the combatant commands, including describing their geographic areas where appropriate.

In the new UCP, Israel was taken from the European Command area and moved into CENTCOM. I had recommended this to Secretary Esper back in the spring of 2020, during our "blank slate review." My view was that all of the threats to Israel emanated from the east—from within CENTCOM. Because of this, CENTCOM maintained a deep and rich dialogue with the Israel Defense Forces. Responsibility for coordinating the defense of Israel was vested within EUCOM. This introduced friction into planning and execution. Aligning *all* responsibilities for Israel with a single commander would simplify the chain of command and avoid the possibility of misunderstanding that always obtained when an operational problem existed across a combatant command boundary. Throughout 2020 the topic was debated. The joint chiefs, otiose as usual, could not agree on a position. As he often did, the chairman saw the opportunity and recommended the move to the secretary. The secretary also saw the utility of the move and embraced it and made it his own, despite strong pushback from within his own policy shop.[7] It went across the river in the late fall and disappeared from view in the White House. Acting Secretary Miller was silent on this matter; I never learned his position. I actually felt that it would not be something that the president signed before he left office, given everything else going on. My very capable J-5, Maj. Gen. Scott "Eggs" Benedict, USMC, was confident that it would be signed. I bet him a Diet Coke. On Thursday, January 12,

I gave him a cold Diet Coke, with a short note: "Thanks for all the hard work on this. You were right and I was wrong about the signature." It was a bet I didn't mind losing.

This move had profound implications. Israel had been placed in EUCOM when tensions were high between Israel and Egypt. Egypt, of course, was a CENTCOM country. We were now well beyond that era, and military cooperation between the two was significant, particularly in the Sinai. The move also aligned with the Department of State's diplomatic grouping of Israel within the Middle East Bureau. Additionally, the signing of the Abraham Accords was the first real break toward Israel among the Arab nations in the Gulf. It was a very strong signal. Since the president signed the UCP at the last minute, there was a widespread belief that it had been a White House initiative, one of many that were trundled out in the waning days of the administration. Instead, this was a recommendation that came up from CENTCOM, was thoroughly reviewed by the Joint Staff and joint chiefs, and gained the full-throated approval of the chairman, and, most importantly, Secretary Esper. The secretary's support was very important, because without it, I'm certain the idea would have died, as ideas had so many times before.

Coupled with the initiative of the Abraham Accords, there was now an opportunity at the military level to integrate Israel carefully and cautiously into the family of Middle East nations. Bilateral relationships already existed between Israel and many of its Arab neighbors. It was my belief that we needed to turn these quiet linkages into a multilateral approach, even if it was sub rosa at the beginning. It would take time to do this, far beyond my own time at CENTCOM, but it was a road worth pursuing.

As we approached January 20, I met twice with the Biden transition team. The guidance from the chairman had been simple and direct: be cooperative, go the extra mile, and help them in any way possible. I felt that we met that standard in our dealings with the transition team. While I read stories of obstructionism within the department, I never saw it, and it certainly wasn't entertained at CENTCOM. It helped that both meetings were chaired by Christine Wormuth, who had been undersecretary of defense for policy when I was the Joint Staff J-5. I knew her to be an exceptionally intelligent, insightful leader—and the meetings bore that out. She went on to become the secretary of the Army in the Biden administration. In the theater, we continued to watch the Iranians carefully, but it now seemed increasingly certain that they were choosing to ride it out and see if their fortunes would change with a new team. I was busy all day on January 20 with meetings, briefings, and phone calls, but I kept the large panel monitors in my office on CNN and Fox. By the early afternoon of January 20, I felt that we had left a deep and perilous valley and had negotiated some of the most dangerous days in the history of the republic.

We had "crossed the streams" in November, December, and January. Despite this, we had avoided total protonic reversal. Simply arriving at the afternoon of January 20 without a major war with Iran under way was a great accomplishment, and it was achieved in two domains: first, the exercise of restraint by the United States, and second, the effective deterrence of Iran. It took all the elements of national power to achieve this. I will always believe that the actions we took—and the actions we didn't take—contributed to this.

The final months of the Trump administration within the Department of Defense were the time of the sorcerer's apprentices: the heyday of temporary appointees who grasped at the levers of power and influence without a deep understanding of the effects of their actions. This was compounded by a frenetic rush to remake the department in the handful of days they were granted before the inauguration. Just as they did for Johann Wolfgang von Goethe's apprentice, things began to spin out of control, and the administration was not mindful of the consequences. In some cases they did not care: they actually sought disruption and chaos. Nowhere was this more manifest than in the hurried attempts to reorder the command and control of special operations forces, the attempt to end support for the Central Intelligence Agency by the department, and the uncoordinated letter directing us to leave Afghanistan. We were saved by the sturdiness of the design of the department itself: it's hard to destroy such an edifice in a few weeks, and we were also saved by the long-suffering and much maligned nonpolitical civilian appointees within the department, who soldiered on and kept the faith, even in the darkest of days.

10

CLEANSING THE TEMPLE

THE NEW TEAM

There is less here than meets the eye.
—*Tallulah Bankhead*

I knew most of the Biden defense team. They cut their teeth under the Obama and Clinton administrations, and I had worked with them closely at the beginning of the Obama administration, when I had served while a new brigadier general as the presidential transition coordinator in 2008–2009 for then-chairman Adm. Mike Mullen, and then at the end of his two-term administration, when I was the Joint Staff J-5 from 2015 until 2017. Much earlier, as a lieutenant colonel, I worked as a fellow for Michèle Flournoy from the summer of 1999 until December 2000 at the National Defense University. The time with Michèle was one of the most formative of my entire career, giving me the opportunity to examine the relationship between politics, policy, and military planning and operations. In 2004 as the commanding officer of the 22d Marine Expeditionary Unit, I had commanded under Lloyd Austin in Afghanistan, when he was the commanding general of the 10th Mountain Division. He had been a good commander in combat: tough, no-nonsense, and conservative. I later worked for him again as a lieutenant general when he was the CENTCOM commander and I was his Marine Forces Central commander. He wasted few words and kept his counsel closely held.

The biggest and most immediate change that attended the arrival of the new team was the rebirth of a genuine and formal policy decision-making process. To an ever-increasing degree throughout the Trump administration, there was no process for systematically addressing problems at the interagency level, arguing them out, making decisions, recording those decisions, and then transmitting orders and guidance to the departments and agencies that would carry out the decisions. It is a truism to say that every president eventually gets the national security decision-making process he wants. That doesn't make the observation any less trenchant. The Obama team embraced process, with an elaborate nesting of committees of ever-increasing weight and seniority. This would be reestablished in the Biden administration. The danger of policy paralysis by extended analysis was real, and it happened, but it was presumably offset by the ability of the machinery of government to provide the president with the best possible options and to pass on his decisions in a systematic, orderly manner. From a process perspective, I believe the uniformed military welcomed this return to "normal order."

A second component of the Biden team's approach would be "cleansing the temple": righting what they saw as the usurpation of civilian control by the Joint Staff and combatant commanders during the Trump administration. There was a certain element of truth to this assertion, but it was more a reflection of the very limited pool of talent that filled the senior leadership positions in the department than actions by the Joint Staff to unbalance the concept of civilian control of the military. The Trump administration would not, as a matter of policy, bring into government any of the many talented Republicans who had either signed a "no Trump" letter or who might have expressed some anti-Trump sentiment on social media. As a result, with some notable exceptions, such as John Rood, who was a very effective undersecretary for policy, and Joe Kiernan, the undersecretary for intelligence, the human talent available for service at the civilian appointee level was neither of the highest order nor very deep. On the other hand, the Joint Staff continued to attract the very best men and women in uniform—joint service was a prerequisite for flag rank. As a result of lengthy gaps in the appointment process, acting civilian leaders and their staffs struggled to compete with the ability of the Joint Staff and the combatant commands to argue positions on virtually everything.

Having said this, there was never a chance that the "unequal dialogue" between civilians and the military would be upended. In my extensive experience on the Joint Staff, I never met any senior military leader who would have disagreed with Clausewitz's lapidary commentary on this matter: "Policy is the intelligent faculty, war only the instrument, not the reverse. The subordination of the military view to the political is, therefore, the only thing possible." In fact, the many articles that circulated among the opposition policy elite about this "problem" during the Trump administration seemed to work very hard in sepulchral tones to draw strained and ominous conclusions from scant evidence. Despite this, we would be in for a thorough fumigation.

Secretary Austin wasted no time in putting his mark on the Pentagon. As a combatant commander, I was removed from the significant reforms that were introduced in the military justice system, promotion practices, and other measures that were designed to improve diversity across the department. I was more attuned to how the new team would execute within the policy/strategy realm and how relationships would be managed between the secretary and his commanders. Of the several secretaries that I observed up close and the four that I worked for directly in the chain of command, Secretary Austin was the most remote and removed from dialogue. I had far less contact with him than any of the others. When we did meet, it was formal and carefully scripted.

His team came into office determined to complete the shift to a focus on China. Like others before them, they found it harder to do in practice than in theory, because there were other significant problems besetting the United States. It wasn't possible to simply flip a switch and send everything to the Pacific—where the vast majority of U.S. military power was and had always been. As I watched them struggle to square this circle, it was my judgment that they disregarded Emile Simpson's definition of strategy, set out so clearly in his excellent book, *War from the Ground Up*: "Essentially, strategy is the dialectical relationship, or the dialogue, between desire and possibility." The new team never argued the proposition as a dialectic process; instead, they applied a bureaucratic approach that sought or more often imposed homogenized consensus—as defined by them. The first real expression of this effort to shift our emphasis was the long-awaited Global Posture Review. Closely held before release, it seemed unsatisfying when briefed from the Pentagon press room in November 2021. A further and more directed review of forces in the Middle East was promised, as if this would bring decisive weight to the China reorientation. Since only a very small percentage of the department's forces were in the Middle East and even fewer were permanently assigned to CENTCOM, it was hard to see how much more blood could be squeezed from a patient who had already been repeatedly bled.

More concerning was the new team's approach to planning and the review process for those plans. All combatant commanders maintain a series of war plans based on guidance received through documents such as the Unified Command Plan, the Contingency Planning Guidance, and other directives. End states for plans—what the theater should look like after execution of the plan, or victory—was assigned in these documents, and other guidance was provided to assist the tasked commanders in developing their plans. I had some expertise in this process, having been the Joint Staff J-5. It was disquieting to see that the new team seemed determined to reclaim a perceived loss of primacy in the planning process. In truth, since all plans required civilian approval and were in fact tasked only by civilian leadership, this was a red herring. They actually had always exercised total control. In an approach that could only be called Orwellian in its nature, CENTCOM was directed to prepare plans where the resources allocated were significantly inadequate for the tasks assigned in the planning guidance. In our planning process, we were used to seeing a series of agreed-upon terms and words that meant very specific things—language such as *seize, destroy, neutralize, suppress*, and so forth. Instead of this clear and recognizable language, terms such as *manage* began to appear as end states and as planning concepts. Words that are not broadly understood in professional practice are prone to misapplication, and that was the result of this erosion of specificity.

These disagreements all came together in how risk was considered and who bore the risk for plan accomplishment or failure. I had first come to study the nature of risk when I worked for Michéle Flournoy as a member of her Quadrennial Defense Review study group in 1999. I contributed a chapter on risk to the book we published in 2000.[1] We included that chapter in our anthology because we all felt collectively that the department had long done a poor job in explaining risk. When I became the J-5 in 2014, not much had changed. We still didn't do a good job of explaining what risk was and how it manifested itself. Secretary Mattis helped correct this dilemma with what he called his "Jesuitical" approach to the concept of risk. By the time he left the department as secretary, his vision had imbued all aspects of the way that the Joint Staff considered risk, and it directly influenced all of the risk assessments that followed. In short, when we thought about risk, we moved away from airy declarations of "high risk" or "low risk," which were usually accompanied by the ubiquitous stoplight chart, with red corresponding to the higher levels. Instead, we began to focus with laser clarity on defining the risk—what was the specific action or threat? Then, who bore the risk? Was it a specific unit or organization? Finally, what was the temporal nature of the risk? What triggered the risk, and how long did it obtain? When a planner began to think about risk in these terms, it became much easier to achieve specificity, and also much harder to support airy proclamations. Specificity is the heart of good risk analysis; broadness is its bane.

Just as important as this is the critical decision about who holds the risk. It was in this discussion that I often disagreed with the new team. In giving planning guidance to a commander, civilian leadership should specify objectives, amplifying direction when necessary, and offer guidance on forces available. The commander takes this guidance, applies both objective analysis and his or her own subjective judgment, and returns to say the given tasks can be accomplished with the forces provided or that the objective cannot be obtained with the forces designated (allocated or apportioned in planning terms). Of course, it's never as completely black and white as this may seem, and there are always nuances in these distinctions, but the general concept is valid. If the commander returns and says that the end state can't be accomplished, then it is the responsibility of civilian leadership to do one of three things: change the objective, making it attainable with the forces provided; provide more forces to the commander so that the objective is attainable; or, tell the commander that the additional requested forces are not available, but the objective remains. In this case, the risk of the failure of mission accomplishment does not rest with the commander—it is now borne by civilian leadership. Any of these outcomes are perfectly reasonable, and they all rest indissolubly on the principle of civilian control and final decision-making.

As we worked our plans with the department, what concerned me was an attempt to avoid making the hard decision about risk in the third category. All commanders understand that it's not possible to get everything needed for the execution of a plan, but it is reasonable to expect a decision and a shared understanding of where risk is held. I did not get this feeling as we worked our plans with the new team. Instead, what emerged was planning guidance that attempted to avoid making the hard decisions, at least in the CENTCOM area of responsibility. It placed me in a very difficult situation. I was being asked to do things that the command wasn't resourced to accomplish, and when we pushed back, instead of crisp decisions, we got vague language about "managing problems." Moreover, it was as if the very process of producing more and more planning guidance would somehow in and of itself change the nature of warfare. In the struggle between nation-states, which is often kinetic and violent in nature, planning guidance, however artfully conceived, with beautiful emendations and caveats, cannot soften a mortal meeting between flesh and fire and metal.[2] As a result, our plans lagged in the process and were not approved or disapproved. A decision either way would have been helpful; limbo was not.

There was another aspect of the new team—they were intent, to a degree that I had never seen before, to protect the secretary from anything that was disagreeable, confrontational, or even hinted at divergence or dissension. The effect of this was, whether intentional or not, a marked inability to deliver clear guidance to commanders. Moreover, as the policy shop became increasingly assertive, the chairman, supported by the Joint Staff, found it harder to give military advice that was not homogenized, and that approach stood at a variance to policy inputs.

Sometimes, civilian leaders in the department equated honest disagreement with disloyalty. There is always an urge within the department to bring a consensus product to the secretary, rather than a staff action where the chairman, the chiefs, or a combatant commander might hold different views than policy. In my experience, both as a key member of the Joint Staff and then as a combatant commander, we often disagreed with policy, and we weren't reticent or retiring about sharing our opinions. In the development and approval process for plans, and as the Joint Staff began to assert the usefulness of global campaign plans, global integration, and the role of the chairman as the global integrator for the secretary, these disagreements sharpened. I found that there was more concern from policy over the idea that we had new and different ideas rather than any objection over the specific merits or faults of our position.

I once created a slide that I used in briefings where I quoted from one of my favorite books, *Eminent Victorians*, by Lytton Strachey. *Eminent Victorians* was written in the immediate aftermath of World War I, and in four character sketches Strachey brilliantly skewered paragons of the Victorian age: Cardinal Henry Edward Manning, Florence Nightingale, Doctor Thomas Arnold, and General C. G. Gordon. In the section on Cardinal Manning, his relationship with another ecclesiast, Cardinal John Newman, was extensively discussed. Newman converted to Catholicism from the Church of England and was sent to Rome to be re-educated as a priest. Once there, Newman, who had many ideas about religion and was a prominent and respected scholar in his former Protestant faith, learned the hard truth about bureaucracies, whether they are secular or of the church: they do not easily accept new ideas. His own words remain the best: "With a sinking heart, he realized at last the painful truth: it was not the nature of his views, it was his having views at all that was objectionable."[3] I referred to Newman's observations frequently in meetings with our OSD colleagues, and there was always a collective sucking of teeth. I made the point for a very specific reason: disagreement is not a bad thing. To disagree is not to dispute the primacy of civilian control, which I've frankly never heard any responsible uniformed officer question. Rather, it is a healthy tension, which in and of itself isn't bad, either. Ideas will compete based on their merits. New and different ideas can come from anywhere, and they can prove valuable for the administration of the department. This friction was less about the merits of our ideas—global campaign plans, global integration, and the role of the chairman—than the thought that we had these ideas at all. That, I did argue then, and argue now as well, wasn't a healthy response.

A relentless focus on achieving incremental internal bureaucratic victories in the pursuit of re-establishing civilian control cannot substitute for the relative lack of emphasis in the hard work of creating a genuine strategic view of the global responsibilities of the United States. The Biden team entered the Pentagon determined to reassert civilian control over what they believed was an unruly and recalcitrant military. They accomplished this task, largely because little correction was needed: civilian control had never been seriously eroded. Regardless, they expended considerable time and energy to this end. The other implied task that they set for themselves was to restore competence and predictability to the entire defense enterprise. At best, this has been partially accomplished.

11

THE NOOSE TIGHTENS IN AFGHANISTAN

I hate the corpses of empires, they stink as nothing else. They stink so badly that I cannot believe that even in life they were healthy.
—*Rebecca West*

Presidents Biden and Trump were as unalike as any two presidents have ever been, but they shared one abiding objective: to end U.S. participation in the war in Afghanistan. As I have previously described, under President Trump we reduced our forces to 2,500 by early January 2021. This was all part of our agreement with the Taliban and, to a lesser degree, with the government of Afghanistan. In the last few days of the Trump administration, it was obvious that his team saw Afghanistan as unfinished business. Ever since the June briefing with him, he sought to further draw down. Unfortunately, while we fulfilled our obligations under the February 2020 agreement, the Taliban were not fulfilling theirs. As usual in Afghan affairs, there were other factors in play. The government of Afghanistan would not—or could not—establish a negotiating position for intra-Afghan negotiations, which were going on in Doha. Over time, the psychological effect of being effectively excluded from the negotiations eroded our Afghan partners' will to fight and, insidiously and perhaps even more importantly, to govern.

When President Biden came into office, it was clear that Afghanistan would be at the top of his list of things to work on. I think everyone was surprised that he retained Ambassador Zalmay Khalilzad as the special representative for Afghan reconciliation. The choice would ensure we had continuity, but there were deep personal antagonisms between the ambassador and

President Ghani, and they ultimately influenced the course of negotiations. We began the process with a series of interagency meetings, which Scott Miller and I were invited to attend.

In January and February, I participated in several principal-level meetings. During these, we laboriously reviewed our positions on Afghanistan, going back over the long road that brought us to this point. I wanted CENTCOM to be first at the whiteboard with potential military options. My long experience in the interagency process taught me that if we provided an initial structure for the military element of power, it would be helpful for decision-makers as they considered broader options, and it would prevent others from doing this work for us. Working with Scott Miller and his team, we developed four alternative concepts for a U.S. presence in Afghanistan. I was gratified that these options, with some slight modifications, remained the basis for discussion throughout the long process of making a decision on our way forward.

The first option was to hold what we had: 2,500 U.S. forces, plus a small number of special operations forces. This posture would allow us to continue advising and assisting the Afghan army and national police at the corps or regional level. We would also be able to continue our counterterror mission. We would maintain eight bases in Afghanistan, including Bagram, which I viewed as a critical location. We assumed our NATO and allied partners would also remain, and their end strength was at about 5,600. While they did not directly participate in combat, the myriad of ministry-level advisement functions they carried out was indispensable. They also participated in some regional advising. Both Scott and I felt that this posture allowed us to continue our work against al Qaeda and ISIS-K while providing critical assistance to our Afghan partners against the Taliban. Our security assistance programs would all be able to continue, including the administration of funds for the Afghan military.

We also believed that at this force level, we could continue these operations even if the Taliban turned against us and began attacks, as they continually promised to do if we did not leave Afghanistan by May 1, 2021. Perhaps counterintuitively, the smaller presence and reduced basing structure that we had at 2,500 not only reduced the potential "attack surface" for the Taliban, it also had flushed a lot of fat out of the country, and the remnant was a lean and lethal force. We could fully support our CIA partners with this force level. We retained Bagram airfield, a key transportation and support node. We would be able to hold Bagram even if the Afghans ceased contributing forces to its defense. When briefing this option, I was always emphatic that this was the lowest level that we could go that was survivable in the event the Taliban turned on us. This was also the lowest level that would permit us to maintain any semblance of a functioning Afghan military.

Our second option featured a reduction to 1,800 and a drawdown to three bases, including Bagram, although our hold on it would be tenuous. Both Scott and I saw the value of Bagram—if we had the forces to defend it. At a force level of 1,800, we would be entirely dependent on the Afghans to defend Bagram, and we would be unable to defend it if they disintegrated. The fundamental assumption for this alternative was that we would have an agreement from the future Afghan government—which would probably be, at a minimum, heavily influenced by the Taliban—that we could remain. I personally did not consider this a likely state of affairs; it seemed a little tautological. It introduced irreconcilable tension into the design. It was a diplomat's solution—elegant in language and concept—but it did not bear close inspection. At this level, we would no longer be able to provide advising and assistance at the corps level. Without this, it was our assessment that it would be difficult for the Afghan army to fight successfully. Of course, if we had some sort of a reduction in violence agreement with the Taliban, things would change, and this would be acceptable. Our ability to support our CIA partners would also be greatly reduced. Counterterror operations would still be possible—but again, only with the acquiescence of the Taliban. We still believed that NATO and our allies and partners would stay with us at this lower level, although their own troop contributions would inevitably decline as well.

Our third and fourth options were variations on a complete drawdown, with some form of over-the-horizon (OTH) counterterror capability. The third option featured a complete withdrawal of all U.S. forces from Afghanistan, with the sole exception of some number of security forces remaining at a still-open Kabul embassy. This option obviously assumed that the government of Afghanistan, whatever its composition, would observe the normal diplomatic practice of allowing—and protecting—foreign embassies. Nothing in the history of the Taliban had led me to believe that this would happen. If this did happen, and they also allowed us to reach into Afghanistan for directed operations against al Qaeda and ISIS-K, then the embassy could enable a CIA platform to run agents and develop leads for these operations. We believed that some NATO and allied partners might seek to keep their embassies open as well under this construct. Of all the options considered, I felt this one offered the highest risk to U.S. interests. We were, in effect, going to place a number of Americans in Kabul, where they would be at the mercy of the Taliban, relying solely on their good word for our protection. I had absolutely no confidence in their good word. We would have no way to come to the rescue of the embassy and our small garrison if the Taliban turned on us. In many ways, we were setting ourselves up for a repeat of the British experience in Kabul in 1841 and 1842, where their entire diplomatic platform and associated security forces were massacred.

The fourth option was a variant of the third. Under this option, there would be no U.S. diplomatic presence in Afghanistan. We would establish an "offshore" embassy, or interests section, in a neighboring country. Any counterterror work would be carried out from over the horizon, based somewhere in the theater. This option would remove completely any U.S. financial support for Afghanistan, both military and civil, since there would be no way to administer the execution of the budget. This is what we ended up with when it was all said and done, but not through any deliberate choice.

In late January I again provided formal written advice to the secretary, arguing that we should hold and maintain our force at 2,500, the first option, and I emphasized the importance of holding the Taliban to the conditions we had negotiated for further reductions. The chairman and Scott were completely aligned with me on this. Since the collapse of Afghanistan, there has been much debate about the viability of a force of 2,500. In the back-and-forth of testimony before Congress, that number has been challenged. Those challenges are reasonable. Typically, the question is this: If we elected to hold at 2,500, wouldn't the Taliban have attacked us, causing significant U.S. casualties and requiring us to bring in more forces to respond? My answer to these hypothetical questions has always been that, first, we didn't know what the Taliban response would have been. We always linked holding at 2,500 to a renewed strong diplomatic press on the Taliban, more forceful than what had been going on in Doha. For too long, negotiations in Doha had been all carrot and no stick. A less supine negotiating posture, coupled with a demonstration of obvious will and the participation of NATO (which we had), could have significantly changed the tone and tenor of the negotiations. We were not seeking a military victory—we were seeking a stasis that would compel genuine talks.

We do know now, objectively, what would result from our withdrawal: complete and utter defeat. Scott Miller always believed that the 2,500 force level was harder and more resilient than some of the higher numbers. I agreed with him. We had significant firepower from external bases that could have been rapidly applied against Taliban targets, and they had grown lazy in their operational practices because of the withdrawal of our support to our Afghan partners. Therefore, I do not believe it was a foregone conclusion that holding at 2,500 would have inevitably resulted in higher U.S. casualties and required the introduction of additional forces. Instead, it was a calculated risk, one that required imagination, redoubled and focused diplomatic engagement that wasn't driven by an overarching desire to gain an exit with a decent interval, and a political appetite for taking the inevitable partisan heat that would attend a continued presence in Afghanistan. None of those things existed. I am certain that we would have sustained casualties had we stayed, but it's just not possible to say how many, just as it is not yet possible to say how many lives will ultimately be lost because of the course of action that we did execute. This option remains an intriguing counterfactual that will be endlessly dissected by future students of the conflict, but I believe it is wrong to cite as a matter of course a "contingent future" that assumes 2,500 wasn't a viable alternative and was, in effect, a door to a larger presence.

Even as we worked these options, CENTCOM turned to address OTH counterterror options in Afghanistan. The idea that we could exit completely from Afghanistan and then swoop in whenever we wanted to attack troublesome terrorists who were plotting to attack our homeland was a shibboleth of many senior political leaders, both Republican and Democrat. It provided a veneer of respectability and comfort for those who wanted it all—a total exit from Afghanistan and total security for our homeland. Like so many expansive dreams of this nature, it looked best from a distance and only upon close and rigorous examination showed its flaws, risks, and contradictions. Throughout, our position remained that it was possible to conduct operations from a distance, but they would be very hard to execute.

I wanted to get in at the beginning with a definitive military view on the viability of this politically seductive approach. Of course, it was only a consideration if we believed that a complete U.S. departure from Afghanistan, coupled with an Afghan state that was unwilling or unable to prevent a resurgence of al Qaeda or ISIS-K, would lead to attacks against our homeland. The intelligence I read throughout all of 2020 and 2021 tended to agree that should we leave completely, the Afghan government would collapse and then fracture. The military would soon follow. A civil war would ensue, warlordism would rise, and the end result, over a period of months to years, would be either an internally divided Afghanistan with no central authority, or an Afghanistan with the Taliban in some degree of, and perhaps total, control. Regardless of which outcome resulted, there would be weak governance and vast ungoverned spaces. The Taliban had never fulfilled their obligation to rein in al Qaeda or ISIS-K, so even if a Taliban government emerged, we had no reason to think that a brake would be put on those groups' ambitions. Moreover, either of these futures would set back, perhaps for many years, all that we had done in Afghanistan for human and women's rights. These assessments informed all the advice that I gave during this period.

I had seen throughout the Trump administration a belief that we could find a way to do effective counterterror operations from afar. The operative word was "effective." I had always pushed back against that view, with limited success. In mid-January I tasked my operations officer to comb through the CENTCOM archives, talk to the Special Operations Command, and collect all of the considerable material we had on the viability of long-range counterterror operations. We would then boil it down to a white paper, free of jargon and the typical soul-crushing military format, that would summarize our position in clear English. As usual, Grynch and his team outdid themselves. By early February I was able to review a draft paper, and by mid-February it was ready to be launched through the chairman to the secretary and, pending his approval, into the interagency. The paper was a direct reflection of my views on this important subject. I believe it had a significant influence on the development of options going forward, at least within the department: hard, not impossible. It was also a good example of the same bureaucratic approach that underpinned the "four options" for presence in Afghanistan—to define the terms of the debate, it is necessary to quickly establish the framework for the debate (i.e., be first to the whiteboard!).

We wrote our paper, and all of our arguments that were in it and that followed, in a deductive style. We used the model of find, fix, and finish that is at the heart of the counterterror process. I felt this would keep our arguments linked to understandable concepts with clear examples. If we began with the assumption that we would be out of Afghanistan with all our forces, then it followed that our CIA partners would also be absent. While they—and we—would certainly continue to run agents and proxies in Afghanistan, the ability to interface with—to brief and debrief—them would be logistically challenging. We would also lose the partnership of the Afghan military, since they would probably not be in existence as the force that we once supported, and if they did still exist, it was hard to foresee why they would be motivated to work with us. After all, we had just fled the country.

Not being physically present in Afghanistan, we would lose most of our human intelligence. Human intelligence is the retail level of the find activity. Without this force on the ground, we would be dependent upon signals intelligence. This would be difficult, since we would find it hard to employ short-range ground-mounted collectors. We could rely on our constellation of satellites, but they might be hampered by the weakness of most of the signals on the ground, and the fact that the satellites themselves were extremely high-value and limited resources and the department wanted them all focused on threats like China and Russia. If we could manage to find a target with these very limited resources, the fix part would be even harder. Fixing a target requires persistent coverage. The coin of the realm for this was the MQ-9 Reaper. Against a target that we were trying to "soak," we would require around-the-clock coverage, often for extended periods of days or even weeks. This ubiquity allowed us to build a pattern of life if we were targeting an individual. It also allowed us to ascertain potential collateral damage and to avoid taking unnecessary life if we struck the target. We launched almost all of our MQ-9s from bases in Afghanistan. If we lost those bases, then the drone's journey would probably be much farther.

To illustrate the point, consider this: with Afghanistan basing, an MQ-9 might fly two hundred miles before reaching its operational area. This allowed for a lengthy period of time overhead actually working the target—twelve hours or more. If we were forced to come from an airbase in the Arabian Gulf, the distance the drone would "commute" to work would be more than 1,200 miles, resulting in a much shorter period of time being usefully employed—perhaps as little as two to three hours or even less. We would need a minimum of two around-the-clock, seven-day-a-week coverage "lines," which would translate into twenty MQ-9s. Of course, these were best-case calculations without considering weather or maintenance problems. We would also require permission from neighboring countries to fly through them to get to Afghanistan. Most likely that would be Pakistan, which might prove problematic.

The object of all this work was to arrive at a finish solution. We could do this in one of two ways. The first solution would be a kinetic strike from an MQ-9, a crewed aircraft, or long-range fires—usually the TLAM. All of these approaches had significant problems, centering around the length of time it took to prepare and execute a strike from a great distance, based on overhead surveillance of a target that could move. CENTCOM had a lot of history with this problem. In August 1998 President Bill Clinton authorized using 109 Tomahawk TLAMs from Navy ships in the Gulf of Oman against Osama bin Laden's purported base in Afghanistan. The intelligence was good at the time of launch, but the four-hour period of time it took to prepare, launch, and transit the missiles to the target allowed bin Laden to move. We could improve on this with crewed aircraft, but they would also be coming from a great distance and would have limited loiter time over the target. Additionally, should we lose an aircraft over Afghanistan, we would have no real options for recovering the aircrew; it was more akin to a gamble than a risk. All of these alternatives, of course, focused on destroying the target with air-delivered fires. The strike against al Qaeda leader Ayman al-Zawahiri in July 2022 is an example of the effectiveness, and the limitations, of this approach. If conditions can be created for a long-range strike, then success is possible. The fact that this was a single strike taken almost a year after we left Afghanistan emphasizes the difficulty of these operations.

The other solution was to conduct a long-range raid. CENTCOM also had a deep history with these types of operations. Assuming that we could work out the find and fix parts of the equation—not a given by any means—we would then execute a raid of well over one thousand miles into Afghanistan. We would need to establish intermediate staging bases to support the force— all of them would be established in hostile territory, and clandestinely. The distances were eye-watering, and the tolerances were minute. We would be employing the national mission force as the raid force for this operation. They were the very best in the world, without exception, but I still expressed in the paper how uncomfortable we were with this option. Part of this is our own success. Everybody, including policymakers, always recalls the success of the bin Laden raid and the Baghdadi raids. These raids were both magnificent successes, but they benefitted from close-range support networks and human intelligence on the ground. We would have neither of those if we went into Afghanistan.

The tyranny of distance brought grave risks into any endeavor of this range. I always felt the best history on this was Eagle Claw, our attempt in April 1980 to rescue our hostages from Iran. In many ways, it was a much better simulacrum of what an Afghan raid would be like. The force launched from extreme distance and had to use an intermediate staging base, Desert One. When conditions for onward execution weren't met and the force had to be withdrawn, a mishap during taxiing operations killed eight servicemen. To me, this was a perfect example of the nature of risks inherent to extended range raid operations. I once got into an argument with Keith Kellogg about this very point. He dismissed my concerns about long-range raids, implying that I was guilty of "old think." A key difference between Kellogg and me was that he could afford to be flippant about the risks. I could not—the difference between an advisor and a commander.

In summary, our formal position was that it was technically "feasible" to undertake any of the operations outlined above. The risks would be grave. Ultimately, only our political leadership could decide what was unacceptable. I've never felt that a combatant commander should characterize risk in that manner, because only the policymaker—not the military commander—can calculate the ultimate prospective gain against the potential loss. This is an important point. An action that to a combatant commander seems too costly or inappropriate may seem very different to the commander in chief, who, in concert with the secretary of defense, must balance global considerations against the gain and the loss predicted. Only civilian leadership can make this ultimate decision.

It might also be possible to use proxies recruited and equipped by the CIA to conduct the operation. The problem here was that because of the complex nature of these operations, it would be very hard to craft a prompt response or to even maintain a timeline, and we would not be able to ensure that the strike would be carried out to minimize casualties and collateral damage—the loss of innocent life.

There were certain unpalatable truths about Afghanistan as a target for OTH counterterrorism. It was a landlocked country. It was far from the ocean—the shortest distance from eastern Afghanistan to the Gulf of Oman was over a thousand miles. None of the countries around Afghanistan—Pakistan, Iran, Tajikistan, Uzbekistan, and Turkmenistan—were particular friends of the United States. The last three countries all had varying degrees of dependency upon Russia. Afghanistan itself was characterized by extremely rough terrain, an undeveloped road network, and an even more immature power, telephone, and wireless network. Nothing in Afghanistan was ever easy. That's why we brought almost everything we used in with us during our long years there.

In late February I was travelling in the theater, and we were in Muscat, Oman. I received word that there was going to be a National Security Council meeting on Wednesday afternoon, February 24, on Afghanistan. Both Scott Miller and I would be invited. Afternoon conferences in Washington were the curse of CENTCOM commanders when travelling in the region. A 3:15 p.m. meeting meant an 11:15 p.m. meeting in Oman for me, and that would be after a full day of work and meetings in Oman, with another full day following. It was a small price to pay for an opportunity to talk directly to the president on a key issue. In a pre-meeting with the secretary and the chairman, it was agreed that Scott would talk about the current situation, and then I would outline the OTH options to the president.

The mechanics of these meetings were always interesting. I was staying in a hotel in Muscat, the Hormuz Grand. In the middle of our comms room, an opaque plastic tent was erected, large enough for one person, a small desk, and several computers, Tandberg video teleconferencing monitors, and phones. The sides of the tent were kept up by air pressure from small motors, and attached to the wall of the tent and scattered about the room were noisemakers that produced a strange susurration—it always sounded to me like voices that were just too quiet or muted to be understood, like people talking in another room. The intent, of course, was to make it harder for anyone trying to listen in with electronic devices.

I took a few hours earlier that evening to lay out what I wanted to say. Briefing President Biden was different from President Trump. The meetings moved crisply, there was an agenda, and National Security Advisor Jake Sullivan ensured it was followed. Vice President Kamala Harris was often direct in her questions, but they were always on point and germane. It was refreshing to discuss plans and options without discursive expeditions into military—and political—grounds that weren't why the meeting was called. I wrote out my notes on hotel stationary that we later destroyed. The quality of the connection was very good, and all parties were able to state their positions clearly. I spent most of my time talking about the difficulty of OTH counterterrorism, but I always noted that while it would be very hard, it would not be impossible. It was clear from my briefing that I did not recommend a complete withdrawal from Afghanistan. There was a good back and forth, and it was obvious that the president was torn by the choices he confronted. He plainly wanted out, but he also understood the steep price we could pay for leaving precipitously.

I left the meeting with no idea what the president's decision would be, but I was also heartened by the inclusive approach that he had taken. As Joe Dunford said many times about meetings like this, "They should listen to your advice. They don't have to take it." After the meeting, I had no idea what direction the president would go with his decision. Our session had been much too large for any president to actually think aloud, so we signed off knowing little more than when we started about where he stood.

There are moments that stick in everyone's mind—when something big happened, where you were, what you were doing. Aside from personal matters, two had always stayed with me. The first was the assassination of John F. Kennedy in 1963—I was in first grade, and I remember the weather, the low, hushed voices of the teachers, and everything else—a hundred small details. The second one that had always stuck with me was the attack on the Pentagon in September 2001. I was there, and I have described my participation in the actions that followed, so it's probably not surprising that tortured and harrowing day still looms large in my memory.

I now have a third memory. It was when I learned that we were leaving Afghanistan completely. The date was Sunday, April 11. I was scheduled to fly to Norfolk, Virginia, to host the Pinnacle course, a small seminar for promising three-star officers designed to expose them to four-star issues. A group of retired four-stars act as the mentors for the small group of students (the seminar I was going to had but ten student officers). I was taking a small staff group up with me in a Gulfstream, and we were planning to take off from MacDill at 11:30 a.m. for a ninety-minute trip to Norfolk. As fate would have it, a ferocious squall line blew through the Tampa area right after we boarded the aircraft; we taxied out to the active runway but were put on hold. It was an impressive storm, with lightning clearly visible. In situations like this, it's best for senior leaders to be quiet and let the aircrew work the problem. Once, many years ago, the closest I had ever come to death in an airplane was when I was travelling with Commandant of the Marine Corps Gen. Carl Mundy Jr., and his senior aide, then-Lt. Col. Joe Dunford, and we were trying to land at Andrews Air Force Base in a snowstorm. It must have been 1994. The runway was icy, but the commandant wanted to get in, and the aircrew sensed it. We executed three or four missed approaches, which were reasonably frightening, at least for me. Finally, we made it—but the memory has lingered, and I try very hard to avoid influencing safety-of-flight issues.

As we sat on the taxiway, my executive officer, Col. Shawn Leonard, came into my small cabin and told me, "The secretary wants you and the chairman to join him in a conference call; they're setting it up." As soon as Shawn said that, I knew it had to be Afghanistan or Iran. The secretary was in Israel, and the suspicious attack on Natanz was being widely reported. I told Shawn to have the aircraft stay in place: it was hard enough to establish the top-secret satellite call from the airplane—and a Gulfstream 550, while fast and comfortable, has extremely poor satellite bandwidth while airborne. The communicators bustled about for several minutes, going through the rituals of establishing a link to the communications agency for the secretary of defense. They then handed the headset to me, and the operator told me that they were adding General Miller to the call. At that second—a little after 1:00 p.m.—I knew that we were going to get a decision on Afghanistan.

At that moment in time, I still had no idea what it would be. I had provided lots of advice, in many fora, on Afghanistan, and my counsel to stay had been consistent and clear, both in writing and verbally. We'd now see what the decision was. I got my notebook out and prepared to listen. It was a very small conference: The secretary, his chief of staff, the chairman and his chief of staff (Kelly Magsamen), me, and Scott Miller. The operator checked that we were all in the call—the quality of the call, I absently noted, was excellent; great work by the crew of the jet—and then she introduced the secretary.

He came on, and said, without preamble, that "POTUS has made a decision." As he spoke, I was reminded of earlier moments in calls like this as the CENTCOM commander—the Soleimani decision, the rocket attack on al Asad—a lot of phone calls. "We will leave Afghanistan. The clock starts on 1 May. We will take the necessary time to leave in an orderly manner. I know your planning has called for 120 days; we will be out before the twenty-year anniversary of September 11." He went on, "The president will announce this Wednesday at the White House at 1:30 p.m. Nobody has been informed. You as the relevant commanders are the only people to know of this decision. Ambassador Russ Wilson in Afghanistan will be informed later today." He went on to discuss the notification process for our allies and for NATO, which would be quite complex. The president would call President Ghani on Tuesday.

I thought it was a great performance by Secretary Austin. His calm, steady presence over the phone with his commanders was a masterful example of leadership. The president had made a decision. There would be significant geopolitical impacts because of that decision. I, and I believe everyone on that call, thought they would be bad. For us, though, the problem had fundamentally shifted, from giving advice and planning multiple options to now faithfully executing the orders of the commander in chief. I know that various pundits have hailed the president's decision as a courageous act by him to push "the generals" aside and have further imputed that there was some form of civil-military crisis at hand. Nothing could have been further from the truth. As the senior commander, I was happy to have had the chance to give my advice—although the president did not have to ask for it. He did, and I know it was subsequently part of his decision-making process. That he did not take my advice was—and is—irrelevant. I don't know of any responsible senior military leader who doesn't firmly understand the concept of civilian control, and we were seeing it in action, in front of us, right now.

The secretary then asked the chairman, me, and Scott for our thoughts and questions. I told the secretary, "I recognize the importance of operational security, so I will be the only person in my headquarters who is aware of this until Wednesday afternoon." I had three questions. First, "Does a complete withdrawal mean we'll try to keep an embassy presence?" Second, "We've seen discussion in deputy-level small group meetings about bringing out up to 100,000 Afghans along with our own forces. Is this in play? If so, it will have a major impact on Scott's withdrawal timeline." Last, I wanted to ensure that Scott did not lose the authorities he needed to defend himself during a withdrawal under pressure—and this would also need to extend to defending our Afghan partners. We continued to discuss the details of the way ahead. Scott was confident and calm as usual, and when asked directly by the secretary, he said that he wanted to retain command through the end of the withdrawal. This didn't surprise me, although Scott would have three years in Afghanistan by the end—the United States was asking a lot of this exceptional officer. As the call ended, I sat back and watched the rain drum against the cabin windows. A key part of the president's decision was the fact that we would not leave at the end of May but rather in September. Of course, by not reaching a decision until mid-April, it was de facto impossible to leave by the end of May, so we had been anticipating a delay. The Taliban's response to this delay would be important.

Scott Miller had developed a solid plan to retrograde from Afghanistan. He had been working it well before my June 2020 briefing to then-President Trump, and his hard work had formed the backbone of my recommendations. His plan was based on speed. We would bring out about 23,000 personnel, consisting of 3,600 U.S. military, 5,700 U.S. contractors, about 6,000 of our coalition partners, and some 7,000 third-country contractors. The number of U.S. military, 3,600, included the special operations forces that we did not report publicly but that were well known within the U.S. government. At the same time, we would be bringing out 422 pieces of rolling stock and more than 6,500 pieces of nonrolling stock equipment. With the withdrawal of our units, we'd be bringing out more than 20,000 additional pieces of equipment and over 250 pieces of rolling stock. We would be turning over thousands of pieces of equipment to the Afghans and destroying more than 200 vehicles and over 25,000 pieces of nonrolling stock. All of this was spread across eleven bases. Some of the nonsensitive equipment we could get out through Pakistan, through our ground line of communication to Karachi. All of the people, and much of the equipment, though, would come out by air, which would require more than one thousand C-17 sortie equivalents. The number of sorties we required in April was less than what we had used for planning the prior year, largely because of the good work the logisticians had been performing, drawing us down steadily. We thought it would take about seventy-four days to execute this plan, and based on presidential guidance, we had established N-day as May 1. Zero day—the time when we believed we'd be finished—would be July 4. This was well before the September "no later than" date set by the president, but we saw no need to go slowly, and by setting an early date for completion we put some shock absorber into the system. This would prove to be a useful decision as the plan unfolded.

Scott's base plan for the withdrawal did not account for the extraction of our diplomatic platform or any Afghans, nor did it include a noncombatant evacuation operation (NEO), which would bring out U.S. citizens.

We weren't bringing out the diplomats because of the president's decision to retain our embassy. We had a plan to do so. For the other categories, this did not mean that we hadn't given this careful thought—only that we viewed it as a separate requirement, which needed a separate plan. We calculated that there were as many as 18,000 Afghans in some stage of applying for special immigrant visas (SIVs), and since it was our practice to calculate this population by adding their families, we tripled the potential size of the pool. This meant we rapidly went up to more than 50,000 Afghans that we might be ordered to bring out. When U.S. citizens and permanent residents were added to this pool, the total quickly escalated to more than 100,000 potential evacuees. As a reference, in the final days of the fall of Vietnam, Operation Frequent Wind brought out more than 80,000 South Vietnamese. The operational problems in Vietnam were much simpler, of course—the distance to sanctuary was much shorter than in Afghanistan. We had branch plans for these eventualities, but it was clear that executing them would increase our risk while lengthening the timeline. We began to refine our existing NEO plan for Afghanistan at this time, updating it continuously.

Finally, of course, it is important to emphasize the fact that the president had directed that we maintain an embassy in Afghanistan even after we withdrew. This was going to be a tough one. Calculating the security requirements for the embassy would depend on the tactical situation in Kabul. The requirement could rapidly climb to more than one thousand personnel, with significant capabilities. Even this would assume that the situation would not be openly hostile, because if the Taliban took power and wanted us to leave, it would take a massive addition of combat power—well above what Scott Miller had now—to protect an embassy platform. I was confident that the president did not want such a large force on the ground. My main concern, which Scott shared, was that we would now proceed along a path that assumed the embassy would stay, and then, at some late point in our withdrawal, the State Department would realize that it wasn't tenable. We'd then need to fold the evacuation of the embassy—about four thousand people—into our withdrawal plans, in addition to the many tens of thousands of other people who might be taken out. This, of course, is exactly what happened.

There were some big unknowns. The most important was whether or not the Taliban would allow us to leave unmolested. It was obviously in their best interest to let us withdraw, but as usual, the Taliban was wrapped up in internal, theologically driven considerations about what to do with the fact that we would be in Afghanistan after May. My gut instinct was that they would want to fight us, at least at the local level, whatever Taliban leadership said. Happily, I was wrong on this issue.

At the very beginning, I also had to consider the role of CENTCOM. Scott Miller would run the retrograde operation. I could count on him and his superb staff to do this effectively. The operation would be conducted within the larger framework of the Central Command theater. At some point in the retrograde, Scott and his headquarters would go away, and CENTCOM would take the reins. More pointedly, CENTCOM would own the OTH problem set from the beginning. This would require detailed planning, coordination across the interagency, and some policy guidance that we just didn't have yet. As Scott and I worked it out, we divided responsibilities like this: he would run the retrograde, and CENTCOM would provide overwatch, assistance, and cover for him. This was natural and obvious, since his headquarters worked for CENTCOM. We also agreed that my headquarters would do all the planning associated with the residual embassy platform—whatever it would be. Should we have to do a large-scale withdrawal of American citizens or Afghans, either I would provide him with a JTF headquarters to run the operation, answering to him, or CENTCOM would command this operation as well. The decision would depend on where we were in the withdrawal schedule and how his command and control capabilities were postured. Shortly before the withdrawal was completed, responsibility for the NEO and all other operations would shift to CENTCOM. Finally, and as already noted, CENTCOM would own the OTH planning.

Scott and I talked frequently during this period, because both he and I felt that we needed to be completely aligned. We both agreed that we needed a decision early on about what the planning factor would be for embassy security. We also realized that the larger question of whether it was even possible wasn't going to be answered immediately—that would be a risk that we would have to carry. Later in April, I participated in a secretary of defense–led rehearsal of concept drill, a session in which every commander participating in an operation outlines what he or she thinks they're doing. It's a great tool for exposing flawed assumptions and seeing what coordination has actually been accomplished. We did ours virtually, and I sat in the newly reopened main conference room at my headquarters in Tampa. In this drill the chairman, Scott, and I did most of the talking, and we had an opportunity to expose our concerns to the secretary in a straightforward manner. I thought the Joint Staff did a great job of orchestrating the exercise. At the end of the two-hour teleconference, I was confident that the secretary knew our problems. We were also very clear that the velocity of the withdrawal was important. This was no surprise to anyone.

One of the key things we determined at the very beginning was that in the execution of the base plan for retrograde, we would not need infantry reinforcements, with one exception. We would need specialized cargo-handling and aerial port-opening units. Mainly, though, we needed firepower. I asked that USS *Eisenhower* and also the *Iwo Jima* amphibious ready group and her embarked MEU remain in the theater through September. I also asked that a bomber detachment be flown into the theater and based in Qatar, from where we could maintain near-continuous overhead coverage by these huge "bomb trucks." Answering a request from Scott, we froze the reliefs of units in Afghanistan so they would not be turning over during this critical time. The one exception to the idea of no more ground forces was the introduction of a Ranger battalion at the very end of our timeline, which would provide airfield security as we made our final exit from Kabul.

On Tuesday, May 4—N+3—I was flying from Tampa to Bahrain to officiate at the Naval Forces Central Command change of command. My old and dear friend Sam Paparo would be detaching to assume command of the Pacific Fleet. I would have the honor of promoting him to four-star admiral as part of the ceremony. I was saddened to see Sam leave, particularly after such a short time in command of NAVCENT, but this was a great opportunity for him, and it was good for the nation as well.

As usual, we planned to stop and refuel in Shannon, Ireland. About two hours out of Shannon, my executive officer let me know that the chairman wanted to talk to Scott and me. He had just come from a meeting at the White House. Cables quickly established the three-way call. Unusually, the quality of the call was terrible, but we were able to work through it. The chairman debriefed us on his just-concluded meeting with the president. The secretary had been in attendance, as were, I inferred, several other cabinet officers. Most significantly, the president affirmed his support for the seventy-four-day plan that we were executing. He also agreed that if we were going to maintain an embassy, there would have to be a level of security that would allow us to defend it with a force of no more than about 650. This option had been our "moderate threat" scenario. This was important news for us because it again narrowed our planning choices. We could now focus our efforts on this single way ahead.

At the same time, the chairman reported extensive discussions about a potential NEO for Americans and Afghans who had worked with us—the numbers that were being tossed around were well over 100,000. This gave me real pause. We could certainly do it, and we had developed solid plans for this contingency, but there would be very real ramifications for our timeline, for the risk that we accepted, and for the additional forces that we would have to flow into Afghanistan to accomplish this task.

As May turned into June, our withdrawal proceeded apace. Scott and his team were simply magnificent. We steadily withdrew from our bases, turning them over to our Afghan partners. I worked hard to keep our allies and partners informed about our progress and pace. Tod Wolters worked the NATO side, and we retained good alignment both with NATO and the countries within NATO that had troops on the ground. Every morning at my headquarters, we would begin my morning brief with staff and commanders with an Afghanistan rollup. My intelligence officer, the operations officer, and then the strategy and plans officer would each brief overnight developments.

The centerpiece of the brief, though, would be the logistics officer, Army Maj. Gen. Jeff Drushall, who would discuss what progress we'd made since the prior day. Jeff had replaced Chris Sharpton earlier in the year. It was a rare moment in the sun for the logisticians, who usually toiled in darkness and bore the brunt of the ire of the operators when they couldn't support operations as aggressively as the J-3 demanded. Jeff was fully equal to the task, and in fact he and his team were now in the driver's seat. All that long summer we were paced by what the logisticians could deliver—and they never failed. We measured throughput with an arcane term: the pallet position equivalent (PPE), which was the weight and size capacity of the standard Air Force 463L pallet. A PPE could mean up to 10,000 pounds of cargo. By the end of June, we had flown out 14,431 PPEs and 984 pieces of rolling stock—a task that required 949 C-17 sorties, plus hundreds more C-130 missions, and also commercial air cargo. Much came out by the ground line of communication through Pakistan as well. This was a herculean effort by everybody—but the flexibility of Army Gen. Steve Lyons and U.S. Transportation Command was particularly invaluable, as was the total commitment of the U.S. Air Force to this complex and demanding mission.

On June 30, we closed both Mazar-i-Sharif and Bagram, leaving Kabul as the only airfield open to us in Afghanistan. In late June we briefly paused the drawdown at Bagram, as administration officials close to the president confronted the reality of losing a key location and base.[1] There has been considerable discussion by pundits and other critics about the decision to close Bagram. The reason we did so was simple: we had received presidential guidance to leave Afghanistan, maintaining only a small security force directly associated with the embassy in Kabul and the international airfield. This force would not number above 650. Holding Bagram would have required thousands of troops, and it would have been inconsistent with direction from the president. In fact, holding Bagram would have pushed us to the 2,500 force level that we had recommended, and the president had disapproved, back in the spring. A course of action that retained Bagram was something that the president had specifically decided not to pursue. Also, it would have been inconsistent with our messaging to the Taliban that we were leaving. The withdrawal had been well conducted by Scott. I believed that our obvious posturing and messaging to the Taliban, including the uncovering of Bagram, had been a big factor in their deciding to allow us to depart largely unmolested. It was certainly in their best interest to do this, but as I've noted, theocratically driven groups do not always arrive at optimum, rational solutions.

Scott and his team have also been criticized by some on how we turned Bagram over—it's been said that we surprised our Afghan partners. This was simply not true. In late June, several orientation tours were conducted for Afghan leaders, including Dr. Najibullah Wardak, the first deputy minister of defense; Abdullah Raqeebi, the deputy minister of construction for the ministry of defense; Lieutenant General Shoaib Khan, the chief of staff for the ministry; Major General Shafi Noori, the deputy G3 for the ministry of defense; and the chief engineer for construction property management. We also provided extensive training on the operation of the water systems, generators, and airfield lighting systems. We did not share the exact time of our departure with local security forces, but this was a reasonable force protection measure. The Afghan chain of command was completely informed.

On Thursday, July 1, we had a video conference hosted by the secretary. Scott Miller joined from Afghanistan, and the chairman participated as well. We were now at the very end of our withdrawal—what was left was the security force that we were keeping for the embassy, a contingent at Hamid Karzai International Airport (HKIA), and the small headquarters element that Scott still retained. If we stayed on our plan, now was the time for Scott Miller to leave. We had a two-star Navy SEAL named Pete Vasely, a very capable officer, who would remain in Kabul as my representative with a small staff. Pete and I had not crossed paths before this operation, but I warmed to him quickly. He had the qualities I wanted in a commander that would go forward into the fight: he was calm, he had significant combat experience, and he wasn't overawed by the task he faced. His staff, while small, comprised what had been the incoming special operations task force element—they were all very experienced in Afghanistan. We could not have asked for a better or more competent group of professionals to go in on the ground in Afghanistan.

We had laboriously established the mechanisms and procedures to conduct OTH counterterrorism operations as well as security force assistance. We also had a good plan to defend the embassy. The chairman, Scott, and I saw our briefing to the secretary as a "battle handover" brief—where one commander says that he or she is ready to be relieved, and the incoming commander says that he or she is ready to assume responsibility for the organization. It was our intent to make this a "four-star to four-star" handover. Scott would not be relieved by Pete, but by me. I would be the last four-star commander in Afghanistan. Pete would be my subordinate, acting in a far narrower sense than Scott had done. I would assume the broader responsibilities that Scott had been fulfilling. Handover at the four-star level would also send a message of assurance to the Afghans that, while we were withdrawing all of our forces and ceasing direct combat support for them, other means of support would remain open.

In briefing the secretary, I spent some time talking about how we would perform security force assistance for the Afghans. The principal headquarters for it would be at my forward headquarters at Al Udeid Airbase, Qatar. There, Army Brig. Gen. Curtis Buzzard, fresh from duty as the commandant at West Point, would supervise a headquarters of more than two hundred military, civilian, and contractor personnel. Curtis was a pleasure to work with, and he waded into the immense challenges of long-distance advising and support with great energy. Curtis would keep a team of twenty people in Kabul at the embassy. They would do the actual liaison with our Afghan partners. This team would administer the Afghan security force fund, which totaled over $3 billion a year—not an inconsiderable amount. This money would pay the salaries of the Afghan security forces, assist in their procurement of equipment and supplies, and provide mentoring and coaching—all from a distance.

A key part of our assistance was the aviation logistics element. We all recognized that the singular advantage the Afghans had against the Taliban was their air force. We needed to keep it flying. We would do this by establishing a dedicated facility in the UAE. There, more than four hundred contractors would rework Afghan airplanes that we brought out of the country to repair. Other damaged aircraft would go farther back in the aviation maintenance pipeline—some to the United States, some to other countries. We also planned to keep more than two hundred contractors on the ground at HKIA until we completed our withdrawal to provide hands-on assistance. This was a risky, fragile, fraught approach. There were many ways we could fail. For the overall security assistance effort, what was missing was any real supervision, training, or coaching below the point where we gave the material to the Afghans. In briefings, I used a practical example to illustrate the point: we could deliver a case of mortar rounds to the Afghans on the ramp at Karzai International. We could be sure that they signed for the rounds. We had no practical way to understand how or if those rounds made it to the mortar platoon that needed them. Perhaps they would all get down there, but perhaps some would show up in the bazaar, or some would even go to the Taliban. We also no longer had the ability to determine if the mortar platoon that was to receive the ammunition had any training or even possessed their weapons. It was a disconcerting thought—and there was no solution.

We also talked about the OTH counterterrorism operations. Our MQ-9s were now based at Al Dhafra, in the United Arab Emirates. We were learning that flying the MQ-9 at extreme range resulted in many cancelled missions. Weather was always going to be a factor, but the combination of searing heat at the runways from which we launched, inclement weather during the transit, and more cloud cover over the places we wanted to look at all increased the friction exponentially. We were going to struggle to keep MQ-9s over Afghanistan with any degree of predictability.

Finally, we talked about embassy security. With about 650 U.S. troops on the ground, we kept almost four hundred of them at HKIA. This was where the embassy's aircraft were as well as the handful of Army helicopters that we would use to defend ourselves in extremis. The remainder were at the embassy proper. Splitting them up in this way reduced the visual signal of U.S. forces at the embassy, which we believed might make the situation more palatable to the Taliban. The key to maintaining an embassy was the airport. Without an airfield, there could be no embassy. The Turks had been operating the coalition part of the airport for several years. They were interested in staying. Over the summer, we had engaged in a tedious series of negotiations with the Turks, negotiations that included everyone on the U.S. side up to the president, and we believed we had arrived at a way to cooperate on defending the airport. They had between seven hundred and nine hundred troops there. We agreed that our troops there—numbering about four hundred—would work together to defend the facility. We had some unique capabilities that they wanted to have in place—the counter-rocket and mortar guns, which were the Navy's short-range cannon air defense system, for example, and some more of the huge, lumbering mine-resistant armor-protected vehicles that provided protection against improvised explosive devices. Their brigadier would exercise tactical command, but we would always maintain a U.S. chain of command. Achieving this was a key step in assuring that our embassy could stay.

At the same time, we all realized that the actual defense of the airfield depended upon the Afghans—they formed the outer circle, and if they collapsed, it would be hard for us to hold on without significant reinforcement. This key fact has been overlooked by many: The airport was not defendable without Afghan military assistance. If they collapsed, our 650 troops and the Turks would not be able to defend it. This was a key assumption in our planning. We devoted considerable thinking to what we would do if the Afghan perimeter failed or disintegrated, and we had a branch plan for this eventuality.

After a good discussion of all these points, we came to the key decision for the secretary: when would Scott leave? It was our view—Scott, the chairman, and I—that he could and should leave immediately, before July 4. In the ensuing back-and-forth, it was clear that the secretary wanted him to stay longer, and that he wanted a visual symbol—an event—to occur that would mark the end of his time in command. We ended the briefing with agreement on all of the details we had briefed on the way ahead, but with no firm decision on the date—and manner—of Scott's departure. The secretary was headed over to see the president, and we expected that guidance would come back to us from that meeting.

None of us were surprised by this. There was a persistent narrative circulating in Washington that our withdrawal had been too fast, too rushed. We should have used every day to get out at the last minute, so the story went. By moving quickly, we—the generals—were trying to embarrass the president. It takes a certain jaded, cynical view of the world and of the purported motives of senior military officers to advance these thoughts, but they had been ubiquitous throughout the high summer of 2021. In fact, the withdrawal had been paced by the dictum that "safe was fast" and that we would also show our intent clearly to the Taliban by moving aggressively and unambiguously. The president was presented with many opportunities to change the pace of the withdrawal, and he always pressed for speed. He was right to do so.

There was a second view as well; as we approached a genuine end to the campaign, what had been aspirational and academic now became firm and corporeal. Since we would no longer be able to support the Afghans in their fight directly, the Taliban was gaining ground, and there was a very real chance that all the advances in human rights that we had paid for in blood were now at risk. The many thousands of Afghans who had assisted us over two decades would also be in mortal danger. Because of these two factors, there was a political desire to prolong support to the Afghans as long as possible. We had been clear that so long as we maintained forces in Afghanistan during the withdrawal, we would support the Afghans in their fight. By early July, our support had dwindled greatly, given the ranges we had to operate from and the lack of U.S. terminal controllers, but it was still a factor, although increasingly a marginal one. We were now proposing to end that support in the next few days. At the very end, and after a clear decision from the president, people were still trying to reconcile the irreconcilable. They were finding that it was hard to execute a strategic withdrawal and still hold to lofty, ambitious societal goals in a faraway country. I knew this was the environment that the secretary would now enter as he talked at the interagency level, and with the White House, about our proposals.

We received our answer later that same day. The chairman called to relay it to me. Scott would stay in command for about another week—until after July 4. I would then fly to Afghanistan to have a ceremony there, memorializing the passage of command. Left unclear at the time of this call was whether we would cease our kinetic support for the Afghans at that time. Scott and I talked, and we worked out the date of Monday, July 12, as when I would relieve him in Kabul. That date would allow him to visit part of the force that had positioned to my forward headquarters, visit NATO in Mons, Belgium, and then be back on hand for the ceremony.

On the morning of July 8, we had another video conference with the president. This one ran two hours. It gave me an opportunity to clearly lay out the risks that we were going to face in the security force assistance and counterterror OTH tasks. It also became clear that we would not declare the end of the retrograde until August 31 and that our kinetic support for the Afghans would continue until that time. There was a risk here that the

Taliban would react to our continued support for the Afghan security forces. It's my belief that some the people in the room for the video conference left with an underappreciation of just how difficult it would be to provide effective air-based fire support for the Afghans and retained an overly optimistic view of how effective it could be. The weather, the extreme range, the requirements of the Doha Agreement to act only in defense, and our need to ensure our strikes were conducted within the law of armed conflict all narrowed the window through which these fires would have to be delivered.

The president delivered nationally broadcasted remarks on Afghanistan that afternoon, affirming what we had discussed that morning. I had no issue with the president's direction to not make the "retrograde complete" announcement until the end of August. We were still moving a few odds and ends around, so it wasn't inaccurate or misleading. I did believe the Afghan government would not prevail in the fight that was now coming upon them like a late summer storm, but I didn't think they would collapse before the end of August.

What I was most worried about after our video conference was what we were going to do with the large number of Afghans that we were talking about bringing out—most visibly interpreters, but also other people who had assisted our efforts over many years and were now in the crosshairs of the Taliban. The potential numbers ranged from a few thousands to tens of thousands. CENTCOM's part of the problem was to prepare to move them from Afghanistan when directed, in numbers large or small. The Department of State would assess their viability for the special immigrant visa program. The SIV process wasn't noted for its speed of execution—it often took years to fully process an application. Furthermore, State had not begun to ramp up its ability to handle the onslaught that was expected. We would need somewhere to hold these people in a transient but livable environment while they were processed for onward movement to their final destinations. CENTCOM would need help with this, because the Department of State would have to negotiate for permission to keep them in the region. We had some good alternatives in that case, beginning with Kuwait and Qatar, two nations that had always extended a helping hand to us when we need assistance of this type. I was more worried about the second-order effects of taking so many inherently valuable members of society out of Afghanistan at the same time we were pressing the Afghans to fight on. It seemed to me that this could act as an accelerant to the Taliban narrative and deprive Afghan society of key talent that could be used for its defense.

Finally, we continued to refine various plans for a noncombatant evacuation operation. This would involve bringing out all U.S. citizens and anyone else designated by the Department of State from Afghanistan. As a Marine and a former MEU commander, NEOs had been part of my professional kitbag for many years. One in Afghanistan would be particularly challenging. The F-77 list, a Department of State document that enumerates the eligible population for evacuation, in late June identified about 12,000 U.S. citizens. With family members and other categories, this could easily triple—although some had left because of the department's warnings, which had begun early in the year. Should the Taliban contest the NEO, we'd have a real fight on our hands. We had been studying the problem for some time, and we stood up a JTF headquarters, built out of my Marine component, under Brig. Gen. Ferrell Sullivan. I knew Ferrell well—he had been my son's battalion commander several years before. He was good under pressure, and that would prove important over the next few weeks. By the end of June, we had solid plans on the shelf, and we had even had the opportunity to have an internal tabletop wargame exercise, speculating about major parts of the plan. As always, our timing would depend on State's ability to make a decision to conduct a NEO. It had been my experience that no chief of mission liked to do this—it was an admission of failure. Resultantly, they often delay too long and don't take reasonable preparatory steps, such as requiring a paced forced drawdown as conditions deteriorated. Embassy Kabul was no different, and they had not drawn down significantly. We would also depend on the ability of State to process potential evacuees. This would prove to be the Achilles' heel of the entire mission.

I flew into Kabul on Monday, July 12, to relieve Scott Miller. His work was done—the retrograde was essentially complete, although, as directed by the president, we would not finalize that process formally until August 31. During my two-day visit, I met with President Ghani and his national security team, Dr. Abdullah Abdullah, and also the minister of defense, General Bismullah

Khan. The meetings with the Afghanis were designed to assure them that although our "boots on the ground" presence in Afghanistan was coming to an end, and in fact it already had, we would continue to support them.

After completing this round of meetings, it was obvious that the Afghan military had finally realized that they needed to get away from the "defend everywhere" approach that they had followed for so many years. Defending everywhere meant a myriad of small outposts, many not mutually reinforcing, and spread across the country. Sticking with this approach had allowed the Taliban to gobble up the isolated checkpoints. Now, there was a growing realization that defending everywhere meant, in effect, defending nowhere. It was the most significant shift in Afghan military strategy that I had observed in my long association with them. Their plan called for the defense of Kabul and a number of provincial capitals, as well as the nine key border crossings into Afghanistan. As our planners worked with the ministry of defense, we recommended a "one plus seven" approach: Kabul, Maiden Shahr in Wardak, Pul-e Alam in Logar, Jalalabad in Nangarhar, Kandahar City in Kandahar, Kunduz City in Kunduz, Mazar-e-Sharif in Balkh, and Herat City in Herat. The Afghans wanted more provincial capitals than the seven just listed. My fear was that unless they ruthlessly prioritized, they would end up with a "checkpoint-lite" approach that would not solve the core problems they faced. In the final analysis, it had to be their plan, so their views prevailed. I found it interesting that in many times over the past decades, we had imposed our planning concepts on them. Now, at the very end, they were ultimately responsible for planning—and execution. We were the onlookers.

I was impressed with the straightforward, soldierly demeanor of Bismullah Khan, the minister of defense. It had been many years since I had last seen him. I felt he grasped the nature of the problem his country faced. He had been sidelined and out of the service for many years, but he looked in good shape to me. His son accompanied him for our meetings. I found him candid and realistic. In our blunt, straightforward exchange, I told him that they needed to get some stability in the leadership of their combat formations. President Ghani had relieved several corps commanders for reasons not related to combat efficiency. This was a destructive practice that sapped morale at lower levels and made sitting commanders risk-averse. If someone wasn't performing, of course they should be relieved. If, on the other hand, the relief was driven by political calculation or cronyism, the quality of senior leadership would inevitably decline.

He had some asks for me—mainly dealing with the inevitable friction that attended shifting to an OTH model. I had heard criticism of him that he did not understand the new capabilities of the Afghan air force, since it had grown significantly in size and capability since he last served, but I found him very knowledgeable on this subject. More close air support from us was one of his asks, and I took pains to explain why it was going to be extremely difficult to get the air support he was used to from the past. In short, it was a combination of numbers of platforms, extreme range, and a requirement, negotiated in Doha, to fly only in direct support of Afghan forces that were in distress. We could not do any deep strike or interdiction; we no longer even had the intelligence resources to develop those potential targets.

Our intelligence was unclear about when the Taliban would start their main offensive. We knew that in their internal debates, there were differences of opinion. Most of the intelligence supported the proposition that they would not start until September, so the government had some six weeks to reposition and get ready for the assault. I spent a considerable amount of time with Pete Vasely, reviewing how we needed to nudge the government in this regard. In a very real sense, this was now their war. We would continue to support them logistically and financially, but our airpower could only have peripheral effects at best—and it would end completely on August 31. We had much less time than this in reality, because the Taliban offensive never really paused, although the degree of centralized direction is still unclear as I write this.

On Monday afternoon, I relieved Scott in a small ceremony in front of the Yellow Building, the old Resolute Support headquarters. It was well attended by the Afghan national security team as well as dozens of reporters. Scott's remarks were personal and introspective; I thought he hit exactly the right tone. My remarks were more formal and were written (and exhaustively vetted by the White House) to assure the Afghans. I don't know that they did. I do believe that the series of meetings I was able to hold around the change of command did some good.

Early on the morning of Tuesday, July 13, I jogged over to the Resolute Support gym, just a short distance away from the headquarters. I had first gone into that gym early one morning in June 2009 as a new one-star reporting into what was then the ISAF headquarters. It was a multilevel building with dozens of cardio machines as well as free weights. In 2009 it was packed, alive, and vibrant. Loud workout music blared everywhere. Men and women bustled about, getting their physical training in before the day got started. When I went in this time, it was completely empty. No music, all the televisions dark and silent. The workout equipment was still there, but it was just me and my security detail. I got an hour in on an elliptical—it may even have been the same one I first used back in 2009. Afterward, I walked around the compound. It looked like a scene from *On the Beach*, Nevil Shute's dystopian novel about Australia and the end of the world after a nuclear war. The streets were all empty, with papers blowing about aimlessly, swirling in the morning breeze—the detritus and wreckage of a large and complex military machine that had died suddenly. Very few people were about. It was quite a change from the hectic, international flavor—proudly emphasized by the NATO national representatives and their office spaces—that the compound had maintained for so many years.

Later that afternoon, I climbed aboard my C-17 and began the long trip home. I was confident in our military leadership in Afghanistan. I also believed we would be able to defend the embassy if it were attacked. I was less confident about the ability of the Afghan security forces to adopt the plan that had been so laboriously worked out. There was a disconnect between the planners around the national security advisor, Hamdullah Mohib, and the uniformed military leaders in the ministry of defense. After my series of meetings with senior Afghan civilians, I was not convinced that the political leaders understood just how critical the strategic situation was: we were literally hanging by a thread. There was nothing inevitable about a Taliban victory, but time was now working against us. The storm was coming—would the Afghans be able to weather it?

12

AN INCONVENIENT TRUTH

REALITY INTRUDES IN AFGHANISTAN

Everybody has a plan 'til they get punched in the mouth.
—*Mike Tyson*

By mid-July my personal estimate of the situation had coalesced to the point that I saw the future path in Afghanistan lying somewhere between two boundaries. The optimistic outcome would be that the Taliban's offensive, now beginning to gather steam, would capture a number of provincial capitals, mainly in the south and west, but the Afghan security forces would be able to hold on to at least half of the thirty-four provincial capitals. Most importantly, they would hold on to the approaches to Kabul: Highway 1 south to Ghazni City, and Highway 7 east to Torkum Gate, as well as Maidan Shahr in Wardak and Pul-e-Alam in Logar Province. As winter closed in, fighting would lose intensity, and the government would be able to stabilize itself and perhaps force international pressure on the Taliban, leading to genuine negotiations. Whatever happened in the winter, the Taliban would renew their offensive in the spring, and then the government would be hard pressed to survive. This was my positive scenario.

My alternative view was that a collapse would come suddenly in the late summer and early fall in a nonlinear manner. By this, I meant that corps formations would begin to disintegrate, provincial capitals would fall, and a sense of inevitability would begin to cloak the Taliban offensive. Warlords and governors would make deals, and the government would evaporate. Under these circumstances, Kabul would fall before the first snowfall. I thought the outcome would most likely be somewhere in the middle, but as each day in July went by, my view began to settle around the gloomier view of the future—although I did not then, and do not now, believe that any outcome was inevitable.

Over the weekend of July 23–24, I held my quarterly CENTCOM commander's conference at our forward headquarters at Al Udeid Airbase in Qatar. This was the first in-person conference with all my commanders that we had been able to pull off in well over a year. The opportunity to see each other face to face was a welcome change from the distance of secure video conferencing. The forward headquarters had been built as an elaborate bunker. I never entered through its armored doors without feeling like I was going into a Maginot line fortress. Building an elaborate forward headquarters in Doha may have been a good move from an assurance perspective for our Gulf partners, but from an operational point of view, it did not stand up well to the changing nature of the theater. We were in very close range for Iranian missiles—less than two hundred miles—which would yield a warning of only two or three minutes at best. The bunker, well protected against tank main gun fire, was vulnerable to missiles falling from the stratosphere. In many ways, the bunkered structure was a monument to short-sighted thinking. On the other hand, the command and control facilities were excellent, and there was ample space for the staff to work. In addition to catching up with my commanders, I used the days in Qatar to further refine the noncombatant evacuation operation (NEO) plan that we were working.

On Friday evening I held a small dinner for my component commanders. It was an opportunity to relax and just spend some time in each other's company. We did this inside the headquarters bunker, which could cater meals. We were about ready for dessert when my executive officer, Shawn Leonard, came in and said that the chairman wanted to talk to me. Excusing myself, I walked back to my office, just a few feet away. I was quickly connected to the chairman, who told me that the president had talked to President Ghani earlier that day, conveying a message intended to stiffen his spine and to encourage him to be more public and positive in his messaging.[1] The task for the chairman and me from the White House was to follow up that call and emphasize the same message to President Ghani at the military level. Jake Sullivan would join us for the call.

I acknowledged the task and sat down at my desk to cobble some notes together while the White House built the call. I thought it was a reasonable thing to do—the public messaging from the Taliban was quite vocal, attempting to create the perception of inevitability. Messaging from the Afghan government was muted, fragmented, and generally dysfunctional, largely ceding the space to the Taliban. Information was half the battle in an environment like Afghanistan. I've seen the many pundits who have weighed in on the nature of the president's earlier call to Ghani, but from a CENTCOM perspective, it was a reasonable action for President Biden to take. The message from the leader of a nation at war—President Ghani—needed to be upbeat and positive. There was nothing underhanded or innately unethical in urging him to be positive when addressing his countrymen and the world. Our own messaging to him dovetailed with this, and I had no compunction about delivering it. He needed to act like a leader in a moment of supreme crisis for his nation.

We were quickly connected, and both the chairman and I delivered our messages to President Ghani, who, as always, was courteous and engaging. The Reuters article that I cited in note 1 of this chapter used information that had been leaked to the reporters—but they did quote me correctly when I told President Ghani that "I do not believe time is our friend here. We need to move quickly."[2] I left the call with a sense that things were trending in a negative way and that the national leadership of Afghanistan did not fully comprehend the precipice they were on.

In subsequent discussions with the chairman that evening, I decided to go to Kabul on Sunday, July 25 (see map 7). I went with three objectives: First, and most important, it would give me a chance to convey to the Afghan national leadership the need to act aggressively if they were to save their country. Second, I would also have an opportunity to talk with Pete Vasely. Last, I would be able to have a media availability while in Kabul, and I could message our continued support for the government of Afghanistan—in keeping with the "spine stiffening" messages we were sending the president of Afghanistan.

In Kabul, I met with President Ghani first in a small room in the palace. In all my meetings with him, this was the most focused I had seen him. Before my arrival, he told me that he had led an extensive planning

Map 7. Kabul

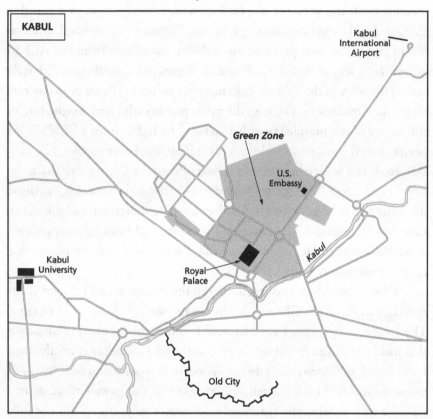

session with his ministers. He emphasized that they had to achieve strategic consolidation. I was glad to hear this, because this was the recommendation we had been making for some weeks. He acknowledged that consolidation would require uncovering some provincial capitals, and he would not be able to support these capitals with either airpower or elite forces. He was also concerned about building political consensus for the plan. For the first time, he did outline an end state that I thought was reasonable: "a stalemate sufficient to force progress on a political settlement." He also expressed displeasure with what he called the narrative coming out of Washington, which he believed was negative and unhelpful. I told him that I was going to hold a press conference at our headquarters later that evening and that

I would do my best to offset that tone. He also wanted us to expand our airstrikes. I told him that we were limited to strikes in direct support of his forces; we could not go against deep targets. Any change there would require new policy guidance from my chain of command. I told him that I would ensure that the secretary knew of his request. As we were finishing our meeting, he looked me in the eye and remarked with clear bitterness that some key Afghan commanders were being approached by U.S. interlocutors with special immigrant visa offers. He then said, "Don't give up on us yet, give us a chance."

As I left the palace, I was struck again by the liminal beauty of the grounds and the severe and unrelenting elegance of the architecture. Men and women walked around in well-tailored Western business suits. People, including men and women together, were seated in a chic glassed-in coffee bar in the outer courtyard. I wondered how long this bucolic scene would last. I was very much aware that this might prove to be the last time I'd be in the palace. As my vehicle pulled through the palace gates to return to our headquarters, I did not look back.

My meeting with Minister of Defense Bismullah Khan echoed many of the same themes I covered with the president. We met in the gardens across from the headquarters building. The sun had gone down, and the sky was soft and beautiful, as it always was at sunset. We sat in a pavilion for our meeting—the same pavilion that had hosted my farewell party in June 2010, when I left the staff in Kabul to go to Tampa. As usual, Khan was a formidable presence, but he seemed to me to be tired. Our discussion was straightforward and businesslike. He was clearly frustrated that the plan outlined by his president had not been created in concert with military leaders who would have to execute it. It was obvious to me that he understood the absolute importance of stopping the Taliban somewhere. Like the president, he asked for more air support. We also talked about things we were doing to increase the availability of Afghan aircraft, and, finally, the provision of more munitions for them—particularly more precision seeker heads for their 2.75-inch rockets, which they were going through at a high rate. I believed then that he had a good understanding of the operational situation, but his receipt of reporting was deteriorating rapidly. More importantly, he simply did not have the ability, either technical or political, to maneuver his forces to carry out the plan that was being discussed at the palace. As we concluded the meeting, I again had the sense that this would be our last meeting.

Immediately after my session with Bismullah Khan, I walked to the front steps of the Yellow Building, the former Resolute Support mission head-quarters, now the U.S. Forces–Afghanistan Forward headquarters. Standing behind a podium, I talked briefly to the media, attempting to give a positive message to offset the many negative memes that were circulating. My basic theme was that a Taliban victory was not inevitable—that there were still things that could happen that would change the course of the campaign. As I stood and read my remarks and then took questions from the twenty or so media still on the ground, one of the many feral cats that lived in the compound walked over and rubbed itself luxuriously against my combat boots. It was below the line of sight of the cameras, but all present could see it. It was probably a fitting addition to the last press conference in Kabul by a U.S. four-star commander.

Flying home, my focus was now on two things: how the campaign was unfolding on the ground, and the NEO planning occurring in our opera-tions shop. We had placed a thoroughly competent Canadian major general, Derek Macauley, as the principal planner and owner of the process. He was a good match as the principal assistant for Air Force Maj. Gen. Alexus Grynkevich, my superb J-3. Since Alexus' call sign was—of course—Grynch, it was inevitable that Derek's nickname at CENTCOM would be "Max," for the dog that accompanied the Grinch in the Dr. Seuss tale. They were a good team, and I spent a lot of time with them and their large cross-functional planning team over the summer as we refined the plan. We had submitted our NEO base plan to the Joint Staff on May 8, and we continued to refine it extensively throughout June and July.

I have always believed that commanders must be intimately involved in the planning process. A commander who issues broad guidance and then leaves the room is defaulting on one of his or her most basic responsibili-ties. Any plan must reflect the personality of the commander, as well as the capabilities of the organization, all oriented on the task at hand. Because of this view, I met frequently with Max's team. We would test assumptions, challenge the data, and sharpen the argument. I enjoyed being challenged, and the dialectic with the planners was always a highlight of my day. Any good plan must tell a story—there needs to be a narrative, and the plan must also account for sequels—what will happen in the future if things go as we intend—and branches—what will happen in the future if things don't go as planned. Since things never go exactly as planned, we spent a lot of time looking at these alternatives.

There is an axiom of planning, attributed to Helmuth von Moltke the elder, that "no plan survives contact with the enemy." This is actually a misquote, because what von Moltke actually said was, "No plan survives contact with the enemy's main body."[3] That's a very big difference. In fact, the structure of a plan can live well into execution. If done insightfully, planning can establish a cognitive framework that will aid future decisions that must be made in the turbulence of operations. The difference is this: In the planning process, you have the luxury of time. The one thing that you do not have in execution is unlimited time; it is the only resource that cannot be stretched, manipulated, added to, or improved. Proper planning in current time can help a commander in future time overcome this temporal tyranny—because time moves at a different, slower rate when you are planning and at a dizzying speed in execution.

The core of any plan is its assumptions. In our planning process, assumptions are assertions about a future condition, upon which the plan is based. We try very hard to turn assumptions into facts, which are immutable, through our intelligence processes. By definition, if an assumption is tested and found to be invalid, then some element of the plan will need to be changed—a branch.

By late July we not only had modified and improved the plan, we had also begun positioning forces for execution. In early July I had sent Ferrell Sullivan into Kabul, with the core of the Joint Task Force Crisis Response. His headquarters would be the centerpiece for NEO execution. In discussing a NEO, it's important to understand that the operation is triggered by the Department of State, and they are responsible for identifying who is—and who is not—coming out in the evacuation. Security and transportation are tasks for the Department of Defense. The Department of State's F-77 list for Afghanistan from June 17, 2021, identified 12,044 potential American citizens and family members eligible for evacuation. It also identified 13,304 non-American citizens who would be evacuated, which, when a coefficient for family members was applied, yielded a total of 55,876. Added to the U.S. citizens, we reached a total of 67,920. We estimated that 4,000 personnel from other embassies would need to be evacuated. Finally, we were working off of a projected total of 20,000 Afghans for the SIV program. Taken together, this was a total of 91,920 evacuees. This did not include potential "at risk" Afghans, and we were getting conflicting guidance about what this category would entail. I directed our team to assume another 50,000 Afghans under this category. We were then left with a potential requirement for 141,920 people to bring out.

It's important to note that the final 50,000 was a CENTCOM calculation, made in the absence of firm direction or guidance from State. Of course, under the SIV program, a few Afghans were already leaving. This program, called Allied Refuge, flew fully vetted Afghans and their families to the United States. By the middle of August, 2,500 Afghans had entered the United States through this program. Clearly, this was just a tiny percentage of those who would need to come out.

Our chargé in Kabul, Ambassador Russ Wilson, had developed a seventeen-point list of conditions that he proposed to use to guide decision-making on calling for a NEO. I thought it was a good product but too complex a tool to use to make actual operational decisions. Centering on at most four events would provide much greater speed and focus. From our perspective at CENTCOM, those events were the loss of half of the provincial capitals, the loss of the approaches into Kabul, large-scale desertions or demonstrations of ineffectiveness among Afghan forces, and, finally, the inability of the government to execute command and control of whatever forces it still commanded. I felt that the display of two or more of these conditions should be the basis for a NEO decision—but it was not my call.

In our planning, we assumed that the outer cordon of security around HKIA would continue to be maintained by Afghan government forces, but we were prepared to introduce additional combat forces to secure the entire perimeter if this didn't hold. In fact, this happened—the Afghans collapsed—so we brought in additional forces that were able to provide security around the airfield for our operations. We thought the primary threat to our operations would be ISIS-K, and this proved to be true. We also assumed that the Taliban would not oppose our efforts, and this assumption also held. In fact, by mid-August, they had effectively replaced the dissolved Afghan security forces as the outer cordon. We also modeled aircraft throughput and capacity. Our base and most stressing assumption was that to evacuate 100,000 people as rapidly as possible, we would require twenty-five C-17 sorties a day, with floor loading, which would extract this number of people in nineteen days. Floor loading a C-17 meant putting additional people on the floor of the aircraft, well above the designed seating capacity. In fact, we exceeded the daily flow of C-17s in the assumption on many days of the evacuation, and we also had the assistance of our allies, who brought out more than 40,000 people. In every measurable way, we exceeded our planning factors for outflow of people.

On August 3 I briefed the secretary of defense by video conference on our plan. CENTCOM had four battalion-sized elements available for employment immediately: a Marine battalion from the MEU, another one from the Special Purpose Air-Ground Task Force, and two U.S. Army battalions. Additionally, I had the carrier strike group, a bomber element of six B-52s, and additional Air Force fighters from across the Gulf for fire support if required. This was a minimal force that could execute a very small NEO of up to 12,000 people. We called this the Blue Force, and it would put about 3,000 personnel on the ground at HKIA and the embassy. We did not see this as the most likely option. The most likely option was a requirement to bring out 100,000 or more people. We called this the White Force, and it brought an infantry regiment or brigade into HKIA and added significant numbers of helicopters, medical support, explosive ordnance disposal, and special enablers such as civil affairs, psychological operations, and cyber teams. Most importantly, the White Force also brought an Air Force contingency response group, airmen capable of maintaining an airfield and even taking over traffic control duties if necessary. The White Force totaled about 2,885 additional personnel on the ground and gave us a total of seven battalions, with a total force on the ground of a little under 6,000. This option provided all of the core capabilities required to conduct a NEO, including the ability to operate up to three entry control centers (ECCs), in support of our state partners. An entry control center is an organization that screens and processes potential evacuees. Security and manpower are largely provided by DoD, but all decisions about who is evacuated rest with the consular staff of the ECC. It's important to understand that throughput was dictated by the ability of Department of State consular officers to process potential evacuees at the ECCs. The number of consular officers, and their ability to work swiftly, effectively, and continuously, was a major pillar of our plan, and this factor was completely outside the Department of Defense's control.

The final package was the Purple Force. This was a security-oriented package that introduced another parachute infantry brigade, the division tactical headquarters and a big part of the combat aviation brigade of the 82nd Airborne, substantial enablers, and the possibility of the XVIII Airborne Corps headquarters. This package of up to 7,803 personnel would give us a total of ten battalions on the ground. I envisioned it as having two methods of entry—we could seize Bagram with a joint forcible entry operation, establish a second airhead, and provide fires and other support if the Taliban attacked Karzai International and the runway there became inoperable. Alternatively, we could introduce the force directly into Karzai International. There was absolutely no appetite from the chairman or the secretary to entertain a forcible entry into Bagram. There was also no appetite for bringing in the corps headquarters. I was a little surprised at this, because the corps headquarters would have given us additional flexibility, but I recognized that the secretary's mind was made up on this. It was obvious to me that he was worried about the risks of an airborne assault into Bagram, so I again emphasized that Bagram would be an option only if we were unable to use the runway at Karzai International.

We had a good plan for command and control. Rear Adm. Pete Vasely would be the overall tactical commander on the ground, with his U.S. Forces-Afghanistan forward headquarters. Brigadier Gen. Ferrell Sullivan would work the NEO as well as the initial security element of the plan. Should we need to take over security for the airfield, then we'd bring in the 82nd Airborne Division tactical headquarters, and Maj. Gen. Chris Donahue would assume responsibility for overall ground security, reporting to Pete. I knew Chris from the Joint Staff, and he was another highly capable and effective commander.

Bringing him in would allow Ferrell to focus on our most important task—running the evacuation. In the event, this was the command and control design we eventually arrived at, and I think it worked very effectively, which was a tribute to the three flag officers involved. This also highlights the importance of personal relationships. You cannot build an organization for combat based simply on a wiring diagram. Any design must recognize the role of personalities, particularly at the higher levels of command. In these three men, we had the right officers for these difficult, dangerous, and demanding jobs.

Our plan also accounted for the presence of the Turks at the airfield. For many years, they had operated and secured that part of the airfield that was used by NATO and other coalition forces. They also served as the senior airfield authority, which organized our flights in and out. We thought the Turks would stay—at least for a while—but we were prepared to assume all of their responsibilities on short notice if that situation changed.

During this brief, and at every opportunity I had to meet with senior leadership inside the Department of Defense, I reiterated my concern that the Department of State wasn't moving as fast as we were on preparations for a NEO. I was particularly concerned about the sheer volume of potential evacuees and how we would care for and hold them over time. I had addressed these issues formally with the secretary on July 21, and I knew that he shared many of my concerns. Nonetheless, I was worried that our departments were moving at different speeds. I received little feedback from the secretary on this brief, but it was clear that he did not support moving the XVIII Corps headquarters into the theater and showed little enthusiasm for the remainder of the forces we outlined. I asked that elements of the White and Purple forces be placed on prepare-to-deploy orders and that the White Force deploy forward to a staging base. I received no answer in the brief, but I didn't expect it. I knew that the secretary would want to talk offline with his advisors before making any decision.

While our planning and approval process continued, the situation in Afghanistan began to deteriorate. On August 2, the day before my brief on our NEO plan, I updated the secretary, through the chairman, with Pete Vasely's running estimate of the situation. In summary, the campaign was approaching a final tipping point from which the government could not recover. Despite the visits, the encouragement, and the pressure from Pete and his team, the Afghans were proving unable to create a genuine actionable plan from their strategic concept—a concept that was one PowerPoint slide deep. Additionally, they were losing the ability to see their own forces, which is perhaps the fundamental requirement of any military organization. You must know where your units are, their state of supply, and their readiness to fight. Largely, by August 1, this quantitative information was no longer available to the Afghan leadership. The one key advantage that the Afghans had, their air force, wasn't even being applied in support of their strategic concept. In the week before August 2, only 36 percent of the airstrikes by their air force supported key areas in the plan: Helmand, Kandahar, and Herat. All other airstrikes were frittered away against nondecisive targets. Pete and I both felt that the fall of multiple provincial capitals was imminent, and once that began, the effect in the information environment would be profound—and perhaps decisive.

As CENTCOM focused on putting forces in place for a potential NEO, a series of tabletop exercises were held in Washington. We were not part of them, because they were focused on interagency actions. The readouts of these exercises that were shared with me painted a picture of an interagency team that did not take the possibility of total evacuation seriously. In opening comments for the August 6 exercise, a senior White House official said: "I don't think we'll have to do this [a NEO], but if we do we have all failed." That's a good summary of the U.S. position. As late as the end of the first week of August, we still wanted to have it all: leave Afghanistan, continue to influence events there through a large and robust embassy platform, and carry out counterterror operations. Reality would soon intrude on these dreams.

To understand what was happening on the ground, it is important to compare it to how the Taliban fought when they took over Afghanistan, and more particularly Kabul, in 1996. The 1994–96 campaign was a conventional military campaign, with large elements of the Taliban (and the government) operating with motorized formations. There was little air threat to the Taliban, so they could mass and maneuver. The campaign against Kabul was far slower, taking almost two years to come to fruition, and the Taliban was never able to bring the northern tier of provinces under their suzerainty. In short, the campaign of the '90s, culminating with the fall of Kabul in

September 1996, looked more like a traditional military campaign, as government strongholds fell in sequence with a period of maneuver transitioning to either a brief or a lengthy siege of major provincial capitals.

It was very different in 2021. There was little actual large-scale organized maneuver in time and space; instead, bands of Taliban attacked across a broad front. In many ways, it was akin to the Tet Offensive strategy of the North Vietnamese in 1968—except that it was actually working in Afghanistan. Their plan, as we observed it, was this: a combination of broad, simultaneous military success achieved with a narrow margin between victor and vanquished, the treachery of regional warlords and governmental officials who wanted to be on the winning side, and a conscious strategy to neutralize what had not been addressed in the '90s—the northern provinces and tribes. Another factor was the imperfect command and control the Taliban exerted over their tactical formations. In many cases, aggressive commanders on the ground were willing to take risks that the Taliban senior leaders were uncomfortable with. This was even more pronounced when contrasted with the attitude of Afghan commanders and their political leadership, who were generally risk-averse and slow to act. It's still too soon to know for sure, but I believe that the Taliban senior leadership was surprised by their own success.

On Thursday, August 5, I took a call from Ambassador Zalmay Khalilzad. I had a liaison officer with his team in Doha who kept me apprised of what was going on with negotiations, although Zal's propensity for extreme secrecy and compartmentation made it impossible to gain a full understanding of his progress along the diplomatic line of effort. He shared nothing more than what was absolutely necessary. It was exactly the opposite of our approach. He asked me for my view of the situation, and I updated him with my assessment, which was consistent with our August 2 running estimate. He then delivered his bombshell: Jake Sullivan wanted me to go to Doha to join in negotiations with him and the Taliban. I was noncommittal. Scott Miller had gone to Doha frequently with Zal, but that had been for specific military input during the lengthy negotiation process. The chairman had gone as well on one occasion. I did not see the value of the chairman going to Doha at the time, although I recognized his desire to provide some energy to the process. With conditions as they were on the ground, it wasn't clear to me that having the CENTCOM commander in the room would change anything. Zal was ambiguous on what I might contribute. Two thoughts struck me as we talked—I did not relish being a potted plant for Zal while he continued to negotiate, with his leverage melting away every day, driven by events on the ground. Second, I wasn't sure where the idea had actually come from. I knew Zal and his methods well enough to believe that perhaps he—not Jake—had suggested this. It was then a small step to call me and to infer that the national security advisor wanted me to go. I did not commit to doing anything during our call, since neither Zal nor Jake had the authority to tell me to go.

Upon hanging up, I immediately called the chairman and passed on the conversation. He was completely unaware of the "initiative." I knew that he would get the information to the secretary—who could direct me to go or not go as he chose. I continued to believe that the time wasn't ripe for me to go, and the mission was profoundly unclear, at least on August 5. I also knew that it wouldn't go away, so I put my team on notice to begin to work a trip into the region. A problem with going into Doha was that I would lose my communications to some degree: even the best-equipped aircraft can't provide the communications structure I had in the United States. After arriving, I would be at my forward headquarters, so comms would be good except for the transit. I make this point to illustrate how important communications were to me at this vital juncture. On average, I was talking to the chairman ten times a day and to my field commanders the same amount. At the theater level of war, the ability to communicate is critical. For the rest of that day, and all of the next, I watched events in Afghanistan. On August 7 Pete called to tell me that the first provincial capital had fallen. It was Zaranj City, in Nimruz province. Nimruz was in extreme southwestern Afghanistan and was hardly key terrain—but it was the first provincial capital to go. This would be the first of many such calls from Pete, as capital after capital went down.

The next day, August 8, I sent the secretary what would become my final estimate of the situation in Afghanistan. It was based on significant input from Pete Vasely, material from my staff, and my own read of the situation. I spent some time alone composing it. At that point in time, it represented my very best judgment of where we were in the campaign and what lay ahead. When I wrote it, the Taliban had captured five provincial capitals and were executing active attacks against another thirteen. Zaranj in Nimruz (the first), Sheberghan in Jowzjan, Konduz City in Konduz, Sar-e Pol in the province of the same name, and Taloqan in Takhar province had all fallen. We expected Fayzabad in Badakhshan, Pul-e khumri in Baghal, and the vital city of Mazar-e-Sharif in Balkh to fall within forty-eight hours. The Afghan defense against this metastasizing threat was wholly inadequate. They were "decisively engaged," which is language from our doctrine, but is nonetheless apt: to be decisively engaged means to be unable to maneuver or to shift forces. The Afghans were no longer able to move forces to threatened areas. In fact, they often had no knowledge of events on the ground. I saw little reason for optimism and said: "At their current pace [they] will have Kabul isolated within thirty to sixty days." I also noted that "it is my assessment that given current policy guidance we have no ability to provide decisive action of the scope and scale required." I was right on that, but I was also wrong—Kabul didn't have thirty days, it had less than a week to live.

I sent the assessment to the secretary via the chairman. The chairman's call back wasn't long in coming. Our views of the situation were aligned. He was going over to the White House for a discussion with the president, and I knew that my assessment would provide a lot of grist for the mill. We also talked about the embassy and its reduction in size. Chargé Wilson had reduced his staff to a smaller but still unwieldy size of 2,070. Pete and I still considered this much too large. We had a plan to get smaller—down to about a thousand—but the embassy was reluctant to take that step. At this time, it seemed to me that we were working with a Department of State that was in organizational thrall—facing disaster but unable to act. They were mirroring the views held in Washington in this regard. Ultimately, at a bare minimum they would need to consider completely leaving the embassy in downtown Kabul and shifting to their compound at HKIA. We could protect them there, and there would still be an embassy presence in Afghanistan, albeit a very small one. In conversations with embassy personnel, they believed they had weeks to make these moves. Our assessment was that their time to move was drawing down, and it was a matter of a few days at best for them to shift to Karzai International.

We still attempted to help the Afghan army where we could, striking two targets with MQ-9s on August 9. The Afghans struck thirty-one times as well, but we had no independent way to corroborate where or what they struck—or the battle damage assessment. For Pete and his team in Kabul, it was getting increasingly difficult to liaise with the ministry of defense. Many times, we had a better picture of what was going on than they did. Also, personal considerations of survival were now becoming obvious at the higher levels of Afghan command: they were leaving the country. In every way, it was a negative synergy where failure begat failure, and a sense of inevitability began to predominate. The margins of Taliban victory were small and often bloodless, particularly when deals were cut on a tribal basis with district chiefs and even governors. At any time during these critical days, a victory of some kind for the government, however small, would have had an effect wildly out of proportion to the actual event. The information space inside Afghanistan was volatile, and it could have swung away from the Taliban, but the Afghans could not manufacture even a small victory or the will to message more vigorously.

On August 11, I asked the secretary to release our forces that were on prepare-to-deploy orders so that I could bring them into the CENTCOM area. We still did not have a State Department decision on a NEO, but it was apparent that the situation in Afghanistan was headed toward total collapse, and we would be facing a NEO, regardless of the position of the Department of State and the national security staff. The secretary agreed, and on August 12, our in-theater forces began to move, while the 82nd Airborne units—the White package—began to move to their departure airfields in the United States.

The same day, the chairman told me that the secretary wanted me to go to Doha. As I had suspected, Zalmay Khalilzad's idea had not died; it had fermented in the growing disaster. The plan was for me to meet with the Taliban political committee on Sunday, August 15. I would deliver a message about staying away from Kabul while we evacuated our embassy, citizens, and other groups of people. While not yet public, we were clearly moving toward a NEO. On Friday, August 13, our first forces—Marine combat units—arrived in Kabul, and we also began to flow the White package into the theater.

The situation continued to deteriorate over the next forty-eight hours. Provincial capitals in Herat, Kandahar, Uruzgan, Badghis, Logar, Zabul, Ghor, and Paktika fell. Additionally, there were indications that the Taliban had freed prisoners in the large Parwan prison facility, near Bagram, which held more than five thousand inmates, including at least one thousand hardcore ISIS fighters. Pol-e-Charkhi prison was also sprung by them. I had had another video conference with the secretary on August 13, where we discussed force flow. I proposed to substitute a battalion of the 82nd, already en route into theater, for another Army battalion that was in the theater. Because of the speed of the 82nd's deployment, it would actually close Kabul faster than my ability to bring the other battalion in with my own organic theater lift. To my surprise, the secretary's reaction was strong and negative. By both body language and tone of voice, it was clear that he didn't want any element of the plan to be changed once it had been briefed at the White House. All I could do was acknowledge his decision, but it certainly didn't give me the feeling that I had much latitude to adjust forces in the theater based on my read of the situation.

I also received guidance on why I was headed to Doha. The secretary's direction was to prepare a map that established a boundary around Kabul on easily identifiable geographic features, at a range of between twenty-five and thirty kilometers from HKIA. It would be a rough circle but would trace against terrain features that could be understood and visualized. My instructions were to tell the Taliban to stay outside this line, which was variously called a no-penetration line or a line of control, until we completed our withdrawal, which would be August 31. In return, we would stop striking them across Afghanistan. We would, however, strike inside the line of control if they interfered with our withdrawal. This was a lot to communicate. I got my team at CENTCOM working a first cut of the product with amplifying text. I iterated it with the chairman very quickly over the course of August 13 and had a workable copy in hand late that evening. I was leaving for Doha early Saturday morning, so we shipped the digital map to my forward headquarters, where they would print it and have it ready for me when I arrived there on Sunday.

By the time I took off on Saturday, August 14, the decision had been made to evacuate the embassy, moving everyone to the airfield. Over a two-night period, Pete Vasely and his team lifted all embassy personnel over to

HKIA and completed the destruction of sensitive material that we couldn't get out. This included destroying four counter-rocket and mortar systems, which we kept up and operational until the final moments of our presence. As I flew east, I worked the phones continually. The airplane was challenged to keep good communications, and my conversations were often like shouting underwater, with frequent stoppages as the system went down. Nonetheless, we did some extremely important work while airborne. We agreed to send the lead battalion of the 82nd straight into HKIA, with the rest of the brigade going into Kuwait, which was a welcome change from the strict adherence to the plan that had been in effect the day before. We would also stand up another brigade of the 82nd back in the United States and increase the readiness of the division's tactical headquarters. We would also speed up the flow of Marine units into HKIA—they were all coming from within the theater.

As the situation deteriorated on the ground, our priority was now very clear: defend the airfield. I didn't feel that I could depend on the ability of the Afghan military to provide the outer cordon anymore, and if they could not perform that function, we would need considerably more forces on the ground. Of course, this was a branch we had foreseen in our planning, and those forces were now preparing to deploy. We also knew that the civilian staff at the airfield were fleeing, so we would need to be ready to take control of all aspects of airfield operations. These forces were also already flowing in, so we would be ready to take over seamlessly. Additionally, I directed my air component commander, Air Force Lt. Gen. "Gooey" Guillot, to begin aggressive demonstrations around Kabul. This included low-level supersonic flights, particularly over the prisons that we felt were about to be opened. We also displayed the B-52s overhead. In my discussions with the chairman that day, I learned for the first time that there was a possibility that President Ghani would step down in a "dignified transfer" to Taliban rule. It was a hectic flight. While I flew, we finally got the decision we needed: to conduct a NEO. The situation Scott and I had been worried about the most back in April—a late decision on a NEO after most of our resources had departed the country—was now the precise situation we confronted. Being airborne, I missed President Biden's statement on Afghanistan, which confirmed that we were bringing in forces to execute a withdrawal. It also referred to my upcoming visit to Doha and the message that I would be delivering when I got there. After we refueled in Shannon, Ireland, I tried to get some sleep, but I was interrupted repeatedly by calls from Washington. We landed in Doha at about nine o'clock in the morning local time. My meeting with the Taliban had been scheduled for 4:30 p.m., but given the catastrophic failures of the Afghan military, I tried to have it earlier—we finally settled on four o'clock.

I spent some time in my office at Al Udeid, talking to Pete Vasely, ensuring I had a current understanding of the fight and reviewing my talking points for the upcoming meeting. I was told I'd be accompanied by Zal and other representatives of the Department of State. My guidance was crystal-clear on the message I was sending. I did receive an email from Kelly Magsamen, the DoD chief of staff, telling me it was important to "show a united front." In my discussions with Pete, it was obvious that the Taliban were now in downtown Kabul and therefore well inside the line of control we were proposing, so our entering plan was already overtaken by events. Pete told me that he thought Kabul would fall within twelve to twenty-four hours. I agreed—all the more reason for me to see the Taliban leadership in the afternoon and to push hard to get more forces on the ground at the airfield as quickly as possible.

The drive from Al Udeid to Doha takes a little over an hour. It's a pleasant drive, and it gave me an opportunity to review my notes yet again. Downtown Doha is a monument to exotic, startling architecture and the relentless drive by the Qataris to improve their infrastructure to get ready for the World Cup, which was held in Qatar in the winter of 2022. Our meeting was to be in the Ritz Carlton. I got there well in advance and went into the U.S. Team's comms room on the eighteenth floor. I had a video conference with the secretary before my meeting, and we reviewed force closure into Kabul. I asked him to flow the second battalion of the 82nd directly into Kabul, and I reported to him that the Afghans were abandoning their posts around the southern side of the airfield. We would have a video conference with the president after my session with the Taliban. I also took the opportunity to go up to the twenty-third floor and do a personal reconnaissance of the room within which we would meet. Zal joined me for a few minutes but then left to work his cell phone. It was a surprisingly small room, dominated by a circular table. There was nothing ostentatious about it. My two liaison officers, Army Brig. Gen. Joe Kline and Marine Corps Brig. Gen. Shawn Selene, talked me through how we would be seated. The Taliban would be there first, and I would be the last to enter. Zal would introduce me, and then we'd begin.

We started right on time. Mullah Abdul Ghani Barader sat directly across from me. To his side were Mohammad Fazl, Abdul Salam Hanifi, and Suhail Shaheen. This was the first time I'd met any of them, but I knew a lot about them. Barader was a key player within the command structure of the Taliban. He had been one of Mullah Mohammad Omar's confidants and had enormous credibility with Taliban rank and file. He had been in prison in Pakistan from 2010 through 2018 and was released largely as the result of U.S. pressure on the Pakistanis. He spoke no English. In the strange world of negotiating with the Taliban, he was assessed as reasonable and worldly—relatively speaking. We were unsure of his actual authority and his standing with senior Taliban leadership. In retrospect, we may have overestimated his ability to deliver on his promises. Mohammad Fazl, on the other hand, had been held in Guantanamo Bay from 2002 to 2014, and we knew he was virulently anti–United States. He also had been severely injured in combat and had a prosthetic left leg. He had been the de facto chief of staff for the Taliban's military arm. He would give no quarter in negotiations. Hanifi was a key assistant to Barader and actually spoke a little English—although he didn't during our meeting. Finally, Shaheen was considered to be media-savvy, and he spoke good English. He also had an academic degree in English from Kabul University. They struck me as serious men, conscious of their battlefield successes and determined to press home every advantage that we had given them in negotiations without any serious recompense on their part.

With me were Zal, Tom West, and Salman Ahmed, all from the Department of State. From the beginning, the tone of the meeting was direct and businesslike. The translation was very good, and Zal jumped in frequently to add nuance or a correction. I began by telling them that our military withdrawal was continuing, and the forces that we were bringing into Kabul were focused on facilitating the safe withdrawal of Americans, other allies, and our Afghan partners. I explicitly told them that they should do nothing to jeopardize this effort, including attacks against us, our allies, or our partners. If they did attack, I told them they would be met by a swift and forceful response. I went on to acknowledge the restraint that they had shown by not attacking us to date, and yet again emphasized that they would be held responsible for any future attacks, and therefore it was critical that they exercise command over their forces to ensure that our withdrawal was not interrupted or delayed.

I then referred to the large map that we had placed in the center of the table. It was a blowup of the line of control map that we had worked so hard on for the past two days. I explained to them that we would consider this a neutral zone until our withdrawal was complete. I told them that if we could come to an agreement on this map, we would undertake to launch no airstrikes anywhere else in Afghanistan. If there was any interference with our withdrawal operations inside the circle, then we would respond with force. I also noted that there were clearly Taliban forces inside the line of control—the best way to deconflict would be for those forces to withdraw to beyond the line of control. In my own mind, I was certain that there was no way that the Taliban were going to withdraw from Kabul now that they were inside the city. Hanafi, through translation, said that the map had obviously been prepared a day or two before our meeting. He was certainly accurate about that. There was, in fact, no chance of the line of control construct being accepted by the Taliban. As they knew only too well, events on the ground had overtaken it—they had forces in the center of Kabul as we spoke.

I felt that there was still an opportunity to get what we wanted: noninterference with our withdrawal. Hanifi then said, "We completely support your withdrawal. Diplomats and non-diplomats." He went on to say that the United States could secure the things and areas it would need to withdraw, "while we do the others." During these exchanges, Barader asked me: if they gave us assurances of safe passage, would we consider employing additional forces to provide security for Kabul? This wasn't a serious question, and in my opinion then, and now, there was no practical way to undertake what he so casually suggested. While I believed his question to have been off the cuff, my response wasn't. It was something we had carefully considered and planned for. I knew the facts inside and out. The introduction of significantly more U.S. combat forces would have been inconsistent with Taliban objectives of getting us out of the country quickly. I told him that our mission was singularly focused on a safe withdrawal, and we would not commit forces for any other purpose. My guidance from the secretary for this meeting was very clear; we were leaving, and our forces would all be dedicated to protecting our withdrawal. I also knew from extensive analysis that it would have required a reinforced division, with a significant package of corps-level enablers, to hold Kabul. The Taliban would never have countenanced the introduction of large U.S. and coalition combat forces into their new capital, even as they proclaimed victory. We would have ended up fighting them, with the potential for significant U.S. casualties.

The matter at hand in the room in Doha was ensuring that the Taliban knew we were deadly serious about protecting ourselves as we withdrew, and that we would strike back ferociously if they chose to interfere. I believe they clearly understood the message I was delivering. Hanafi told me, "We will not allow any hostile act. We will ensure ISIS and others do not strike." I told them again that if we were not attacked by the Taliban, then we would not undertake any strikes against them. Barader then said, "If you give this assurance to me, I give it to you." I then reiterated, "If we are not struck, then we will have no strikes on anyone else." Mohammad Fazl then said, "We will provide security. We will try to stop others." We talked for a few minutes about establishing procedures for coordination. Pete Vasely would be my man on the ground for this coordination. Hanafi closed out the meeting for them by saying, "This is our policy. We will support your withdrawal. We will never jeopardize this. This is clear if all agree. We will assign a liaison." We all stood up, I nodded at them, and then I walked out. We signed nothing, there were no handshakes, and there were no official photographs. As I rode the elevator down, I played it back through my mind. It had been a cold, hard, straightforward meeting, with no pretensions of anything else. They knew where we stood.

I was confident that at the political level, they would do everything possible to allow us to leave. There was some risk in their ability to command their forces, but the real threat would now be from ISIS-K—a threat made far more real and tangible by the opening of the prisons across the country. I was also forcibly struck by the fact that in order to maintain this relationship of convenience, we would need to get out as planned: by August 31. To stay beyond that date would require us to plan to fight the Taliban again, and we would need significantly more forces for that course of action.

I arrived back at my forward headquarters just moments before the president's video conference. He was at Camp David. The entire National Security Council was on the video conference, including the vice president. It was a long meeting, and I debriefed him and the rest of the participants on my meeting with Barader and his companions. There was no interest in the Taliban's idea about us assuming security for all of Kabul, and Zal and his team did not raise the point. We could also report that most of the embassy move to HKIA had been completed. The residual security element would be recovered tomorrow. I learned in that meeting that President Ghani had—literally—taken flight and was out of the country. The collapse of the government was complete. There was a strong interdependency between the government of Afghanistan and its security forces; the self-decapitation of the government destroyed any vestigial hope that the military would fight on. It was a complete rout, not made honorable or more palatable in any way by resistance from the Afghan security forces. While military realities had outpaced any ability of the Afghan government to defend Kabul, it was still remotely possible that a determined stand by the president of Afghanistan might have bought a few more days. The cost would probably have been high for that last stand, so perhaps he was right to leave—it certainly resulted in a near-bloodless takeover of the city, far different than in 1996.

In different conversations throughout the day, I became increasingly concerned about the speed of our force flow into Karzai International. It was obvious that the security environment in and around Kabul was collapsing, paced only by the ability of the Taliban to advance to fill the void left by evaporating government forces. The 1–504 parachute infantry battalion of the 82nd was already inbound to HKIA. We had planned to hold the two sister battalions at Kuwait and flow them in later. Over the course of the late afternoon in Doha, I ordered two more battalions directly into HKIA. That would give Pete seven battalions to work with, and I was considering requesting the second brigade of the 82nd as well.

13

NO SAFETY
OR SURPRISE

THE END IN AFGHANISTAN

This is the end
My only friend, the end
Of our elaborate plans, the end
Of everything that stands, the end
No safety or surprise, the end.
—*Jim Morrison and The Doors, "The End"*

On Monday, August 16, it was my intent to fly into Kabul. It would give me an opportunity to meet face to face with my commanders, see the status of the processing, and gain a first-hand appreciation of the complexities our people were facing. We took off out of Qatar in a Charleston-based C-17, crewed by airmen from Joint Base Lewis-McChord. It was an interesting testimony to the truly global nature of our operations. The aircraft had a Moose callsign, meaning that it was allocated to Central Command (but not assigned, since CENTCOM owns no forces). The crew had been working hard over the past few days, coming in and out of Karzai International. As usual, a large box-like structure was tied down forward in the huge cabin, giving me the ability to sit and work in a little room with near silence. On most flights, I ended up working my communications—either emails or calls—from the moment I entered the aircraft until after we landed, without ever looking outside. This time, though, I wanted to watch the approach into Kabul so I could listen to the Air Force controllers, see the aircraft in the pattern, and get a good airborne look at the airfield. It wasn't to be on this day, though. About an hour into the three-hour flight, my communicator, Army Capt. John Jensen, banged on the door of the box—"Sir, Admiral Vasely needs to talk to you immediately—it's urgent." A momentary glitch in our comms made it impossible for me to take the call inside the quiet box, so I followed John out into the cavernous and noisy cargo bay of the aircraft. Putting on a headset, I was patched to Pete. He was always calm and steady, and this was no exception, but I could sense the tension in his voice. Desperate Afghan civilians had breached the southern entrances to the airfield, where the civilian terminal was. All of our infrastructure was on the northern side of the runway. There were thousands of frantic Afghans trying to get to C-17s that were parked on the north ramp. This had happened because the Afghan security forces, responsible for the boundary security, had simply melted away. We had about two thousand U.S. military forces on the ground, which was not enough to establish a boundary that would keep these frightened people away from our aircraft. We did have a solution, though. We were in the process of bringing in about 1,200 Afghan National Strike Unit (NSU) personnel aboard HKIA, elite Afghan commandos who had been thoroughly vetted. Over the years, they had proved to be very effective in combat operations, and we had come to depend upon them. In the meantime, we would use them to work to secure the inner boundary. They would prove to be invaluable in helping us establish security on the ground. Pete would speed up their arrival, and we would deploy them directly onto the runway to dam the tide of people. We also had several C-17s inbound with paratroopers from the 82nd and more Marines. We needed to clear the runway so that we could get those jets in. It was during this hectic time on the runway that a C-17 took off with people clinging to it. This tragic event would provide an iconic image of our withdrawal. Pete recommended that I turn around and not attempt landing. I took his advice, and we turned around, heading back to Al Udeid. While Pete reestablished control over the airfield, we were stacking up inbound C-17s, and this would slow our buildup of combat power. We needed more infantry on the ground immediately.

As the afternoon wore on, the combination of NSU elements, our own infantry, and Taliban activity at the South Gate pushed people off the runway, although a significant number still clustered around the terminal

Map 8. Kabul International Airport

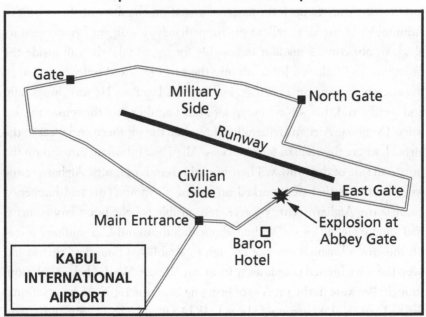

buildings on the south side of the airfield (see map 8). This was the first case
of the Taliban responding to a request to assist us in establishing security.
They answered with about four hundred fighters, and they were useful in
pushing the crowd back, although their indiscriminate use of sticks to beat
people produced even greater fear among the Afghans.

If there was a crisis in the operation, these few hours were it. The sudden
collapse of Afghan security allowed the breach to occur; while we were still
building up the combat power, we needed to defend the entire perimeter.
Pete Vasely and Ferrell Sullivan coolly maneuvered U.S. units, incoming
NSU forces, helicopters, and loose coordination with the Taliban to recreate
order. From the breach to the reestablishment of a solid perimeter took about
sixteen hours. Lives were lost, and that was tragic—but the larger disaster was
averted, and we would never again face the threat of overrun at the airfield.

This was one of the few times I intervened at the tactical level. I learned
that C-17s carrying paratroopers circling over Kabul were reaching the end
of their crew day. The plan was to bring them to Al Udeid, then launch

again tomorrow. I didn't think we could wait that long to get more infantry on the ground. Speaking directly to my operations officer Grynch, and then Lt. Gen. "Gooey" Guillot as the air component commander, I told him to bring the jets to Al Udeid but to have fresh crews immediately available, so that we could hot-turn them and get the paratroopers on the ground. I know it was a miserable experience for the troops in the back, but it saved a lot of time in building up our strength on the ground.

In my midnight video conference with the secretary, I could tell him that the airfield was open for military traffic and that we were landing C-17s and C-130s. We expected a steady flow of reinforcements throughout the next day. I considered the field secure, thanks to the great work of Pete and Farrell. We were also beginning to process American citizens and third-country nationals and had flown out about 390 over the past few hours. We all knew this wasn't a good enough pace, but I was confident the flow would increase. I also asked for the deployment of the division tactical headquarters of the 82nd, and the secretary approved my request. This command element had always been on my list of requested forces, and now seemed an opportune time to bring it in. The division commander, Maj. Gen. Chris Donahue, would give me someone to focus on ground security, while Pete Vasely retained overall command and worked the "up and out" problems. Farrell Sullivan would focus squarely on the NEO itself. As I've noted earlier, the team-oriented attitudes of the three flag officers involved made this complex arrangement work.

The next day, I planned to go into Kabul again. The day began with an early morning conversation with Pete from my office at the forward head-quarters—things were better on the ground. We had pushed two companies of Marines down into the South Gate area. The first ECC was operational at the North Gate, and a crowd was gathering there. Pete had worked with the Taliban to establish a rough security posture outside the gate, and this was beginning to take form, although it was not very well coordinated on the Taliban side.

This time, we weren't forced to turn around. I went up into the cockpit after we went into Pakistan and sat in the jump seat behind the pilots. When the weather cooperates, the flight deck of a C-17 is a bright and sunny place, with great visibility. I put on a headset and plugged into their communications. As a visible sign of how fast we were pushing forces into HKIA, ahead of us by fifteen miles or so and slightly lower was another Moose C-17 inbound. We were operating under visual flight rules (VFR) around Kabul. The airport's radar had been destroyed when the control tower operators had fled. There were lots of planes operating around the field: our C-17s, and also military aircraft and charter flights of many other nations. It gave me a real sense of the risks we were running. The Air Force controllers on the ground, along with their Turkish counterparts, worked to maintain procedural control since we had no sensors to give us a radar picture. The clouds were mixed as we began our descent, but we took a straight-in VFR approach and were on the ground shortly.

On the airfield, it was a scene of intense, controlled activity. Several U.S. C-17s sat at ramp 8, the northern loading and unloading area. A Czech Republic 737 was loading people. Long lines of Afghans, led by Marines, airmen, and soldiers, snaked toward the waiting aircraft. Since 2009 I had been in and out of this field many times, but it had never looked so busy. I got off the aircraft and gave a bear hug to Pete Vasely, and then we went into his operations center, where Farrell Sullivan was waiting to brief me. We spent about an hour leaning over a large-scale map of the airfield, where Farrell talked me through what was going on. His brief was clear and to the point: we were bringing people in at the North Gate and the East Gate, but the crush of the crowd outside the perimeter made it hard to get American citizens up to the front. We were also limited by the number of consular officers that the embassy had on hand—we started with nine, and decisions on who came in or not were made by these State Department officials. More were coming with Ambassador John Bass, an old friend, and his energy and drive would undoubtedly help, but the pace was still too slow. We would have thirty-six consular officers by August 23, which would be a great help. The threat streams from ISIS-K were very real and concerning. We spent some time talking about those. It was obvious that they wanted to attack us. I was now less concerned about breaches of the perimeter by crowds of Afghans than I was about ISIS-K opportunities to attack us, either by indirect fire—mortars or rockets—or by slipping a suicide bomber into a screening point, or worse, past a screening point and onto an aircraft. Something like that would results in the loss of hundreds of lives.

After the brief, we went out to the North Gate to observe the screening process. It was here, at this small entrance, that U.S. policy, politics, and national decisions—and the inevitable outcomes of those decisions—became human reality. The North Gate was being used because it had T-walls—large concrete walls that served as blast attenuators—and ample space inside for a serpentine processing facility that allowed Marines and diplomats to spread out just a little. The stench was overwhelming, and the ground was covered with discarded water bottles, partially eaten brown plastic packets of food, and human waste. It was loud as well: instructions were being shouted, babies were crying, and outside the gate, thousands of people were shouting to get someone's—anyone's—attention. The Marines and diplomats that I saw there were preternaturally calm, focused completely on their mission. They were tender in how they treated families, and particularly children. To do the job they were doing, for hours at a time, exposed to potential attack at any time, required persistent courage—the very hardest kind of courage—and it humbled me. Even more, it was the kind of courage that required the calm and patient execution of a repetitive and difficult task over an extended period of time, while the threat of sudden attack hung over them like the sword of Damocles. I knew that I was in the presence of the greatness of the American spirit in that dirty, concrete-walled entry point. In all my long years of service, I don't know that anything I've ever seen touched me so directly and deeply with what it meant to be an American in uniform, far away from home, and in such a white-hot, searing eternity of danger. This was the point on the ground where national decisions merged with human beings: Afghan and American. As I went back to conduct a video conference with the secretary at Pete's headquarters, I swore to myself that I'd do everything in my power to get them all home safely. That I was unable to get them all back will haunt me for the rest of my life.

As the sun began to go down in Kabul, I had several conversations with the secretary and then the president. There was widespread dissatisfaction with the pace of the evacuation. Pressure was growing to set aside the careful categories that State was working to use to define how people were processed; instead, there was a rising chorus that went something like this: Get people on the planes. After the American citizens, prioritize the vulnerable: women and children. If that meant they brought their families with them, including men, then so be it. Don't sweat the details of special categories or visas. Just get them moving. Move whomever is there to move. Over the next twenty-four hours, this guidance would solidify, and it would result in the vast numbers of people that we brought out over the next few days. It did, however, mean that we were not directly addressing our special visa and other designated at-risk populations. Instead, we were bringing out people who were at the front of the line. With the virtue of hindsight, it is easy to criticize this decision. Given the reality of the facts on the ground, though, it's hard to see a viable alternative. The situation was simply too overwhelming to solve a meat-axe problem with a micrometer's measurement. We did not have the consular processing capacity to screen appropriately. It took some time for the Department of State to implement the president's guidance, and we probably could have moved even more people had that internalization occurred more rapidly. This was an inevitable result of the decision to withdraw U.S. forces and delay a decision on embassy closure and evacuation.

We also discussed staying beyond August 31. From the beginning, I wasn't in favor of considering an extension. It would require extensive negotiation with the Taliban, and I didn't think they would be disposed to allow us to do so. Of course, we had options to stay without their forbearance, and they were well developed and ready to execute. It would mean bringing significantly more combat power in and then possibly fighting the Taliban and ISIS-K while we continued the evacuation. It would probably mean many U.S. casualties. From my perspective, adhering to our timeline would preserve future options to bring those U.S. citizens and Afghans out that we couldn't get to by August 31.

I had told my team that I wanted the C-17 that took me back to Doha to be filled with evacuees, so we brought out 136 people with us. During one conference with the president, the crying of babies was so loud I told him about it and held the headset away from my ear so that he could hear as well. As we flew back to Doha, three things were at the front of my mind. First, we had to reduce the crush of people at the gates. To do this, we'd need the

Taliban to establish a perimeter away from the gate. Doing this would mean accepting some form of pre-screening by them, but I thought this was a risk worth taking. The danger of an attack at the gates by a vehicle- or vest-borne improvised explosive device (IED) was more significant to me than whether or not the Taliban kept some of the population we wanted to fly out away from the gates. We could continue to work the issue of access with them. Second, we needed to increase our processing efficiency. The new consular officers would help; opening other gates would also create greater flow. Third, we needed to complete the flow of forces in and, at the same time, begin to refine how we would withdraw. The withdrawal was probably the most immediate and demanding tactical problem. It was a lot to think about in that C-17, flying south while I listened to the babies cry.

On the morning of Thursday, August 19, I went out to Qatar's Camp as-Sayliyah, where we were building accommodations for up to eight thousand evacuees. The Army Central team was working it hard, and I had a good long conversation with our energetic chargé in Qatar, Ambassador John Desrocher. We agreed that as soon as possible, we needed to get the State Department's specialized migrant affairs elements engaged, which would bring their expertise to the multifaceted demands of running such a large camp. Later that day, I flew to Sharm el-Sheikh, at the southern end of the Sinai Peninsula, where I cohosted a regional chiefs of defense conference. This was the first time we had included Israel, so it was a momentous occasion. My fellow generals were surprised that I could find the time to attend this meeting, but I felt it vital to show up. I still spent about half of my time on the phone or in various secure video conferences during the two-day conference. It did illustrate the multifarious and complex demands a combatant commander faces. Theater responsibilities do not go away, even during a pressing contingency operation.

I arrived back in Tampa before dawn on Saturday, August 21, and went directly from the aircraft to my office. The pace of that Saturday was an exemplar of what would happen for the next two weeks. At about eight o'clock we would hold a video conference with the secretary for at least an hour. Two or three hours later, there would be a video conference with the president, lasting at least an hour and often two. In the late afternoon, usually around five o'clock, we would have another video conference with the secretary. The presidential video conference would involve all of the relevant cabinet agencies, the intelligence community, and much of the White House national security staff.

Most of my day was spent preparing for or participating in conferences. I never minded that; interacting with the interagency and the secretary and others was what combatant commanders did. I wasn't happy that Pete Vasely was typically pulled into these conferences as well. He had actual on-the-ground tactical responsibilities, and these lengthy sessions dragged him away. Additionally, the final video conference with the secretary was usually well after midnight in Kabul. After a day or two, we were able to get him out of the evening updates, but he was still required to attend the first two conferences of the day.

To understand how things worked at Karzai International, it's important to know that it was all about the gates to the airfield. At different times, we operated six gates: North Gate, East Gate, Abbey Gate, South Gate, West Gate, and Northwest Gate. We rotated among them, based on how we were messaging people to come to the airfield and on our assessment of the ISIS-K threat. At each gate, the tactical mission was screening people, ensuring they had credentials, had no weapons, and were safe to enter. The screening was done by Marines and soldiers, and the vetting was supposed to be done by State Department consular officials, but because of their very low number, young servicemembers with minimal training were pressed into this difficult and often heart-wrenching work. Crowds of thousands of Afghans pressed against the gates, seeking entry and making it difficult for people who had credentials—or who were Americans—to get to the front of the line. Furthermore, consular officials were unable to work on a twenty-four-hour cycle. At each gate, security teams were in overwatch, and on several occasions over the course of the evacuation they were forced to use deadly force to protect the screeners. It was a messy, ugly process. Our overriding priority was to get people onto the airport and get them ready to depart. At the same time, we had to prevent a suicide bomber or someone with a weapon from gaining access to an airplane. Underlying everything was a concern for our own force protection.

These priorities existed in tension, causing commanders on the ground to continually assess threat reporting, the size of crowds at the gate, and how many people were already inside the perimeter and waiting to board aircraft. The secure area inside Karzai International was relatively small, and it wasn't equipped for holding large groups of people. On August 20 we had 11,960 people—men, women, and children—inside the wire, awaiting evacuation. They were distributed across the northern part of the airfield that we occupied; some were under cover, but many were exposed to the elements. We were able to bring in non-pork meals ready to eat and bottled water on the many empty flights that were coming in to pick up evacuees, so food and water weren't a problem. Sanitation was a problem, and it grew with each passing day. We were also very worried about the threat of an Islamic State rocket or mortar attack—something like this would have created mass carnage inside the airfield when we had high numbers waiting to get out.

Our throughput was limited by how many aircraft we could get in and out of the airfield. With each passing day we became more efficient. For example, on August 19 we were able to get only nine U.S. C-17s out. Our partners were able to fly sixteen out the same day with a mishmash of military and charter aircraft. Five days later, though, on August 24, we were able to "turn"—land, load, and launch—an astonishing thirty-seven aircraft, carrying 12,917 U.S. and Afghan evacuees. All of this was being done at an airfield that had no radar or other landing aids. An Air Force crisis response group provided all of the support necessary for talking to aircraft as they approached, deconflicting their landing, getting them to safe places where they could off- and onload, and then getting them airborne and gone. It was a remarkable technical achievement, made even more impressive by the fact that we incorporated the aircraft of our coalition partners as well, with occasional language and cultural barriers.

Another important capability that we established was the multinational military coordination cell. This element, located at the airfield, conducted real-time coordination between not only U.S. forces, but those of our allies and partners as well. This was invaluable in ensuring that we minimized the inevitable friction that attended the large number of flights coming in and out and the many thousands of requests for evacuation that we received from multiple quarters. We tried to screen these requests in Tampa, but the nature of communications in the twenty-first century meant that organizations and people could reach directly down to people they knew at HKIA, to plead their case for the Afghans they were trying to extract.

As we balanced moving people out of Kabul, it became clear that our temporary safe havens in the theater, composed of Al Udeid Airbase and Camp as-Sayliyah in Qatar, and other, smaller facilities in the UAE, Saudi Arabia, and Kuwait, were becoming overrun with evacuees. Our partners in the region, led by Qatar, had stepped up to the crisis wonderfully, but we were still struggling to house and maintain this crush of people. On one day at the height of the withdrawal, we had over 17,000 Afghans on the flight ramp at Al Udeid. My staff wanted to slow the movement out of Afghanistan until we could expand our facilities. I understood their logic, but I would not entertain their recommendation. Here was why: We had thousands of people awaiting evacuation in Kabul. Conditions there were not good. Additionally, they were extremely vulnerable to an ISIS-K rocket or suicide attack. Conditions weren't good at our safe havens, either—but the people at those locations were not under the direct threat of an ISIS-K attack that could cause mass casualties. I told my staff and commanders that we would maximize the flow of people out of Kabul without consideration of impact at the receiving locations in the theater. The choice was discomfort by moving or possible death by delaying, and the choice seemed very simple and clear to me. The component commanders, and their Department of State colleagues, did superhuman work to improve conditions at the safe havens, and this rapidly improved the comfort and security of the evacuees.

The Islamic State threat was very real. The Taliban's short-sightedness in opening Parwan and Pol-e-Charkhi prisons around August 15 put about a thousand hardened Islamic State fighters immediately back into circulation. We knew that ISIS fighters were coming to Kabul both to attack us and to grapple with the Taliban for control of the city. We processed almost three hundred specific, credible reports of ISIS planning. From the beginning of the operation, I saw these threats as the most significant challenge to our forces and the evacuation. Our partner intelligence agencies focused many of their resources against these developing plots, and we were able to pass warnings, often quite specific, down to tactical commanders.

A key element of this was our decision to pass carefully screened information to the Taliban about these pending attacks and to also use them to establish an outer cordon around the airfield. Both of these things required coordination with the Taliban. The idea of coordinating came from my Doha interaction with them on August 15. Beginning shortly after that meeting, at my direction, Pete Vasely reached out to Taliban military commission liaison officer Mullawi Hammidullah, who was in charge of Taliban forces around the airfield. This channel of communication allowed us to pass them warnings about ISIS-K activities. Over the period of time that we interacted with the Taliban, we shared eighteen imminent threat warnings. Our success in this effort was mixed; sometimes they responded and looked at areas we felt held ISIS-K members, sometimes they did not. In balance, it is my judgment that this practice did more good than bad.

At the same time, I also directed Pete to work with the Taliban to establish an outer perimeter around the airfield. Of all the things we did, I believe this may have had the most effect in helping our force protection. We pushed hard for the Taliban to establish their perimeter about one kilometer away from the airfield gates. We wanted them to do the initial screening, particularly the search for suicide bombers, either walking or in vehicles—we had plenty of warnings about these impending attacks. This cordon would also have the effect of reducing the press of people at the airfield gates. The downside of this cordon would be that the Taliban would be in a position to screen or limit those Afghans that we did want to get through our gates. I was certain that American citizens would have no problem with passage; I was less certain about Afghans. Even considering this, I believe even now that it was the correct course of action. The task of any commander in a situation like we confronted in Kabul was to balance force protection against the reason we were there—evacuating people. I am confident that using the Taliban reduced attacks on our forces; I am also sure that it reduced by some number—and perhaps a significant number—the Afghans that we wanted to get out. To mitigate this problem, the Department of State provided examples of travel documents to the Taliban and also names and lists of Afghans that we wanted to evacuate. In some cases this helped; in others it did not. I would make the same decision again today. The execution of this plan by the Taliban was halting and uneven, reflecting the hodgepodge of Taliban fighters that existed in Kabul and the informality and inefficiency of their chain of command. Based on what I thought then and know now, I am certain that the Taliban did not cooperate or assist any ISIS-K attacker with their planning or execution over the course of the evacuation.

While the majority of people evacuated came to the airfield, we also planned to go "outside the wire" to pick up people under certain circumstances. In two cases, facilities existed adjacent to the airfield where evacuees gathered and then we brought them in. One of these was a British-associated location, the Barron Hotel, which was just a few hundred meters from Abbey Gate and East Gate. The other was a little-known location a few kilometers northeast of the airfield. On August 19 we used helicopters to move 169 U.S. citizens a short distance from the Barron Hotel to the airfield because the roads were severely congested between Abbey Gate and East Gate and the hotel. We also used a combination of buses and helicopters to move 8,105 people from another location to the airfield between August 16 and 25. On August 22 we used helicopter-borne special operations forces to retrieve sixteen members of an American family from a rural location outside Kabul. On August 24 we paired U.S. and German special operations forces in another helicopter-borne rescue, bringing in twenty-one German citizens and family members. Aside from these operations, there were no other missions to retrieve either Americans or any other nationals. We planned several more of these operations, but in most cases the evacuees made their way to the airfield independently. Contrary to press reporting of the time, partner special operations forces did not range widely across Kabul rescuing people while U.S. forces sat at the airfield. As a practical matter, nobody had the resources to execute these operations without U.S. support.

One little-known but highly successful aspect of our outreach beyond the wire was our phone bank, which we used to reach out to both U.S. citizens and at-risk Afghans. We had their phone numbers from their registration documents. If we could establish telephone communication with them, then we would "talk them in," providing directions and guidance about how to avoid congested areas or other dangerous terrain. We brought in 3,363 people, 1,219 of whom were U.S. citizens and 2,017 were at-risk Afghans. The remaining 127 were citizens of other countries.

As we became more efficient at screening and moving evacuees, and the output increased, the question of when to end the operation resurfaced. We were easily meeting our goal of five thousand per day, and our partners were also performing very efficiently. On August 24 this came up in the presidential briefing. My position from the beginning had been that we needed to leave by August 31. To stay beyond that date would ensure that we would be fighting not only ISIS-K, but also the Taliban. There were a number of conversations about approaching the Taliban at the diplomatic level; these all came to naught. I further believed that if we stayed beyond August 31, we could continue to fly Afghans out for another sixty days at the same rate—the simple fact was that lots of them wanted to leave. The Taliban were, however, already clamping down on access to the airfield for Afghans. Since we had made a conscious political decision to end our participation in the war, I had no problem recognizing that the inevitable outcome of that decision would be to give up our ability to dictate, at least militarily, what happened inside Afghanistan. The Taliban would now determine that; defeat in war has consequences. By leaving by August 31, we would hold open future diplomatic options for the retrieval of U.S. citizens left in Afghanistan after we departed, as well as at-risk Afghans, although I did not hold an optimistic view of our ability to get them out. Finally, to stay beyond August 31 would mean bringing in significant additional combat forces; we would need to consider seizing Bagram airfield, and we would be fighting the Taliban. The Department of Defense held this view from top to bottom, but there were other views in the interagency and within the White House.

In the meantime, we finalized our plan for the tactical endgame. Nothing would be more dangerous and weighted with risk than the manner of our final exit. As early as August 22 we began to draw down equipment and materiel. I entrusted the tactical planning of this to Maj. Gen. Chris Donahue, and I decided that his paratroopers would be the last force to leave. On August 24 the chairman called a JCS executive meeting on short notice. The president wanted to know where not only the chain of command, but also the joint chiefs, stood on the issue of withdrawal. This had been done before, most famously in January 1968 by President Lyndon Johnson. After his commander in Vietnam, Army Gen. William Westmoreland, told the president that he intended to hold and defend Khe Sanh, a besieged Marine fortified outpost in the north of the Republic of Vietnam, the president directed that the joint chiefs sign a letter agreeing with his plan. Johnson's concerns were sparked by memories of the disastrous French defense of Dien Bien Phu in the First Indo-China War in 1954, and he sought political cover. I was struck by the parallel and what it said about confidence in our military advice and judgment. On the afternoon of August 24, I briefed the chiefs by video conference about our withdrawal plan, and why I strongly recommended that we leave as agreed—by August 31. As always, a short-notice JCS Tank was hard to pull together. The Chief of Staff of the Army, Jim McConville, was well read into the problem and asked a number of pertinent questions. I wasn't surprised, because the Army had always been a full participant in our operations in Afghanistan. Interest and situational awareness varied widely across the rest of the chiefs and their representatives, for not all of them could find the time to be present, either physically or virtually. The chairman was direct and forceful with the chiefs, and all agreed with the proposed withdrawal timeline. Subsequent to the Tank, the Joint Staff prepared an advice memo for them all to sign. The next day, I also forwarded my own advice memo, which encapsulated nothing more than my recommendations on this matter and a recap of what I'd briefed the Tank.

There was a twist to the withdrawal. In our meeting with the president on August 25, he asked me if we could modify the plan to keep his options open for another two or so days, and also to maintain the flow of people through the gates. We had originally planned to begin to reduce access on August 27, beginning to focus on getting our equipment and people out. He wanted to adjust this to the right—to August 29. I was sitting in my headquarters at Tampa for this conference, in our main conference room, with all of the planning material immediately at hand. Quickly reviewing the documents, I told him that we could make the adjustment; while it would increase risk slightly, our performance in the withdrawal up until now had made it possible to use fewer C-17s than we had originally thought necessary, so we would be able to delay extracting the evacuation control centers for the time he desired. I include this vignette only to emphasize the point, which I've made before, that planning and operations must ultimately suit the ends of policy. We briefed the president on a good, solid plan, and we were executing it. He heard us out, and then he wanted some more flexibility. It's Panglossian to believe that national leadership will issue broad directives and then stand aside while the military executes the plan without continuous oversight. That isn't the tradition of the United States, and it shouldn't be. The military actions that we take must suit the political end in view and must be readily adjusted when there is a gap between the two.

As we worked hard to screen people, load and move aircraft, and keep track of the ever-morphing threat stream, out of the sky on August 24 dropped two members of Congress—literally. They were Representative Seth Moulton (D-MA) and Representative Peter Meijer (R-MI). Their visit was unplanned and uncoordinated, and we were completely unaware of their presence until they walked off the aircraft that they had commandeered. Their presence took vital resources away from our core problems and also took time and attention away from on-scene commanders. They had to be protected while they were on the ground during a time of considerable tactical stress. During the entire month of August and our lengthy evacuation, I can think of no act by anyone that was so completely self-indulgent and unhelpful to our mission. They left the next day, on a U.S. military aircraft, with tweets and pictures in hand. A couple of days later, we were able to prevent an uncleared and uncoordinated Gulfstream 5 from landing that carried—so we were told—Representative Markwayne Mullin (R-OK) and a group of mercenaries, who were planning to conduct their own wholly uncoordinated rescue operations. The quick work of our air controllers denied their request to land, and we last saw the aircraft heading to Tbilisi. I do not describe these episodes to complain about oversight. Congressional oversight is very important, and Central Command has always worked very hard to support travel into the theater. In this case and considering requests from House leadership to not travel into the region, these visits were much closer to self-aggrandizing, grandstanding combat tourism than any form of sober, mature oversight.

As we worked our final withdrawal plan, we also completed the demilitarization of Afghan military equipment at the airfield. There were seventy-eight Afghan aircraft at HKIA when the government collapsed, ranging from C-130s to H-60s. Most of them weren't flyable. We had no way to get the aircraft out given the competition for space on the departing C-17s, so we asked for guidance and were directed to demilitarize them. We had the experts and the capabilities with us to ensure that none of those aircraft would ever be able to fly again. There were also a number of vehicles at HKIA, and we took steps to ensure that none of them would ever be able to be driven again. This included more than seventy mine-resistant ambush-protected vehicles that had been used by our forces for many years in both Afghanistan and Iraq. The size and weight of these huge, hulking vehicles would have meant dedicating a single C-17 per vehicle—again, we simply didn't have the capacity to get them out. We also demilitarized thousands of small arms at the airfield. I'm confident that we left nothing of value at HKIA after our departure.

Unfortunately, the thousands of weapons ranging from M4 and M16 rifles to D-30 artillery pieces that were in the hands of the Afghan military away from the airfield were all lost. They had been distributed across the country, and we had no ability to either retrieve or destroy them. As the Afghan forces who owned them disappeared, so did these weapons. This included more than 12,000 high-mobility multi-wheeled vehicles and 21,000 Ford Ranger trucks. Finally, thirty-seven aircraft that weren't at HKIA fell into Taliban hands at airbases like Kandahar. Others were flown to neighboring countries by defecting Afghan pilots. A total of sixty-four airplanes were flown to Uzbekistan and Tajikistan. Our best estimate was that the equipment lost totaled about $18 billion. The only good thing about this bad news story was that the Taliban would struggle to maintain the equipment, with none of the support available that the Afghan military required.

By August 25 we were tracking several Islamic State threat vectors, and all of them involved some form of suicide attack by foot or by car or a rocket attack. The rocket attack was particularly worrisome because of the number of vulnerable people we had on the airfield. At the same time, we never took our eyes off the most vulnerable part of our entire operation: the gates that enabled actual entry onto the airfield. As I've noted before, the work at these gates was dangerous and chaotic. It all came to a head on August 26 at Abbey Gate, on the southeast side of the airfield. It was close to the Barron Hotel, which both we and our British partners had used as a rally point before moving evacuees the short distance to the gates. We had opened Abbey Gate on August 17; on August 25 both North and East gates were closed because of the threat streams that we were seeing. We still used some other gates at the south and west side of the airfield, but these gates were now used primarily for groups of precleared people that we were bringing in on an established schedule. The only "walk-up" gate that remained open was Abbey Gate. It was going to be held open for another few hours as we processed the last of the evacuees from the Barron Hotel. The gate and the ECC were staffed by Marines, which included a female engagement team. British forces were also in the area. Several hundred meters away from the gate, the Taliban were conducting screening operations. By five o'clock in the afternoon in Kabul, a crowd of between two to three thousand Afghans were outside the gate. We had successfully processed over a thousand Afghans and some Americans through the gate on this day by this time. Since this was the only gate open, the crowd was restive, and the Marines were employing loudspeakers to tell them to stay calm and to stay back.

At 5:36 Kabul time, an individual we suspect was named Abdul Rehman al-Loghri, an ISIS-K fighter who had been freed from prison by the Taliban just days before, approached the gate and detonated a suicide device—probably a vest. He had possibly used a fake ID to clear the Taliban security checkpoint, or he may have avoided the checkpoint completely by taking an alternate route. We were not able to determine with precision his movements prior to the attack. The device was large for a suicide vest—twenty to twenty-five pounds, made from high-grade explosives, with embedded ball bearings. This was a single suicide vest attack, expertly delivered. The carnage was horrific; eleven Marines, a soldier, and a Sailor would die, twenty-two would be injured, and 169 Afghans would also perish. There was no follow-up fire from any Islamic State fighters, and our Marines and soldiers did not fire back into the crowd after the blast. Despite the horrific casualty count among the Afghans from the blast, no civilian was killed by any return fire from the overwatch elements—a remarkable bit of self-discipline. Our mass casualty procedures took over. We had conducted a mass casualty exercise the day before, so the medical response was swift and effective. Our main hospital at Karzai International was a Norwegian "Role II" NATO facility. It had two operating rooms and a small intensive care unit and intermediate care ward. More importantly, there were 180 medical personnel distributed across the airfield at the moment of the attack. Their immediate response saved lives, both U.S. and Afghan.

I was talking to the president at the moment of the attack. We were in the middle of his morning update. I took these updates from the main conference room in Tampa. I sat at the head of a large semicircular table, with ample space for secure phones and all of my supporting material. Since this was a presidential conference, we strictly limited anyone else in the large room—it could hold more than seventy, but it was empty except for key staff members bringing in material and reports when I was with the president. Under Secretary of Defense Colin Kahl was talking in the brief when my secure phone rang. Pete Vasely's operations officer was on the other end—he told me that we had a "blast with small arms fire" at Abbey Gate. There were indications of a second explosion as well. There were no reports of U.S. injuries. Since we were in a video grid presentation in the White House Situation Room, I held my hand up, knowing that I would be quickly recognized. I told the president what we knew, and the brief went on. I knew that the secretary and the chairman, who were physically present in the White House, would realize that early reporting with these kinds of events is almost always wrong. Tragically, that proved the case at Abbey Gate. My phone continued to ring at intervals of several minutes, and each report that came in was worse.

Over the course of the next ninety minutes or so, I updated the president on our casualty figures. Even as I did this, my primary focus was now on ensuring that commanders on the ground had everything they needed for further attacks—those threat streams were still very active. At the same time, I wanted to be certain that we were flexing to get the aeromedical evacuation enterprise up and running. While I wanted to be sure we were doing everything we could, the Air Force was already far out ahead on their response. They quickly launched three aeromedical evacuation-configured C-17s, from Al Udeid, Qatar, Ali al Salem, Kuwait, and Ramstein, Germany. The efficient medical evacuation chain got all severely wounded patients out of HKIA within twenty-four hours of the attack. We also brought wounded Afghans into Karzai International for treatment, and many were subsequently evacuated. Hundreds more were taken to hospitals across Kabul.

As I look back through my notes of this dark day, I'm struck by the conflicting nature of the information that we were receiving and how fast we had to push it up to the White House. Usually, a combatant command headquarters has time to refine information before it is passed up the chain of command. In this case, as in the al Asad attack of January 2020, I was dealing directly with the president when I passed information. The chain of command was completely flat and was contained in the Situation Room at the White House, my headquarters, and then our commanders on the ground in Kabul. It was vital that our information be correct. I was worried about giving the president incorrect information that might lead him to make a decision that would be hard to adjust later. While this was going on, commanders on the ground tried hard to piece together what had happened, even as they girded themselves for more attacks. We closed Abbey Gate for walk-up processing after the attack, and it never reopened for the movement of large groups of people. We replaced the Marine rifle company that had been attacked with a company of paratroopers, and the United Kingdom brought its last group of people through Abbey Gate from the Barron Hotel late that night.

In the immediate aftermath of the Abbey Gate attack, we looked at all our security procedures again. Clearly, we had to let people in if we were going to evacuate them. After August 26, though, our bias for force protection, even if it severely limited access, was even more pronounced. On the day of the attack, we brought out a total of 13,390 people. I consider that number any time I reflect on the loss of these thirteen brave Americans. I do not believe their deaths were in vain. Something good and tangible was enabled by their sacrifice.

I subsequently assigned my Army component commander, Lt. Gen. Ron Clark, to conduct an investigation into what happened at Abbey Gate. It was a thorough, well-done investigation, one that took over six weeks to conduct. The results of that investigation have informed my description of events in this narrative, but there were also some key points that need to be emphasized. Most importantly, the attack was not preventable by the forces on the ground unless we stopped bringing evacuees inside the perimeter. The corollary, of course, is that had we shut down all the gates, we could have prevented this attack—but that wasn't why we were there. The tactical risk was in the fact that large numbers of Afghans needed to be processed into Karzai International, and that gave an opportunity to the Islamic State. The attacker did not enter the gate; he was outside Abbey Gate when he detonated his explosives. The investigation also found that commanders on the ground had done everything they could to reduce the chances of the attack, and that the conduct of our men and women was magnificent during and after the attack. We also found, contrary to some media reports, that no Afghans were killed by small-arms fire from our troops after the explosion. One of the big lifesavers was the density of medical support personnel and equipment at the airfield. We had built on the framework of our Norwegian partners, and on the day of the attack we had nine surgical teams available across the airfield, all of whom were quickly integrated into the care of our wounded. In short, the medical team was remarkably effective.

We continued to look for opportunities to proactively reduce the Islamic State threat to Karzai International. On the evening of August 27/28, we struck an Islamic State facilitator, who was involved in real-time plotting to attack us. He had been involved in prior attacks, including a particularly lethal attack on Kabul University back in November 2020. We tracked him down to an isolated location in Nangarhar Province and then struck him from an MQ-9. The strike produced no collateral damage, and his death had a significant impact on Islamic State efforts to attack us.

By the next day, August 28, we had shifted into our withdrawal plan with energy. We were now dividing the outgoing flights between those carrying evacuees and those loaded with our own forces and their equipment. We were still able to evacuate 6,828 people, even with reduced capacity. In a lengthy session with the president, I reviewed our final withdrawal plan—what we called a joint tactical exfiltration. He asked a number of detailed questions, and I was able to give him a sense of comfort that we had a good, solid plan. Weather became a factor for this first time on this day—the meteorologists were now predicting bad weather for August 30. This would not impact our C-17s, but it would limit what our helicopters could do, and it would also reduce our ability to see the environment with our overhead intelligence platforms. It was another factor to consider. I talked with Pete and Chris Donahue about advancing the withdrawal by twenty-four hours. On August 28 our best weather prediction was that we'd have adequate weather the following day. I gave this a great deal of thought and told my commanders that we'd stick with the original plan; I wasn't prepared to recommend that we shorten our timeline. This was a decision based on my assessment of the effect of leaving early in our strategic messaging. Also, I wanted to maximize the number of evacuees that we could get out. Finally, the weather predictions, while creating additional friction and narrowing our options, did not create hard no-go criteria. In the event, we were lucky—the weather turned good and didn't impact our final operations. On August 29 and 30, we were able to bring out 6,845 evacuees.

Morning in Kabul was before midnight in Tampa. By the time I got in my office on Sunday, August 29 (and I had been awakened several times throughout the night), we were seeing a high number of Islamic State attack plans, all seemingly nearing execution. They ranged from rocket attacks to vehicle-borne attacks to motorcyclists. There was also extensive discussion about moving IEDs and suicide bombers around Kabul. We had all seen the result of one of these attacks, and that memory was fresh in everyone's mind throughout the day. This reporting, which was very real and immediate, was the backdrop for all else that happened on this day.

Mr. Zemari Ahmadi's car came to our attention when his white Toyota Corolla was picked up by an MQ-9 near an area of interest to us based on Islamic State activities. Over the course of the day in Kabul, we tracked him while he made numerous pickups and drop-offs around the city. There appeared to be corroborating intelligence that matched his various stops. Finally, in the late afternoon, he headed toward the airfield. At a little before five o'clock in Kabul, he pulled into a gated driveway just west of the airfield. Thinking that this was a hide sight and that collateral damage would be very low, we struck his vehicle with a Hellfire missile. As we know now, we were wrong from the beginning on Mr. Ahmadi. He had no connection to ISIS-K and was a long-tenured and treasured employee of Nutrition and Education International, a major nongovernmental organization that worked to reduce malnutrition in women and children through soybean cultivation. In striking his car, we killed not only him, but also nine other family members, including children as young as three. This was an unalloyed tragedy. No one who died that afternoon in Kabul had anything to do with the Islamic State. There have been many public pronouncements on what went wrong and what it means for future drone strikes. The strike itself was a self-defense strike, an action where we were prepared to accept higher collateral casualties if the action we were preventing by striking was a clear risk to those we were defending. At no time during that long day did we ever consider this strike to be "payback" for the Abbey Gate bombing.

The bottom line, though, was this: the mistake was at the beginning, when we locked in on his vehicle. Everything that followed stemmed from this initial judgment, made by harried, stressed drone operators, analysts, and commanders on the ground who were trying to avert another Abbey Gate. The apparently corroborating intelligence that came in during the course of the day certainly confirmed that somewhere in Kabul, nefarious activities were going on—just not in this white Corolla. In the heat of the moment, we never stepped back and considered, with a cold analytical eye, if it all added up. It did not add up when considered later by highly trained investigators, who had the luxury of endless reruns of the video. It can also be described as confirmation bias: a state of mind where the original premise is so strong that conflicting information is either made to fit in with the hypothesis or discarded if it doesn't. One thing I'm sure of—nobody involved in this got up that morning with any appetite or desire to kill ten innocent men, women, and children. I said at the time that I was responsible for the strike, and I feel that responsibility just as strongly now as then. There's nothing we can do to recover those innocent lives, even as we are unable to recover all the other lives—American, Afghan, and coalition—lost in Afghanistan over the past twenty years.

It all came to an end the next day. At 1:30 p.m. in Tampa on Monday, August 30, I was back in the focal point operations center, one of the small rooms connected to my operations center. It was a familiar place for me—I'd been in this room for the Soleimani strike, the Baghdadi strike, and the Iranian attack on al Asad. It was the same small room, and as usual my staff were all gathered around me, each at their workstation. At the end on the table were two huge video monitors, and just as they had shown the last minutes of Baghdadi and Soleimani, now they would show the last few minutes of our participation in the war in Afghanistan. The images we were looking at were from our MQ-9s, orbiting over the airfield. What I could see were the five C-17s parked at various points around the runway. What we couldn't see from the images were the—literally—dozens of Air Force and Navy aircraft, ranging from B-52 bombers to F-15 and F-18 fighters, all stacked overhead and ready to unleash staggering firepower should we need it. The threat streams were loud and pronounced as we quietly withdrew from our few remaining positions and drew back to the waiting C-17s. The 82nd Airborne would be the last unit out, just as the Marines had been the first in. A withdrawal such as this is an extremely delicate operation, perhaps the most professionally challenging of all combat operations. As I sat at the head of the table, I was in a communications bridge with the 82nd's commander, Maj. Gen. Chris "CD" Donahue. I also knew that the chairman and the secretary were watching from the Pentagon, and I'm sure the White House was also piped in. The dialogue, though, was between CD and me. In one of my first conversations with him that afternoon I told him that he was "conditions-based," not "time-driven."

His operations officer would come on every few minutes and give a codeword for an event from the execution checklist. Execution checklists can give a false sense of control, an idea that order can be imposed on combat, but I knew that in CD we had a commander who would be able to think on his feet and act swiftly if something unforeseen arose. Every few minutes he and I would share a few words, but I didn't want anything to distract him from the task at hand. While the troopers methodically worked their way back to the jets, the drones looked out at rooftops that could observe the airfield. Several times, they focused on groups of people who looked suspicious. Nothing developed from these gatherings. At 1:36 p.m., we began to break down the perimeter and demilitarize the close-range antirocket guns. They had provided vital protection, and I hated to leave them, but we had decided that it was important to have their coverage to the very end, and that meant we couldn't get them out. This was the witching hour. We were at our most vulnerable right now—our forces were moving back from the perimeter to their aircraft, our antirocket and indirect fire protection was no longer in place, and nothing is quite so fragile and breakable as a fueled and loaded C-17 sitting on the ramp.

Occasionally the yellow top secret phone would chirp; the chairman was just checking in. He and the secretary were seeing the same images we were, but they didn't have the access to the online chatting that was going back and forth between the operators. The chairman would ask about the groups of people gathered on rooftops—I had to agree that at first glance they seemed worrisome, but the operators saw no threat from them, and I agreed. CD reported there were some individual leakers—Afghans who were climbing over the fence—but nothing significant. My attention was split between the images on my monitors, the cyber chat screens, and listening to the reports that my intelligence officer was relaying. We continued to see intent by the Islamic State to attack us, but nothing was happening. At 2:14 p.m., CD reported that all equipment had been loaded—this included helicopters that we had kept aloft until literally the last minute, flying overwatch. We were now finishing with the infantry. At about 3:19, we had all jets completely loaded. Overhead were AC-130s, MQ-9s, F-15E Strike Eagles, and Navy F-18 Hornets, all stacked, ready to pour death and destruction on anyone who interfered with the operation. We watched as an MQ-9 carefully flew and scanned the length of the runway, verifying that the field was clear for takeoff. Then, as we had rehearsed and planned, the C-17s began to move in a noisy and complex ballet to the end of the runway. In turn, one after another, they rolled, achieved takeoff speed, and were off. The last jet was off the ground at 3:28 p.m. EST. I couldn't relax quite yet—I wanted to ensure that the aircraft got up to altitude and out of any lingering surface-to-air missile range. I knew that CD was probably tired of talking to the theater commander, so my last message to him was pretty low key: "CD, can't say enough about you and your team—get some sleep on the plane." I then passed my congratulations to everyone else on the bridge—the AFCENT commander, the special operators, and all the others who had come together to exfiltrate our forces.

As the C-17s pushed south to the Makran Coast, we began to bring the armada of fighters and other support aircraft out. About an hour later, the last crewed U.S. aircraft exited Afghan airspace. As my air component commander pointed out to me, the actual last American to leave Afghanistan wasn't Chris Donahue walking up the C-17 ramp; rather, it was the backseater in the last F-15E. I don't know for certain, but I'm confident that this was probably the first time since the early fall of 2001 that there weren't crewed U.S. aircraft performing some mission somewhere over Afghanistan. As this happened, I held a press conference with the Pentagon press corps via Zoom from my office in Tampa. At that time, and even now, I have strong feelings about the end of our engagement in Afghanistan. That afternoon, what I regretted most was that we had been unable to get every American out, but I felt we had done as good a job as possible, given the conditions we were operating under.

We also didn't get out all of the Afghan partners we wanted, and that perhaps stung even more, because while I was confident that we would eventually be able to get any American out of Afghanistan who wanted to come, I did not believe the same would apply to the Afghans. Under it all, of course, was the human cost—a cost that spanned two decades. Not just the thirteen who died at Abbey Gate, but those who died before in that long war, in battlefields from Uruzgan to Kunar, from 2001 to 2021. No life is worth more than any other, and those who died in Afghanistan in the fall of 2001 and in the twenty years of conflict that followed were worthy of the same honors we have rendered those brave men and women who died at Abbey Gate. It was a curiously conflicted moment.

My Afghanistan experience had begun on a September day in 2001 at the Pentagon—the very start of this long and tortured war. It was now ending, and certainly not in a way that anyone who served there would have wanted or envisioned. I couldn't get out of my mind the closing lines of a book about Vietnam that I had read as a lieutenant; it had so impressed me that I'd dragged it around with me throughout all of the many moves Marilyn and I had made. The book was *Dispatches*, by Michael Herr. There was much in the book that I disagreed with, but his closing lines created for me at least a parallel sense of history, and although they were about another war, they spoke to me across time: "And no moves left for me at all but to write down some few last words and make the dispersion, Vietnam, Vietnam, Vietnam, we've all been there."[1]

14
ACCOUNTABILITY

Before a war military science seems a real science, like astronomy; but after a war it seems more like astrology.

—*Rebecca West*

On September 28 Secretary Austin, Gen. Mark Milley, and I began testimony before the Senate Committee on Armed Services. It would be followed by testimony before the House Armed Services Committee. These were long, grueling sessions. Going by strict seniority, members of each committee were allocated five minutes to ask questions and for the witnesses to respond. In the Senate, members were allowed two five-minute opportunities for questions, a relatively uncommon occurrence. The tone was partisan and unpleasant. More of it was directed at the secretary and the chairman than at me, but there was plenty of ire to go around. For me at least, nothing new was uncovered in those marathon hearings. I was a veteran of congressional testimony, inured to the wild swings and attacks that were common—but the personal vitriol was exceptional, even by those standards. While I prepared for these sessions, inside CENTCOM we also began the investigative processes for the August 29 drone strike and the Abbey Road attack.

I also had a lot of time to consider what had just happened. In the press of execution, there's little time for introspection. Every day brings a new crisis, and a commander must keep relentlessly focused on current and emerging problems and solutions. In the aftermath, though, there is time for reflection. I set aside some time for that in September as I prepared for testimony. Afghanistan had become a large part of my life. I wanted to understand as much as I could about our painful journey in that distant country. For me, that odyssey is still incomplete. I'm still trying to assemble it all into a coherent, understandable picture. I don't know that I will complete the journey.

Why were we unable to achieve success in Afghanistan, despite trillions of dollars and thousands of lost lives? In the spring of 2020, why were we in negotiations with the Taliban, whom we had routed in 2001? Anyone who served there has their own rationalizations for what did or didn't happen and why we failed. I am no different, and these words represent my attempt to make the war understandable, at least to me. Despite all the plans and concepts of all of the leaders—military and diplomatic—who served in Afghanistan, we never achieved the most fundamental condition necessary for counterinsurgency success. We never cut off sanctuary for the Taliban in Pakistan. Taliban leaders lived comfortably in Pakistan. They met openly in Quetta, and farther north, even the most hard-core elements of the Taliban—the Haqqanis—could exist without real fear of genuine pressure from the Pakistanis. We never conducted military operations against the Taliban in Pakistan, despite threats to do so. Our CIA partners kept up pressure on al Qaeda, striking in Pakistan with drones, but never against the Taliban. Occasionally, the Pakistanis would either arrest or take minor action against some elements of the Taliban, usually as the result of strong pressure from us. In no cases, though, did they ever undertake operations against the core capabilities of the Taliban or prevent them from basing in Pakistan.

There were good reasons for this reticence, from a Pakistani perspective. Most significantly, they viewed everything through the lens of their existential rivalry with India. The depth of this enmity is difficult to calibrate until you have spent time with the Pakistani military. It is very real to them, and we have consistently undervalued its importance in their calculations. Afghanistan thus became an arena of competition for Pakistan and, counterintuitively from a purely geographic perspective, a source of operational depth. The Pakistanis always doubted our staying power in the region, so every accommodation, every deal, every negotiation with the United States was founded on an unspoken assumption that we would eventually leave the region. They were far more clear-sighted, strategic, and true to their thinking than we ever were to ours. Speaking objectively, the Pakistani assumption proved correct. We left.

This doesn't mean that playing both sides was the right decision for the Pakistanis in the long run. In staying with a dual approach that appeased the United States while continuing to aid the Taliban, they paid a steep price, and one that has not yet fully come due. The Taliban gave Pakistan a lever to control what happened in Afghanistan, but it also opened the door for the Pakistani Taliban and other extremist groups to enter and flourish inside Pakistan—a story that is long from being finished. The monster that they created and nurtured may yet turn on its one-time master. The role of Pakistan in Afghanistan has also poisoned our relationship to such a degree that a path to normalized relations is hard to visualize. This is a policy failure at the highest level of our government, across multiple presidential administrations.

We—and by "we" I mean the U.S. military—had an excellent opportunity to capture or kill Osama bin Laden at the very outset of the campaign, in actions in the Tora Bora mountains. A tactical opportunity existed to go after bin Laden in late November and early December 2001 in that high ground. Operations there failed to accomplish their objective, and the blame for that lies with senior military leadership, particularly at CENT-COM. The CENTCOM commander would not release the forces necessary to flesh out the operation. Had bin Laden been taken off the board at the onset of the campaign, it is possible to envision that things might have developed very differently. Counterfactual arguments like this always open more questions than they answer, but it remains the single greatest missed opportunity of the campaign on the military side. I believe this was a military, not a policy, error.

While we had great success with initial operations to topple the Taliban in late 2001, we never had a plan to move beyond and to take advantage of that purely military action. Part of this was driven by the decision to invade Iraq, which took the focus off Afghanistan. Invading Iraq is appropriately viewed as one of the most disastrous and negatively consequential foreign policy decisions ever taken by this country. The immediate and practical effect on Afghanistan was a loss of focus in the immediate aftermath of our invasion. Troop levels declined, and Afghanistan became an "economy of force" theater in every sense of the term. I was in Afghanistan in 2004 and saw the pernicious effects of this neglect. This allowed the Taliban a respite and gave them an opportunity to reform themselves and reemerge as a capable military force in the field. At a time when the Taliban were literally on the ropes, we had an opportunity to continue to go after them, aiming for a complete elimination of their threat, or we could have attempted to coopt them through a political approach. That we did neither is a profound indictment of our interagency decision-making process—but it was not a military error.

The governmental structure we put in place in Afghanistan as a result of the Bonn Conference in 2002 featured a strong president, with local leadership at the provincial level and even below, all appointed by the president. It was an idea that did not stand the test of time. It bred massive corruption, inefficiency, and disaffection, because it never even remotely aligned with the tribal and ethnic structures that were at the core of the concept of Afghanistan as a state—even if this vision of a state did not align with what Westerners thought it should be. We continued to pour vast wealth into Afghanistan in an attempt to create a society with at least some Western values. These decisions, again, were not military ones. At the same time, we did not attempt—or allow—any meaningful outreach to the Taliban in 2002 or in the years immediately after to see if they could be coopted into the government. This was a policy error.

One of our most important mistakes from my perspective, at least, was that we forgot why we were there. We entered Afghanistan to remove the source of an attack on our homeland and to prevent future attacks. This morphed into an exercise in nation-building. It was a remarkable exercise in American arrogance to believe that we could create a democratic society in Afghanistan. Afghanistan is not ungovernable, but it is ungovernable within the structure of an imported Western model. To attempt this was not a military failure, but rather a failure of political imagination at the highest levels of our government. It was certainly enabled by successive generations of commanders and ambassadors who tried to read any change in the situation as a sign of success.

While not discounting the error of their optimism, the ultimate responsibility lies beyond local commanders and ambassadors. The Taliban were not in 2001 and are not now an existential or even a serious threat to the United States. They ascribe to a very narrow and fundamentalist interpretation of

Islam, and their treatment of women in particular has always been repre-
hensible—but there's never been the slightest chance that they could export
their views outside of Afghanistan. We waged war against them for two
decades to seek to establish governmental structures in Afghanistan that
would allow us to continue counterterror operations against the real threats
to the United States—violent extremists such as al Qaeda and eventually
ISIS-K. In doing this, we lost sight of the relative relationship between the
two propositions. Counterterror operations were and are a vital national
interest. Good governance in Afghanistan was not and is not. It's a case of
not keeping the main thing the main thing. This was a shared failure, and
it touches every element of all of the departments and agencies that were
involved in Afghanistan.

The Doha agreement signed in February 2020 was, to use a phrase from
our operational jargon, the proximate "defeat mechanism" that brought down
the Afghan government. It placed requirements on the Taliban and on us
and, through us, on the Afghan government, although they were largely
excluded from the negotiations. It was the operational expression of a plan
for a speedy exit, and one that did not preclude accepting defeat so long
as there was a decent interval. The Taliban saw the agreement as a fixed,
inviolable roadmap for our departure. Strangely, so did senior policymakers
within the Trump administration and later, the Biden administration. Only
isolated pockets within the Department of Defense, the Joint Staff, the field
commanders, and the government of Afghanistan viewed the agreement
as genuinely conditions-based, requiring actions by not only us, but also
the Taliban. We were finally talking to the Taliban in this process, but the
timing couldn't have been worse. The time to talk was when your opponent
was weak—not when he was resurgent. The systematic disconnect from the
Afghan government, while perhaps tactically useful in the negotiations process, was a fatal flaw that couldn't be overcome by any negotiator. Responsibility for this is distributed between the Department of State and the executive
branch, but it's largely external to the Department of Defense.

While it will probably be some time before historians unearth the truth
of the matter, I have always been puzzled at the speed of the Afghan government's collapse in August. Was there more to it than met the eye? In the fall of

1963, the United States gave a de facto green light to coup plotters in South Vietnam, a permission that inadvertently ended in the murder of President Ngo Dinh Diem. At some time in July or August did we give—either explicitly or implicitly—some signal to the Taliban that we were leaving, regardless of conditionality? At the same time, on or about August 15, did we signal to President Ghani that he needed to leave, and in such a way that the abruptness of his departure materially contributed to the fall of his capital? It's an interesting theory, and I saw nothing in my considerable interactions with all parties to make me think it was what actually happened, but there is just a small sliver of doubt in the back of my mind that creates a parallel to the situation in 1963 in South Vietnam.

The disaster in Afghanistan that unfolded in July and August 2021 had roots going back more than twenty years—to decisions that we made at the beginning of the campaign and to long-festering diplomatic problems that were never addressed. Some of those are identified in the preceding paragraphs. What set conditions to bring it all to a head was the decision to completely withdraw from Afghanistan, first codified in the Doha Agreement and pursued by two presidential administrations. What irrevocably accelerated the trajectory was President Biden's decision, made in April 2021, to withdraw while still maintaining an embassy platform and not undertaking a withdrawal of American citizens and at-risk Afghans concurrently. I think this is an important point. The decision to withdraw completely merely affirmed the agreement his predecessor made. The part of his decision that did not simultaneously bring out our diplomats, citizens, and at-risk Afghans with our withdrawing forces was entirely his.

Not mandating an early evacuation of U.S. citizens or Afghans at risk created irreconcilable tension in our planning. That's why I can't agree with those who argue that the decision to leave completely was correct, but poorly executed. The decision itself contained contradictory goals that could not be accomplished. In fact, it was impossible to achieve success with the decision that was made. That we did as well as we did is a tribute to the men and women on the ground, who had to deal with harsh battlefield realities, not aspirational goals. By the time we belatedly recognized that we needed to get our embassy, citizens, and at-risk Afghans out, in August, the tactical situation was irretrievable, and we were forced to reenter a country we had just abandoned, at very high risk. Perhaps some lingering vision of American exceptionalism drove us to believe that we could avoid the uncomfortable fact that the Taliban won their war. We were wrong. Not even the United States can escape the harsh realities of the judgment of the battlefield. Another view might be that it was American arrogance that drove us.

It's wrong to view this as primarily a military failure, although it is convenient for many to do so. Afghanistan's collapse was the destruction of a nation-state, not just an army. Analogously, our defeat—and it was a defeat—as its patron and supporter was far more than military in scope. While there were many things that went wrong for us militarily in Afghanistan, the big mistakes were not solely or even primarily within the Department of Defense. Successive presidents thought they could manage Afghanistan, keeping the war in bounds while limiting casualties and their corrosive effects on internal U.S. politics. No single example of this is more pertinent than President Obama's decision to surge forces into Afghanistan in 2010 while also setting a firm timeline for ending those operations. This decision completely destroyed the strategic utility of adding forces in the first place and gave a lifeline to the Taliban. Wars are not always susceptible to dispassionate, remote, cerebral management. Certainly, politics must be a factor in any presidential decision, but to attempt to manage a war like a business school case study, bloodless and elegant, is to misunderstand the very nature of human conflict.

As a result, we were in, but not all the way in. Because of this incremental approach, we muddled along for many years, without clear direction. As I noted earlier, Trump and Biden may have shared only one political impulse in common—a clear desire to get out of Afghanistan. The confluence of their presidencies allowed the departure to occur. Time alone will tell if it was a wise decision. I did not agree with the decision to completely exit Afghanistan, and the manner of our departure will leave scars in Afghanistan, inside the United States, and among our friends and allies. Our potential adversaries will also draw some coolly considered lessons from our actions, and we may regret that in the future.

In spring of 2021, I testified before the House and Senate armed services committees. Two senators asked me directly what I would tell a mother or father who had lost a son or daughter in Afghanistan. As usual, questions of this type say more about the senator than the witness, but it did prompt me to address this question head-on in a press conference I gave late on the afternoon of April 22 for the Pentagon press corps. As I finished answering their questions, I said that I wanted to make a few closing remarks. I had taken the time between coming back into the building from my visits to Capitol Hill and the press conference to jot down some thoughts on sacrifice. I don't know if they were profound or even useful, but they did sum up my own thinking on the matter. I said,

> No words of mine are equal to the task of comforting someone who has lost a loved one in war. It would be presumptuous of me to try to do so. What few words I can offer would attempt to tell those who must deal with the empty seat at the table, the voice that will not be heard again, the missing laugh at the center of a gathering, is this: we fought to protect our country and to give others a chance to choose their own destiny. There is no better, higher, thing to fight for. It's why I went to war; I do know that. That's why my son went to war. Their deaths are not in vain. If I can paraphrase 2 Timothy: "They fought the good fight. They finished their race, and they kept the faith, even unto death." Semper Fidelis.[1]

I stood by those words then, and I stand by them now.

15

IRAN, IRAQ, AND SYRIA

The essence of strategy is choosing what not to do.
—*Michael Porter, "What Is Strategy?"*
Harvard Business Review, *1996*

nlike Afghanistan, when the Biden team came into office, it was clear that their approach to Iran would be the opposite of that of the Trump administration. It was less clear what this would mean for our position in Iraq and Syria. Throughout 2021 it became obvious that Iran wasn't interested in returning to a status quo ante joint comprehensive agreement. The lead diplomat for the United States was Robert Malley, whom I had known from the Obama national security staff. It was hard to find any common ground with the Iranians. While the Biden team did bring new flexibility to the table, the president's dictum that Iran would never achieve a nuclear weapon was clear and unambiguous. Negotiations, never directly between the United States and Iran, dragged on throughout the year without any significant changes to anyone's posture.

From my perspective, it seemed obvious that Iran sought sanctions relief from the onerous financial penalties we were inflicting upon them. It was also clear to me that they wanted some sign from the United States, and action that would relieve some of the sanctions, acknowledging our error in leaving the Joint Comprehensive Plan of Action, as a precursor for any serious negotiation. Both parties simply remained too far apart. Another obstacle was the fact that the Iranians persisted in targeting current and former U.S. government officials that they viewed as culpable in the strike on Soleimani. As one of the officials targeted, this was—and is—a matter of personal interest to me. The Iranians were also hobbled by pending elections, which occurred on June 18, 2021. The returns were historically low and disappointing for us; they brought into office Ebrahim Raisi as president—a true hardliner. In our own diplomatic circles, always seeking something optimistic in Iran, there was a vestigial hope that a hardline regime would find it easier to negotiate with the United States—but this hope, like so many others, was misplaced.

I had a slightly different view of Iranian priorities from many in the intelligence community. The Iranians valued the ability to build a nuclear weapon. It seemed to me that they valued the idea more than the actual physical act of building one. By holding some degree of ambiguity, they could leverage the United States and our European allies, always playing for more concessions, while staying coyly just below the threshold of breakout. In my opinion, what they really valued was their ballistic missile program. When considered with their relatively recent advances in land attack cruise missiles (LACMs) and uncrewed aerial systems (UAS), they had almost four thousand highly accurate weapons that they could employ against their neighbors. Some of these missiles could reach Israel. We knew from hard experience at al Asad and At Tanf just how accurate they could be. When coupled with their ability to employ proxy forces in the near abroad—Iraq, Syria, Lebanon, and Yemen—they had significant and powerful asymmetric capabilities. I found it very interesting that when President Biden, early in his presidency, said that after we reached some form of a nuclear agreement with Iran, we would then address reductions and controls for their missile force, the response was swift from Iranian leaders. In an excellent article on Iran's military capabilities, *New Yorker* journalist Robin Wright quoted President Raisi: "Regional issues or the missile issue are non-negotiable."[1] In other words, there would never be a linkage between nuclear negotiations and their missile force.

From a CENTCOM perspective, some things seemed clear. The Iranians did not seek a war with the United States or our allies and partners. We had achieved deterrence for state-on-state attacks. What they wanted was sanctions relief and the ability to expand their economy. At the same time, and typical of the baffling and complex nature of Iranian decision-making, they also were pursuing the ejection of the United States from the region. As previously discussed, they saw Iraq as the principal battleground for this. For most of 2020, the Iranians believed that they could achieve our departure through political action, forcing the government of Iraq to ask us to leave. This didn't work out. In fact, the ascent to the prime minister-ship of Mustafa Al-Kadhimi in May 2020 was a clear blow to their hopes. He would never have been the prime minister had Qassem Soleimani been alive. Soleimani's successor, Esmail Ghani, proved unable to mobilize the various Iranian factions to achieve any significant political outcomes. At the same time, through some convoluted process, the Iranians had convinced themselves that they could erect a firewall between actions taken against U.S. forces in Iraq and Syria and negotiations about their nuclear program and the possible revocation of sanctions. In fact, militant groups in Iraq were given the green light to pursue low-level attacks against us, without asking Iran for specific permission for each attack. Their definition of a "low-level" attack seemed to be a handful of U.S. servicemembers killed or wounded. This was dangerous thinking. Any attack with casualties in Iraq would draw a swift and strong response, although the nature of our response would be decided politically, not militarily.

The other factor that began to impact Iraq in the spring and summer of 2021 was their parliamentary elections, which were to be held as sched-uled in October. Attacks against us were reduced greatly in advance of the election. Nobody wanted to create a cause célèbre that would tip the elec-tion. At the same time, our departments of State and Defense convened a high-level consultative process with Iraq, known as a strategic dialogue, that allowed both countries to talk about expectations, grievances, and the way ahead. As part of this, Prime Minister Kadhimi visited the United States and saw the president on July 26, 2021. As a result of the strategic dialogue, we adjusted our posture in Iraq to give the prime minister a little more political cover, but there was strong Iraqi interest and support for us to remain in their country.

I flew into Iraq for the change of command of Operation Inherent Resolve in September and took the opportunity to see the prime minister. It was one of the best meetings I'd ever had with him, and I left Iraq confident that we had political backing for the continuation of our presence. By this time, all of the tactical work against ISIS-K was being done by the Iraqis; we provided intelligence and other enabling support. Most of our actual energy was now being directed toward force protection, with an eye to the various Iranian-aligned militia groups that had plans to attack us.

The Iraqi election of October 10 was a defeat for Iran. Overall, Muqtada al-Sadr and his Sadrist movement captured seventy-three votes, while the Iranian-backed share fell to 17 seats of the 329 possible. Many smaller parties received the remainder of the votes. We were cautiously optimistic in the days following the election that the Iraqis would be able to seat a new government. Our confidence was badly misplaced. Muqtada al-Sadr indicated in November that he would form a majority government but proved unable to gather the required support. As a result, to the present day there has been little movement in this process. We are not in a good place in Iraq, but neither are the Iranian-backed militant groups. It remains unclear whether the Iraqis will forge a path forward.

While all this occurred in Iraq, we maintained our steady presence in Syria, partnering with Syrian Democratic Forces against ISIS remnants in the Euphrates River valley. We had about one thousand troops on the ground in what we called the eastern Syria security area. This was a north-south piece of Syria that ran generally along the Euphrates River, east to the Iraqi border. We also maintained a defensive position at At Tanf, a miserable little desert crossroads about twenty kilometers inside Syria, along the tri-border area between Jordan, Iraq, and Syria. We typically manned this position with about two hundred soldiers.

In truth, our military presence in Syria had outrun our policy objectives. As a matter of record, we were there to complete the defeat of ISIS. In fact, our presence also suppressed Iranian activity and kept the Syrians and their Russian patrons from seizing the oilfields east of the river. We were in a constant state of low-grade friction with the Russians. We had a formal deconfliction channel that we used when events occurred that needed to be discussed, and generally it was an effective tool. By the fall of 2021, there was an increasing sense within the interagency that we needed to reassess why we were in Syria—what were our policy objectives? What level of risk were we willing to live with to pursue them? Those were policy questions. The interagency was unable to provide any of that strategic guidance for our forces.

The other player in Syria was Israel. Because the Iranians used Syria as a land bridge to convey sophisticated weapons in Lebanon, the Israelis struck Iranian—and occasionally Syrian—targets with near impunity. In 2021 this became an increasing source of friction. The Israeli strikes were typically precise and carefully designed to minimize casualties, but occasionally they would launch a big strike package and cause significant damage to the Iranian convoy system. Most of their attacks were in western Syria, but sometimes they struck in the east, closer to our forces. The Iranians chafed under these attacks, but they did not have the ability to strike against Israel with any effectiveness.

On October 13 the Israelis struck an IRGC facility at Palmyra, killing several people, including—we believed—Iranians. It was clear that the Iranians would respond to this, and on October 20 they struck our garrison at At Tanf with five drones. We were able to detect the incoming drones and take action to rapidly redeploy our personnel, so there were no casualties. It was clear that the attack was designed to kill. I was travelling in the theater when this attack happened, which put me in the same time zone as our forces in Iraq, but it also meant that I was eight hours ahead of policymakers and the Joint Staff in Washington. Over the next three days, the interagency deliberated on a response to this brazen attack. It was clear that the reason for the attack was the ongoing pattern of Israeli strikes into Syria. It was also clear that the Iranians considered us complicit with the Israelis on the conduct of the strikes.

Central Command rapidly refined our large target deck in Syria. We had targets ranging from IRGC-affiliated airfields to storage facilities and training facilities for the Shia groups, improving their combat skills under the tutelage of skilled IRGC instructors. We also were tracking a number of key IRGC leaders. The Iranians believed that they had attacked us to stop the Israeli strikes. This was a direct result of their determination to see us and the Israelis as indissolubly linked. The view from Washington was different. We had very little actual control over when and where the Israelis struck in Syria. They informed CENTCOM shortly in advance of their strikes, but they didn't ask permission. Since they were striking against the network that carried precision advanced weaponry from Iran to Lebanon, where they were potentially to be used against the cities of Israel, they had little interest in stopping.

Through intervention at the secretary of defense level, we could possibly persuade the Israelis to temper their pace—to slow down their strike operations. We would not be able to convince them to stop—they viewed the threat these missile parts posed as a matter of life and death for their citizens. If we did not respond, then we would be tacitly messaging the Iranians that we understood their concern, and it was likely that they would draw the conclusion that we would stop, or reduce, further Israeli strikes. More importantly, when—not if—Israel struck again in Syria, they would have established a precedent of attacking us in response, and we would see more attacks like At Tanf. It was an interesting policy dilemma, and we talked it over in several video conferences, including one with the president on October 21.

Nobody wanted to be in a tit-for-tat exchange of fire with Iran. On the other hand, to not respond was in and of itself a response, and not a useful way forward. My position was that we needed to take action, but that we should scale it proportionally. Our own strike should be carefully nested within a strong message to Iran, telling them that we were not responsible for Israeli strikes and that they were wrong to suppose that we could control Israeli actions. Our strike would have been against facilities that were unmanned and, unlike the Iranian attack on us, designed to cause no casualties. It was my view that not responding ultimately carried a higher risk than responding. Over the next forty-eight hours, I watched as the political will to respond deflated across the U.S. government. By October 23, we had talked ourselves into what we called the "Dean Wormer solution" from the movie *Animal House*. We would put the Iranians on "double secret probation" and give them a good talking-to. If another attack was executed against us, we'd really, no kidding, do something bad to them. How the Iranians would respond to these jejune words was unclear, but that was all they would receive from us in response to the At Tanf garrison attack.

The real and fundamental question that the attack posed was this: Why were we still in Syria? As noted earlier, our military position was that war-torn country had outstripped our policy objectives. Our response to the Al Tanf attack clearly demonstrated that there was no appetite to stand up to the Iranians there. Since the winter of 2021–22, Israeli attacks in Syria have continued. So far, there has been little response from Iran. If the current situation continues, there will come a time when the Iranians will feel compelled to attack us again. The fact that they are on "double secret probation" will probably not deter them. Their understanding of deterrence is based not on words, but on actions. I remain very concerned about the situation in Syria.

These events highlighted the essential bipolarity of the Iranian approach— the idea that they could push for sanctions relief and some form of nuclear negotiation with us, while at the same time attacking us directly in Iraq and Syria. I had always thought it a dangerous idea for them to have, but after the October attack, I began to suspect that they might be wiser than me. Regardless, by the summer of 2022, it became increasingly obvious that there was no possibility of a return to the JCPOA. We were simply too far apart. Moreover, the Iranians were creeping closer and closer to the point where they would have enough fissile material for a bomb. This was concerning, but it's important to remember that having enough fissile material is only part of the equation. The bomb would need to be weaponized: made small enough to be transported. A delivery system would have to be built. This would take at least eighteen months and possibly longer.

It remains my opinion today that the best way to keep the Iranians from possessing a nuclear weapon remains through a diplomatic agreement, however unsatisfying and incomplete parts of it may be. The worst way is through military action against their nuclear program, either by us or by what we call euphemistically a "third party": the Israelis. The less one knows about the problems and risks inherent in such a strike, the more positive about its potential success one tends to be.

In 2011 this was a vastly different and easier problem. The scope and size of the Iranian nuclear program, the nature and hardening of the targets, and their air defenses were all less developed than what is in place now. Having worked our plans for this contingency for more than ten years, I consider myself a subject matter expert on this problem. Today, and in the future, it would be very hard to destroy their entire program with all its components:

fissile material, warhead research and design, missile design and construction, and human capital. It will get harder with every passing day to achieve the results that we would want if directed to strike.

Importantly, any such strike would undoubtedly trigger a significant response from the Iranians. A strike against their nuclear program would be an act of war, and they would almost certainly release their large ballistic missile, LACM, and UAS fleets in response. The lesson is this: we should not talk about striking Iran's nuclear program unless we are prepared for the inevitable theater war that will follow. It will be a bloody and violent "fires war" where our bases and the cities of our regional friends will be targets. It's wishful thinking to believe that we can decouple an Iranian counterattack from a nuclear strike. This means that we need to prepare the theater for such a war in advance. Many of the capabilities and resources we once enjoyed in the region have been removed. Uncertain and often conflicting signals about our plans for long-term presence in the region have eroded our ability to gain access to basing and overflight. We will have to be able to base in the region and overfly several countries if we ever need to fight Iran. If it continues to be our national policy to deemphasize the region and to reduce our posture and relationships accordingly, then we should also suppress our appetite for potential kinetic action against Iran. To not resolve these tensions if we contemplate a strike is strategic malpractice of the highest order.

There is one bit of good news that has come about as a result of the rise of Iranian capabilities, their provocative actions, and the drumbeat of messages from the United States about drawing down in the Middle East. Countries in the region are increasingly worried about Iranian capabilities, particularly ballistic missiles, cruise missiles, and uncrewed aerial platforms. These same countries place less and less faith in their relationship with the United States as a protector. This has had the effect of drawing them together. The final component of these new developments was the addition of Israel into the Central Command area of responsibility in 2021. It was far more than symbolic. The air and missile defense domain is an area where countries can cooperate to varying degrees. It's mainly about the prompt sharing of information: radar sensor data, signals and imagery intelligence. A nation does not have to either accept foreign forces on its own territory or station its own forces abroad to participate. This fact, and the imminence of the threat, created a sweet spot for cooperation. Since my days as the CENTCOM strategist in 2010-12, increased cooperation in this area had been a goal of CENTCOM. In 2012 our then-air component commander, Lt. Gen. Dave Goldfein, worked hard to bring nations together. We were never able to get beyond the discussion stage, despite his considerable force of personality and energy. Dave would go on to be the chief of staff of the Air Force.

In 2021 and after, it was different. First in August 2021 and then again in March 2022, I met with chiefs of defense of many of the nations in the Gulf, and Israel, Jordan, and Egypt.[2] Our goals were to find actionable, practical ways to share air and missile warnings and to develop a set of responses that we could employ rapidly. What set these meetings apart was the fact that there was significant preparatory work conducted. Staff officers met and conferred, information and capabilities were shared. The final meetings that I attended represented only a snapshot in the long continuum of planning that had begun in early 2021. We did not meet just to meet. This cooperation offers great opportunities to deter Iran and to create a structure upon which nations in the region can continue to build. For example, cooperation at sea is another domain that is ripe for exploitation. Moving ahead will require additional political buy-in from the nations involved. As with everything in the region, the process will be halting and uncertain, but I believe we have taken the first nascent steps toward a regional collective security architecture.

16

CONSIDERING PHLEBAS

O you who turn the wheel and look to windward
Consider Phlebas, who was once handsome
and tall as you.
—*T. S. Eliot*, The Wasteland

In this book I have tried to describe what it means to be a commander at the highest level of war—the command of a theater—during some of the most tumultuous days in our national history. For some events, I was an observer. For others—in fact, most—I was a practitioner. I gave advice; sometimes it was taken, and sometimes it was not. Ultimately, I took orders from civilian leadership, digested the tasks and policy guidance in the language of diplomats, presidents, and the secretary of defense, and turned them into actionable military plans. I then gave orders to my subordinate commanders and saw that my orders—the orders derived from civilian decisions—were carried out. The role of a combatant commander is unique. The commander gives advice and participates, to varying degrees, in policy debates. The combatant commander then becomes the person who takes those decisions and carries them out. The joint chiefs do not do this. They are outside the chain of command. The chairman occupies a unique position, but he is ultimately not in the chain of command. No other uniformed officer stands at that hard place: the unique point where policy, military operations, and responsibility merge into one.

What Is Going to Happen in the Middle East?
From Egypt in the west to Pakistan in the east, every country in the Central Command region is concerned about the long-term U.S. commitment to

the region. They see our intent to focus on China, and they realize that there is a price to be paid for that decision; they believe it will largely come from the Middle East. These concerns have been exacerbated by the clumsy and maladroit way that we have communicated these very necessary adjustments to our strategic posture to our friends in the region. One of the advantages, it was presumed, of a return to "normal order" in the Department of Defense would have been a heightened level of performance in our alliance management; that has largely fallen short of the mark in the Middle East. There is, in fact, a way to do both things: confront China and maintain a presence in the Middle East. To do so will require more agility of thought and action than we have shown to date.

There is an argument that the United States should completely withdraw from the Middle East—ironically, in the name of great power competition. This is a reflection of our lack of nuance and our historical short-sightedness. More directly, it reflects a failure of strategic thought. It's predicated largely on the idea that our interests in the Middle East began on 9/11 and are at odds with the imperative of great power competition. In point of fact, the Carter Doctrine that eventually led to the creation of U.S. Central Command in 1983 was based on an appreciation that the Gulf region was a central theater of great power competition of that era—just as it had been for the hundred years before that.

This is unlikely to change in our lifetimes. Today, the Middle East provides China with an attractive market for economic investment and infrastructure projects under the banner of its Belt and Road Initiative. In Syria, it also provides Russia a stage on which it can act out its fantasy of restored imperial greatness. More importantly, the world's major shipping routes all run through the region and its strategic chokepoints at the Strait of Hormuz, the Bab al-Mandeb, and the Suez Canal. The 2021 six-day blockage of the Suez by the merchant vessel *Ever Given* affected 12 percent of global trade and cost an estimated $9 billion per day. That the security and stability of this region remain a core interest of the United States should be obvious.

Any consideration of the future of the region must begin by recognizing three unpalatable facts. First, Iran is going to be around for a long time, and it is going to continue to increase its military power relative to its neighbors.

The maximum pressure campaign of the Trump administration failed to break Iran. The softer approach of the Biden administration is almost certainly going to prove ineffective as well. Recognizing this, countries in the region are making their own accommodations with Iran. The UAE and Saudi Arabia are leading the way, and others will certainly follow. These are uneasy relationships, but they are all based on the growing uncertainty with which U.S. security guarantees are viewed. They also are practical reactions to the significant drawdown of U.S. capability in the region. Iran has internal stability problems as well—but it is a proud imperial state with a heritage that goes back thousands of years. The bottom line is this: Iran will weather the storm, and we need to find a way to integrate it into the region in a way that serves our purposes as well as theirs. That used to be the working definition of practical statecraft. I don't want to overstate the possibility of this happening: Iran will have to change if this is to happen—most significantly in its implacable campaign against Israel. The protests in Iran in the winter of 2022 and spring of 2023 are not capable of threatening the center of gravity of the Iranian state. In many ways, they are a false hope.

The second unpalatable truth is that Bashar al-Assad has won the Syrian civil war. He and his murderous regime are going to be around for a while. We had numerous opportunities to change the course of the war in Syria, but in every case, and under multiple administrations, we refrained from acting. Now, we must deal with a badly damaged Syria, one that cannot feed its own people, but one that will be increasingly recognized by its Arab neighbors. The real losers here may well be the Syrian Kurds, our Syrian Democratic Forces partners who fought so well against ISIS. Nonstate entities are often rubbed away when states smash up against each other, and that is increasingly the trend in Syria.

The final truth involves violent extremists. ISIS-K and al Qaeda are also going to have long-term presences in the region. Our withdrawal from Afghanistan was a huge victory for international terrorism, giving a booster shot to a variety of organizations who delight in what they perceive as a defeat for us. The strike against al Qaeda leader Zawahiri in late July was a powerful blow, but the fact that he was in Kabul in a Haqqani safehouse when struck is sobering. Practically, this means that al Qaeda has a platform in Afghanistan, with the support of the Taliban. We will need to continue to focus on their abilities to organize attacks against our homeland. For ISIS, we will increasingly lose the ability to undertake actions to resolve the root of the problem, which is the appalling living conditions and economic opportunity for Sunnis in many Arab states. Syria is at the forefront of this list, but the return of the Afghanistan platform for terrorists will also prove increasingly problematic for us over time.

It's not completely a bad news story. We have had modest success in Iraq, where the Iraqi security forces have proven able to take on ISIS with lower levels of U.S. support. Our NATO partners are also involved in Iraq, and the trends for their continued engagement are favorable, although the war in Ukraine has slowed this process. Iraq can become an island of relative stability in the very center of the region, but it will take not only continued engagement by the military element of power but also sustained economic and diplomatic assistance. The entry of Israel into the region in a military sense, as they join CENTCOM, also provides opportunities. Coupled with the Abraham Accords, there is slow but certain momentum on the part of Arab states to open up to Israel. It will not come quickly, but all in the region realize the immense military capabilities that Israel brings, and those may prove useful in a region with reduced American presence. In the back of everyone's mind is the need to balance against Iran, since they will not be able to count on the United States to do so. There is a path forward here for us, and it is centered on air and missile defense. The primary and growing threat from Iran is that of ballistic missile, land attack cruise missile, and drone attack. Nations in the region need modern, capable air and missile defenses to confront this threat. The actions described in the preceding chapter give us real opportunity here.

Underpinning all these activities is the entry of China. The Belt and Road runs through the central region. At the same time, a significant fraction of China's hydrocarbon imports come from the Central Command area. In many ways, the region is the cockpit of strategic competition with China. Its strategy has been to use economic inducements with a variety of countries in order to gain a foothold in the region. Bases inevitably follow, as we have seen in Djibouti and potentially in the UAE. Countering China in the Middle East is not an exercise in hard power—at least, not yet. We have a variety of tools that we can deploy, but they must be used cleverly. The recurring theme is that we have opportunities to compete and prevail in this region, and they don't require hard power or large, permanent military forces, but we must seize them, and think far more nimbly than we have done to date.

What should we expect from the region? What are reasonable goals? First is a stable order among states, where international norms are observed. Second is the free flow of commerce through the region. Third is preventing Iran from possessing a nuclear weapon. Fourth is preventing the development of terror attacks against our homeland from the region. These are attainable goals. They may not be broad enough for some, but we have very clearly seen the limits of maximalist approaches in the region. To accomplish these objectives, we need to signal that we are going to stay in the central region. We are going to have a smaller military footprint, but it will still be significant, and we will always retain the ability to rapidly redeploy overwhelming combat power when necessary. The three enduring problems will be dealing with a still-dangerous, unpredictable, and resurgent Iran, the management of a growing Chinese presence that will be increasingly military in character, and the threat of violent extremism. These are solvable problems, but we need to see beyond binary, bureaucratic policy solutions that do not reflect the inherent dynamism and instability of the region.

The Next War

The next war will be driven by information. Collecting it, using it efficiently, and denying an adversary's ability to do the same will be the central calculus. Artificial intelligence and machine learning applications will be vital to the ability to distill essentials from the metaverse of data that will be collected. Counterintuitively, the ability to operate in an information-denied environment will be decisive, because the ability to disrupt and cause chaos is inherently stronger than the ability to cohere.[1] Much of this fight will occur in two new domains of warfare: cyber and space. We are still defining the practical limits of how to operate in the cyber domain. As for space, for too long the United States has viewed the domain as a safe and unchallengeable place—a true global commons—where our activities could continue unmolested. This time is over, and space will be a highly contested domain in any future conflict.

The use of uncrewed platforms and the application of artificial intelligence are going to dominate the tactical battlefield. We already see the ubiquity of uncrewed platforms in the Central Command region as well as Ukraine, and this is only going to grow over time. They will become increasingly semi- and then fully autonomous in the future. This is posing grave ethical challenges now in the United States. It is unlikely that the Chinese, the Russians, and several other actors will concern themselves with these niceties. Regardless, today in CENTCOM we do not have unchallenged air superiority. Uncrewed aerial systems overfly our bases frequently, and they have been used to attack us as well. This trend is going to increase.

As I have discussed earlier, nuclear weapons are going to be a big part of any future battlefield. It's interesting to consider that for most of the Cold War, the Soviets held a significant conventional force edge over NATO. To compensate for that fact, we built and deployed thousands of tactical nuclear weapons and also made it clear that we would use them in a defense of Europe. Today, that concept has been completely stood on its head. The Russians realize that we possess conventional overmatch against their forces in Europe, and they have chosen to compensate for the deficiency by maintaining a large inventory of tactical nuclear weapons (we now have relatively few of these weapons) and by holding to a doctrine that emphasizes early use—the idea of "escalating to de-escalate." The poor performance of Russian conventional forces in Ukraine only heightens this imperative for them.

The United States has always considered nuclear weapons tools of last resort, and our thinking about employing them has tended to focus on the political effects that obtain from nuclear use. The Russians and the Chinese are not burdened by these considerations, and they have thought deeper and harder—and more clearly—about how to use nuclear weapons on the battlefield. Nuclear weapons are coming back as battlefield weapons. We cannot ignore this fact, and we need to take practical steps to be able to prevail in a nuclear battlefield environment. This includes pursuing real tactical nuclear capabilities, instead of the bare and perhaps inadequate minimum that we possess today.

When speaking to military audiences in particular, I have tried to find a way to talk about the imminence of the nuclear threat. I found a useful way to do this was to speak about two phrases: a "dying" phrase, one that was leaving our lexicon, and a new or "reborn" phrase. The dying phrase was the term "golden hour." For most of my career, from the end of the Cold War until very recently, an organizing principle of military medical care has been that we would get wounded servicemembers to an appropriate aid station within sixty minutes of being injured. This was a daunting task. It required an enormous expenditure of resources, careful planning, and relentless attention to detail. Particularly in environments like Afghanistan and parts of Iraq, it also required routine bravery and skill from the responders. Our track record has been very good overall with this principle, and in places where we have struggled to maintain this standard—sub-Saharan Africa, for example—we work mightily to get as close to an hour as possible.

Unfortunately, this kind of exquisite medical care will not be available in a large-scale conflict with either Russia or China, or even potentially North Korea. The skies will be contested, and our medical evacuation aircraft will not be able to fly freely. Casualties will be significantly higher. Chemical and nuclear contamination will be routine, and this will drastically slow the process of evacuation. In short, speedy aeromedical evacuation, a thing we have taken for granted for decades, will no longer be a constant.

On the other hand, the return of nuclear weapons to the battlefield will bring with it a reborn phrase: immediate transient incapacitation, or the amount of acute ionizing radiation that a soldier would need to receive in order to make him or her unable to accomplish any basic soldier task. For planning, that number is in the three thousand–roentgen range. To state it plainly, someone subjected to this dose will be immediately ineffective to continue to fight. Death may be days or weeks away, but the soldier will be effectively incapacitated. Mortality would be 100 percent, and it will be a horrible death. In the 1980s this was a significant concept in our tactical planning against the Russians. As a young captain, attending the armor advanced course at Fort Knox, Kentucky, I spent many hours working on a large flat desk with 1:50,000 tactical maps, templates, and whiz wheels at my side and laid out, carefully measuring how to achieve maximum immediate transient incapacitation against advancing Soviet formations. In that era, the United States would think nothing of employing a hundred or more tactical nuclear weapons in an attack on a corps front—a front that could be thirty miles in length and with a depth of fifty or sixty miles. I was taught well by my instructors at Fort Knox. Even today I can remember how we would choose between different warhead sizes and delivery means in order to gain maximum effect on the enemy, while minimizing risk to our own forces. It wasn't lost on any of us that somewhere in Russia, other captains were doing the same thing.

Why are nuclear weapons returning? The Cold War ended. The United States rapidly divested its huge tactical nuclear weapons arsenal. The Russians did not. To this day, they still retain several thousand tactical nuclear weapons—weapons that are not covered by any limitations such as the Strategic Arms Reduction Treaty. We retain tactical nuclear weapons in Europe—B-61 gravity bombs, to be delivered by tactical fighters—but nothing on the scale of what we had in the Cold War. The Russians have many more choices and types of tactical weapons. The use of nuclear weapons has always been an integral part of their doctrine. We didn't see all of this in 2015, but recent events in Ukraine have driven home the point that the Russians view nuclear employment as a technique to flip an adverse conventional engagement. For these reasons, I am convinced that the next large war we fight will have a nuclear component.

Any future war will also touch our homeland in ways that we have never seen before. The ranges and speed of modern missiles, whether they are hypersonic or not, have made the great oceans that border the North American continent little more than river barriers. These weapons do not have to be nuclear-armed to have significant effect. Additionally, our Internet backbone, the wholly unclassified great cyber architecture that underpins literally all activities in the United States, is fragile and vulnerable to attack. It would be very hard to actually deploy our forces overseas if a large-scale cyber disruption occurred.

Despite all of these concerns, the United States is today the world's preeminent military power. To remain so, we must do better at balancing the competing demands of the present with the requirements of the near and distant future, all on a global scale. In his classic work *The Rise and Fall of the*

Great Powers, Yale historian Paul Kennedy has shown that all great powers throughout history have struggled to do this. The bad news is that, eventually, they become overextended and cease to be great powers. How do we, presently at the top of the heap, avoid this fate? As a global power we have responsibilities around the world. We need to be able to ruthlessly prioritize, but we also need to be able to think in nuanced terms. There has been far too little nuanced thinking, particularly in our global response to the rise of China.

The capability advantage we have enjoyed for many years against any putative adversary has eroded. This was in part due to our focus on the Middle East since 2001 but also to declining or steady-state budgets that forced the services to trade readiness and force development for current operations. Most importantly, though, the narrowing capability gap was due to the actions of two nations: China and Russia. Both of these nations had carefully studied the development of the joint force that defeated Iraq in 1991 and 2003. From that study, they developed their own defense programs—aimed directly at what they perceived to be our weaknesses. It would be an overstatement to claim that they snuck up on us while we were fixated with the wars in Afghanistan and Iraq, but it would be fair to say that they made up a lot of ground that we had taken for granted. The Chinese program, in particular, was pointed at our ability to rapidly deploy the force and to command it effectively in battle. For all of the years after the end of the Cold War, while we had focused on regional warfighting, the Chinese kept an unwavering objective of being able to fight globally and across the entire spectrum of conflict. In the case of the Chinese, this was supplemented by intellectual theft of many of our critical defense capabilities, freeing them from a lengthy development timeline. Nowhere was this more damaging than with stealth technology and in cybernetics.

The capacity advantage that the United States had known for so many years had also eroded. "Things, and numbers of things" remained a key part of any discussion of military might. We now had fewer "things" than before when we confronted potential adversaries. This was exacerbated by the underfunding and occasional mismanagement of readiness programs. As a result, the United States did not have much of a shock absorber when global problems were considered. There weren't enough aircraft carriers, submarines, maritime patrol aircraft, airborne early warning platforms, and many other high-demand/low-density assets in the inventory to support our planning. This was aggravated by the regionalization of planning, which made it very hard for the chairman to give advice on a global scale about resource allocation to the sole decision-maker on these matters: the secretary of defense.

To address these challenges, we need to think more broadly in space and time, taking a measured approach to competing demands and varying the tempo with which we pursue change according to the circumstances. Too often in the past, we have oriented on "one big thing" at a time, pivoting only in response to climactic events like the collapse of the Soviet Union in the early 1990s or 9/11. When we do pivot—shifting our perspective—everything looks new to us. And so, we often exaggerate the novelty of the "new" security environment in which we find ourselves. This leads us to mistake recurring and inevitable age-old phenomena such as "gray zone competition" and "hybrid warfare" as some radical new departures from the past.

It is obvious that the world is changing. We would do well, however, to appreciate continuities from the past and to distinguish that which is truly new from that which we have merely forgotten. Taking a longer historical view enables us to do this. There are no eras so old that we can afford to ignore them. If examined carefully, the Cold War, for example, contains nearly everything assumed to be novel about the supposedly "new" era of great power competition upon which we're presently embarking: paradigm-changing technologies, the use of various media to sow dissention among the populations of adversaries, economic and diplomatic competition for influence with third parties that control key resources or terrain, and a constant struggle to maintain freedom of movement in the global commons.

Certainly, there are new tools and even new domains in which this competition plays out—cyber and space—but the fundamental dimensions of great power competition are genuinely ancient. There is a structural continuity in the development of competition between states that stretches from Athens and Sparta to the United States, China, and Russia. Also obvious is the fact that we today live in an interconnected world in which there are global implications to seemingly regional problems. But here again, we shouldn't exaggerate the novelty of globalization. It's been around for well over a century and predates the rise of the United States as a truly great power. During the Cold War, we very much understood that what happened in Asia would have consequences in Europe and at home—and we practiced grand strategy accordingly.

Unfortunately, with our victory in the Cold War, many assumed we had reached the "end of history" and that we wouldn't have to bother any longer with this difficult craft. In a world without an obvious, singular threat to focus on, we settled into a habit of dividing resources *equitably* rather than *strategically* among our services and combatant commands. Bureaucratically, it was the easy thing to do—but it's a poor substitute for strategy. Recognizing this, at the direction of the chairman, the Joint Staff under Gen. Joe Dunford introduced the concepts of global integration and dynamic force employment, which provided the secretary of defense the tools to break free from the chains of allocation and assignment and send forces where they are most needed while weighing and mitigating risk across the globe. I'm a big fan of these concepts and have often described them as the way of the future—but the truth is, they're also a throwback to the days of George Marshall. When the stakes are high and resources are inadequate, there is no option but to think globally and strategically. Marshall had a term for the malady affecting commanders and strategists who could only see what was directly in front of them: *localitis*. It's a good phrase to remember.

On that point, I should add that—when it comes to technology—history is finally catching up with us. Because our ascendance as a great power depended on our technological supremacy, the United States has always assumed that we have a special relationship with technology—that it conveys advantages to us and not to our adversaries. In fact, technology has served as a great leveler throughout history. We can see this playing out in real time. Iran, for example, is not a great power by anyone's estimation. Despite pretentions to regional hegemony, it can't even manage its internal affairs. But Iran has invested tremendous resources into its ballistic missile and drone programs—and through them is able to threaten the peace and stability of the entire region. In so doing, it also preserves the spaces—such as in Yemen and Syria—where violent extremist organizations can reconstitute and stage external attacks. We should also recall their ability to use our own technology against us—as in the 9/11 attacks.

This isn't to say that only lesser powers are reaping the benefits of the silicon revolution. China, especially, has made significant, alarming advances in artificial intelligence, quantum computing, hypersonic glide weapons, and what we might call "new-fashioned" naval power. Meanwhile, it competes across the globe—including the CENTCOM area of responsibility—for influence and access to resources. The next war, even if it's a regional engagement, will have global effects. It will be bloodier than what we have come to expect, and it will range from the silicon pathways of the "vast and infinite" web to cislunar space. Other nations are assiduously preparing for this war, and in so doing they are targeting us. We need to realize this and recognize the shape and contour of what the next war will be. It's not necessary to get it exactly right, only to avoid making mistakes of such significance that they can't be overcome when war comes. It's coming faster than we realize.

Civil-Military Relations

A central theme of this book has been the interaction of civilian and uniformed leaders at the highest levels of government and command. Throughout my narrative, it might be possible to discern a sense of frustration at how this relationship has worked. That's probably true—at various times over the past seven years, particularly since I became the Joint Staff director of strategy, plans, and policy, and subsequently the director of the Joint Staff—I was sometimes frustrated at the process and output of our decision-making process. It would be wrong, though, to infer that I favor any alternative to our current system. Problematic as it occasionally is, the concept of civilian control is fundamental to our republic, and there is no alternative. There have been numerous articles written by academics describing what they allude to as an ascendant Joint Staff within the department that has tended, so the argument runs, to mute or quiet civilian voices. There have even been attacks on the use of the phrase "best military advice," which, it is claimed, is inherently damaging to civilian control, since it infers that the advice of the chairman is "better" than other advice that might be offered by nonmilitary advisors.[2] This particularly fine distinction may seem a little academic, and indeed some of these arguments are lost on everyone except the small group of people who circulate in and out of government in midlevel defense positions. No senior military leader would disagree with the proposition that to work properly, the dialogue at the highest levels between the military and the civilian must be, as Eliot Cohen has written, "unequal."[3] Civilian advice and counsel must speak last.

Of course, there's more to it than that. What makes an effective strategist or policy advisor? It is the ability to understand what is desired against what can be done to achieve that end, and an appreciation for the costs of pursuing that goal or choosing not to. The higher the level of the advisor, the larger the canvas upon which she or he conjures. At the highest levels of the Department of Defense, the setting is the globe. I do not believe that uniformed officers are intrinsically better at this than civilians. Likewise, an advanced degree does not confer any particular strategic insight in and of itself. The one advantage that a senior uniformed officer brings is the technical knowledge of how the vast machinery of war works and a sense of how strategic decisions may play out in time and space: an appreciation for what Clausewitz called friction. In general, and depending on his or her background, the civilian advisor brings a more nuanced appreciation for how the military element of national power fits into the broader government of the United States, and a wider sense of the art of the possible, which is the essence of political art. The danger for the military advisor is fixating too strongly on the technical aspects of the problem and not understanding that military plans and concepts do not exist in a vacuum; instead, they are part of a far larger process and must ultimately yield to policy imperatives. Some—not many—senior military leaders do not always choose to accept this and find it difficult to accept that a plan, while operationally feasible and acceptable, may not serve the larger political requirements of the United States: this is localitis. On the other hand, since the creation of policy is uniquely difficult and may well be the most intellectually taxing task of all that is done in government, sometimes it is easier for civilian leaders to not deal with big policy decisions and to instead look deeply into DoD, substituting tactical micromanagement for policy creation, decision, and enforcement. This is the self-abnegation of civilian control, while avoiding the truly hard choices. Whether these choices are made or not, events across the globe will progress. When it is all said and done, it is the secretary who owns the risk for the Department of Defense. How this is allocated, and mitigated, is ultimately a decision only he or she can make.

The Joint Staff is a very effective and capable organization, but the excellence of its staffwork in no way alters who makes the final decision. The Joint Staff will ensure that the chairman is well prepared to give best military advice, and he will be heard. The chairman does not get to make *any* decision, and in my years as the J-5, the director of the Joint Staff, and then as a combatant commander, I never saw civilian advisors boxed out or unable to offer their opinion. Of course, opinions and advice are no better than their quality, and in the secretary's office, there can be a quiet, fierce competition to prevail in the dialectic. This is not a bad thing; the thing to be avoided is the homogenization of advice, so that only precooked, highly adulterated solutions are presented. When all is said and done, civilians must make the final decisions. Even more importantly, as Peter Feaver has written, "In a democracy, civilians have the right to be wrong. Civilian political leaders have the right to ask for things in the national security realm that are ultimately not conducive to good national security. The military should advise against such policies, but the military should not prevent those policies from being carried out."[4]

Resigning

What are the limits of protest, and when should generals or admirals resign if they disagree with an order? It is seldom done in our system. There's a good reason for that, and it strikes to the essence of civilian control—the very act of resigning to disagree with an order can become a political act, and that is contrary to the U.S. view of what officership entails. Again, Peter Feaver is instructive: "Even if an individual judges a lawful order to be immoral, it still must be obeyed. The *Manual for Courts-Martial* provides that 'the dictates of a person's conscience, religion, or personal philosophy cannot justify or excuse the disobedience of an otherwise lawful order.'"[5] This is a very high bar to resignation, and it effectively makes it impossible to do so unless the order is unlawful. The United States requires a great deal from its officers; this may be the most demanding requirement of all, and it is often misunderstood, inside and outside of the officer corps.

Over the course of my career, I've written four or five letters of resignation. Writing them always made me feel better. I would admire them, polish them, review my carefully crafted arguments and criticisms . . . and then put them away. The only time in all of my career that I seriously considered offering to resign was in the aftermath of the August 29, 2021, drone strike in Kabul. As I said publicly in its aftermath, I was the responsible commander. I felt that responsibility very strongly. I also felt that my subordinates had all acted in good faith, with the best of intentions, and had gotten it terribly wrong. For those critics who spoke with the casual certitude of an antiseptic view of the world and demanded that everyone be fired, I had little time. As I interacted with the secretary on the matter, endorsing the investigation that Lt. Gen. Sami Said, USAF, had conducted, I kept in the back of my mind the promise to myself that, if against my advice and recommendation, administrative or disciplinary action was taken against my subordinates, I would ask to be relieved from command. My reasoning would have been simple and direct—I was responsible, and while the friction of combat explained to any reasonable observer what had happened in Kabul that dark afternoon, if sacrifices were required, then it would be necessary for me to join my subordinates. That did not come to pass.

On the other hand, I have never contemplated resigning because of a policy difference with civilian leadership. When I was confronted with decisions that I strongly disagreed with—and there have been several of these—I found it helpful to pull from my bookshelf the Michael Sorley biography of Army Chief of Staff Harold K. Johnson, *Honorable Warrior*.[6] During the height of the Vietnam War, Johnson considered resigning. He didn't do so and later in life came to regret that decision. It's my belief that he made the right decision not to resign and that his later regret was misplaced. His initial instinct—the instinct he acted upon—was right. The republic does not need generals who quit because they disagree with civilian leadership. I did not choose to resign when President Biden elected to make a decision about Afghanistan that was counter to my recommendation. I never considered resigning. It is obvious that the president did not take my recommendation in making his decision, but it would have been irresponsible to quit because my views did not prevail. The president deserves better from his military leadership. Armchair analysts and critics have the freedom to virtually quit whenever they want—a senior commander must be made of sterner stuff. Perhaps most importantly of all, a president—any president—should be able to expect that lawful orders will be executed aggressively and properly, regardless of contrary advice given by the commander or that commander's personal views.

It is always easy to be a critic: to opine freely, without knowledge of all the facts and with certainly none of the responsibility. Armed with a relentlessly Manichaean view of the world, the choice is always crystal-clear to these refugees from responsibility, and they would have generals ripping stars off their collars and flinging them onto desks over a wide variety of disagreements. This view, while having the single dubious consistency of an almost child-like simplicity, isn't good for the republic. No general should ever wield veto power over a political decision by an implicit or explicit threat to quit if she or he doesn't get what they want.

Two events in the modern history of the republic clearly show what the role of the military is in politics. On April 12, 1945, President Franklin D. Roosevelt died in Warm Springs, Georgia. Late that afternoon, Vice President Harry S. Truman was sworn in as the thirty-third president. What's interesting in all the literature dealing with that tragic day in Washington is the lack of any specific mention of the military. Nobody was interested in what George C. Marshall or any other senior officer thought—and that was exactly correct. The same thing happened in November 1963, when President John F. Kennedy was assassinated and Vice President Lyndon Johnson took the oath of office in Dallas, aboard Air Force One, under painful and emotional circumstances. Nobody sought the opinion of the chairman or the joint chiefs. They were there only to be the loyal executors of the orders of the president—whomever he was. These two vignettes capture the role of the military in our government—invisible, without political power, and completely subservient to civilian control. If we ever get into a situation where we're asking, "What does the chairman think about this?" when it comes to political issues, then we are on dangerous ground. That principle has been tested in recent years, but General Dunford and General Milley have done brave and courageous work in keeping the military establishment out of politics. Their successors will have to be equally adept. I do not think the risk is over, and it has the potential to pose a grave threat in the future.

On the other hand, this doesn't mean that generals should not be fired. We probably fire too few generals at the highest level of command, and here

I am talking about four-star officers in command or as service chiefs. Service chiefs typically aren't fired for operational reasons, because they have no chain-of-command responsibilities. Usually, they're fired for speaking out against a policy position of the administration, or because of mismanagement—real or perceived—within their service. For commanders, it's a little different. Gen. Dave McKiernan was brought home early from Afghanistan by Secretary Robert Gates because he did not seem to be able to implement the administration's plan—and there are varying views about the correctness of that decision. His successor, Gen. Stan McChrystal, was fired more abruptly because of his immediate staff being openly disrespectful to the president and the vice president—among others. Firing a general isn't and should never be an inherently political act. The president can do as he or she wishes. The resignation of a senior leader, however, can be inherently political unless it is very narrowly based on a refusal to carry out a patently illegal order, and there are very few of those.

The Joint Chiefs of Staff

In our home, we have a reproduction of George P. A. Healy's painting *The Peacemakers*, which captures a meeting between Abraham Lincoln, Gen. Ulysses S. Grant, Gen. William T. Sherman, and Rear Adm. David Dixon Porter. The meeting occurred in late March 1865, at the very end of the Civil War. I like the painting for two reasons—first, it captures the essence of civilian control of the military. Lincoln had gone to see Richmond after it had fallen to Grant and his army. After touring the city, he came aboard the Navy steamer *River Queen*, anchored off Grant's headquarters at City Point, Virginia. While aboard, he conferred with his commanders at the end of a terrible, costly, and successful war that they had conducted under his direction. There is a sense of poignancy about the meeting, of course, because Lincoln has less than a month to live, and these men would never gather again.

The second reason that I like the painting is because a copy of it hangs in the Tank—the Joint Chiefs of Staff conference room.. Over the course of my career, I've spent a lot of time looking at that picture while attending meetings with the JCS. Because of that, I have many strong associations with the picture, both in terms of what it means and also what it has represented for me personally as well as for the generations of officers who have passed through the Tank.

Unfortunately, the Joint Chiefs of Staff are ultimately a committee, and like all committees, the sum is often less than the component parts. The members of the JCS wear two hats—as their respective service chiefs, and then as JCS members. This is the original sin of the JCS, and it is why the body has never been able to genuinely assert itself in policy deliberations and why it is always an organization that appears to underachieve. Members of the JCS are consistently unable to resolve the tension between the requirements of being a service chief—recruiting, training, and maintaining military forces—and giving insightful advice on employing the forces they have created. While over the years many of the structural defects in the JCS have been resolved, and there is no longer a need to seek consensus in their deliberations, there is still a strong bias for unanimity, almost a herd instinct, that often produces less than optimal corporate advice. The rise of the authority and power of the chairman, supported by the Joint Staff, as a separate entity has also weakened their ability to speak authoritatively as a body. Finally, it's important to understand that the Joint Staff is not the JCS. The Joint Staff technically does support all members of the JCS, but in fact and practice, the Joint Staff serves the chairman first.

I found working with the chiefs to be a complex art as the J-5 and the director, but as a combatant commander, they were almost irrelevant to the process of employing military force. Any time I interacted with them as a commander, I saw the harsh and inescapable tension between someone who builds and trains a force, with an eye to deep time (and for whom preservation of the force comes first), and someone who must employ the force in current time, even if that means damaging it. I found them to be a Greek chorus of woe on most substantive issues, unable to overcome their parochial service interests to consider problems as a whole and from a global perspective. In general, the joint chiefs were better looking into the future; they were considerably less effective in confronting immediate military problems. They were also better when they did not have to put programmatic service considerations first and could examine problems from the chairman's or the secretary's position. This higher-level thinking happened less often than one might expect. Part of this was because service staffs were unable to operate at the pace of the Joint Staff, so unless a product was provided by the Joint Staff, service preparations for their chiefs often lagged. As individuals, they were immensely capable leaders, but when they sat down in the Tank, the output of their discussions often could be best summed up by Winston Churchill's famous description of his own chiefs during World War II: "You may take the most gallant sailor, the most intrepid airman, and the most audacious soldier, put them at a table together—and what do you get? The sum of all their fears."

A reasonable question might be: "Is there an alternative to our current system?" Chairmen, JCS members, secretaries, the president, and Congress have asked themselves this question for more than seventy years. Various schema have been introduced to heighten their power or to decouple them from their service chief responsibilities, which would, in theory, relieve them of their parochial perspectives. I see no way to break free of the inherent contradiction between service chief responsibilities and their role as advisors as joint chiefs. Their gravitas—their weight—comes from running the massive service enterprises that they represent. That's where they provide good and powerful leadership in the development, culture, and operational approach of their services. To sever them from this linkage would be to make them no more than a committee of old soldiers, who would have no standing. Unfortunately, keeping them as service chiefs—giving them standing—robs them of the ability to advise independently as joint chiefs. There's no way to cut this knot—it is the original sin.

After years of interaction with this body, it is my considered judgment that the current system is the best we can possibly have, and there is no viable alternative. The real strength of the current system is in its almost inadvertent reinforcement of civilian control. There is no possibility that the chiefs can ever band together to assert themselves as an independent power center within the interagency or the Department of Defense. Too much keeps them apart. The chiefs of the novel and movie *Seven Days in May*, dreamt of by breathless academics who warn each other endlessly of usurpation of the constitutional processes of the department, the squeezing out of civilian control, do not exist.

Instead, it's a committee. It does much good, some bad, some that is indifferent. Like most things that work in American public life, it's a compromise, with inherent checks and balances that prevent extreme positions, and perhaps most importantly, it ensures that civilians always get the last say. While their collective advice may not always be of the highest caliber, their potential for challenging the supremacy of civilian control is quite limited. In the long arc that is the history of the republic, the fact that they have been relegated to live outside the chain of command has done more good than bad. The system that has evolved, with a strong chairman and a capable, effective Joint Staff, both also clearly subordinated to civilian control, is the best possible solution. Even so, the chairman is powerless to act independently, and that is quite clearly the intent of both Congress and the executive branch. There have been opportunities to make the Joint Staff a general staff and to make the chairman a commander. Those options have been decisively rejected, and they are, in fact, alien to the American way of war.

It is interesting to speculate about how this system would function in a major global war. I believe it would tend to deemphasize even more the role of the joint chiefs, while increasingly empowering them in their "man, train, and equip" roles as service chiefs. It's simply not possible to do both with the same degree of effectiveness. The role of the chairman will become even more pronounced, and the Joint Staff's role will be enhanced as well. The speed of decision-making will require the rapidity of staff action that only the Joint Staff can deliver. The secretary will be making many decisions on a global scale, and I believe that the offices of the secretary—particularly policy—will be strained to function in a continual around-the-clock rhythm. Combatant commanders will remain the key executors but will have to understand the global nature of a major fight; comfortable assumptions about presence forces in economy of force commands will need to be continually revisited.

Do Generals Matter?

Another central theme of this book has been the singular importance of senior military leadership, both as a source of specialized professional advice for policymakers and then as the actual executors of decisions about the application of violence in the service of the state once decisions are made.

The endless arguments about the relative weight of their advice are interesting, but they can't conceal the very important fact that the civilians are in charge. Most generals, and myself to be certain, are interested in the advice part of our job, but the actual ultimate satisfaction for a professional soldier is in the execution of large and complex tasks in an arena of potential and real conflict. Directing the vast machinery of war at a high level of command remains one of the most intellectually satisfying tasks that any human being can undertake. Command remains a unique responsibility; the commander is responsible for everything the organization "does or fails to do." It cannot be shared. A lifetime of preparation, education, and hands-on experience is the precursor to successful high-level command. There is no shortcut on the path.

At the highest levels of government, one of the side effects of the desire to reassert civilian control has been the self-conscious forced erosion of the perceived value of military expertise. This is unfortunate, because military advice, whether it is characterized as "best" or with some other adjective, is a vital input to policymaking. Military advice is different than advice from a nonmilitary professional. That doesn't mean it is better—only that it is different. Bringing a specialized perspective that has been reached through years of experience and education, it offers a unique insight and should not have to be one of many inputs in a cacophonous process that devalues its importance systematically. It is always subordinate to broader considerations, but it needs to be heard. Military advice should not be civilianized or edited in some levelling process until it is bent to whatever philosophical viewpoint is held by policymakers. I see more of this tendency now than I have at any time in my career.

Generals do matter, and they will continue to matter, even in an era that values flat hierarchies, the devaluation of expertise, and the perception of total transparency. Organizing violence in the service of the state requires experience, judgment, and an ability to routinely look into the abyss without, to paraphrase Friedrich Nietzsche, having it "look into you" to such a degree that the ethical compass that should guide one is lost. It is an individual act, and it can't be done by a committee or by a gifted amateur. Adolf Hitler was a gifted amateur, and he ultimately failed spectacularly as a military commander.

The personality of the commander matters, and the commander is alone. Almost unique to the military, the biases, foibles, and affectations of a commander are imprinted on the command. Good, bad, or indifferent, they show up. At the level of theater command, which is what this book is about, the translation of political decisions into practical military action is at the core of what the commander does. The experiences that brought me to Central Command were the basis for everything I did. In command, I tried to apply something I once read many years ago, written by Vice Adm. James B. Stockdale, a genuine American hero: "A properly educated leader . . . will avoid the self-indulgent error of seeing himself in a predicament so unprecedented, so unique, as to justify his making an exception to law, custom, or morality in favor of himself." There were plenty of predicaments in CENTCOM over my three years of command. None of them were new; none of them were without some form of precedent or guide. U.S. senior military leaders have confronted many stern and demanding tasks across the history of the republic. I worked very hard to find those earlier historical examples, and they were always quite useful. I never saw myself as a leader of the scope and scale of the great captains of World War II, but it was occasionally comforting to sit alone in my office, usually at home and late at night, and read and think about them.

The leader who influenced my approach to command the most wasn't an American. It was British Field Marshall William Slim. He commanded two different corps and ultimately the Fourteenth Army in the China-Burma-India theater in World War II. He saw defeat at the hands of the Japanese and finally a stunning and complete victory by the end of the long campaign. It was an economy of force theater, and he never had enough personnel, equipment, or supplies. His book, *Defeat into Victory*, remains the very best first-person account of what it was like to command at the highest operational level of war. One of his key leadership principles was to "communicate energy with affection." This is a simple concept, but as with so many pithy slogans, it bears a lot of unpacking. For me, it meant that one of the basic tasks of any commander is the need to ensure subordinates understand the nature of the problem and how the organization plans to overcome it, and to make certain that everyone is fully committed to the solution. This is particularly important when "everyone" begins with an audience of senior but subordinate military leaders—two- and three-star officers, who naturally have their own views of any problem, and their own historical, conceptual, emotional, and even doctrinal baggage. It is far easier to gather a thousand junior servicemembers together and explain a problem than it is to sit with a handful of subordinate commanders and explain a plan to them, while taking into account their own views and reservations. It is a dialectic process, and ultimately everyone in the room knows whose views will prevail—but it is far better to carry them with you, rather than impose guidance by stentorian diktat. I don't mean to imply that on occasion you don't have to simply tell someone to do something, and to do it quickly and without any discretion.

That leads to the second part of the phrase—"with affection." At the theater level, there are many short-term problems that must be solved immediately. Additionally, there will be problems that arise tomorrow that haven't yet been envisioned. In giving orders and direction, it's important to recognize that a collegial, interactive command atmosphere is the most effective. Subordinate commanders must know that they can offer differing views and that they will be heard with respect. I've found this to be a very effective technique, and it is particularly useful at the highest levels of command. When I sit down for any initial meeting with either a new commander or a primary staff officer, I tell them that in my career, there have been several officers I've worked for that said at the beginning of our relationship: "I'm an easy guy to get along with, you're going to love working for me." Unfailingly, those officers turned out to be jerks. I go on to tell my subordinates that I don't know whether I'm easy to work for or not, or whether I'm a jerk, but I do know that we're going to accomplish the missions we're given, and it will take both of us, working together, to make that happen. For me, there's the realization that there will always be another mission and another task, and the relationship between senior and subordinate must continue, through the fires of present crises and drama and into the future.

I have tried to prove a case throughout this book that generals, admirals, and commanders do matter, and the personalities of those flag officers are vital to success in war. I've also tried to reinforce the point that the military element of power must always be subordinate to civilian control. I've always enjoyed participating in the creation of policy but have always been aware of the side of the table on which the ultimate decision-maker sits. There is also a requirement that lies with civilian leadership to listen to the military professional. There is no responsibility to agree with that advice. Acting in this manner requires self-confidence by the civilian leader. When that self-confidence or assurance of purpose is lacking, problems arise. Senior military leaders typically don't have overt self-confidence issues, but that doesn't make their opinions better or right. In something of a reaction to this interplay, in our current era it has become fashionable to dispute the value of professional military expertise and to shovel the counsel and knowledge of generals into a larger bin of advice that is not different, specialized, or unique from which it must compete to be heard. If this trend continues, the military advice the republic's leaders receives will suffer, and the performance of our forces in the field will reflect this.

The title of this book was taken from *The Guns of August*, Barbara Tuchman's eminently readable popular history of the causes of World War I. I like the phrase because it draws out the importance of the individual commander. Sometimes we overlook the importance of that one man or woman who has to make a decision upon which an entire campaign turns. Those decisions can come quickly, and often without the opportunity to exhaustively debate options or courses of action. At that point in time, it is the will and character of the commander that will carry the day. The planning, the preparation, the interaction with the staff and subordinate commanders all set the stage for these rapid-fire moments—but they cannot give additional time in the crisis for the decision-maker. All of my military life, and certainly the past fifteen years, I have fought every day to avoid being drowned in the suffocating minutiae and volume of material, files, plans, and briefings that can obscure the essential truths of any situation. No wiring diagram or directive or academic preparation can completely capture the human element of command. It is that time and place where base metal can be transformed into something more—something that conjures a decision in the form of time, space, and purpose. It will always be the melting point.

GLOSSARY

amphibious ready group (ARG): The ships that carry deployed Marines. A typical ARG has three to five ships, including a big-deck amphibious carrier.

Assistant to the President for National Security Affairs (APNSA), also known as the National Security Advisor (NSA): The senior White House advisor to the president on national security matters. Typically, the APNSA runs the "process" of committee meetings that uses the interagency to arrive at recommendations for the president. This is a non–Senate confirmed post. It is also not in the chain of command.

chain of command: In the United States, the statutory authority to give orders to the combatant commanders. This emanates from the president and passes through the secretary of defense. It does not go through either the chairman of the Joint Chiefs of Staff or the Joint Chiefs of Staff. The chairman does have responsibility for assisting the president and secretary of defense in the transmission of orders, and the Joint Staff assists him in this role.

Chairman of the Joint Chiefs of Staff (CJCS): The nation's senior military officer. He is the principal military advisor to the president and the secretary of defense. The CJCS is a member of the Joint Chiefs of Staff. The CJCS exercises no command authority and is not in the chain of command. He does have a statutory responsibility to assist the president and the secretary of defense in the execution of their command responsibilities.

combatant commands: There are eleven combatant commands. Seven are geographic commands, responsible for a designated portion of the world, and the other four are functional commands and provide essential capabilities globally. They are joint organizations. Combatant commands are always led by a four-star officer. These combatant commanders are in the chain of command and receive the orders of the president and the secretary of defense. In usage, the commands are referred to as CENTCOM (for Central Command), EUCOM (for European Command), and so forth.

Global Force Management Plan (GFMP): The aspirational plan for how the joint force will use units and resources to meet vetted requirements over a future fiscal year. Theoretically, it aligns under the National Defense Strategy and the National Military Strategy. In practice, because of the tension between planning and reality, the GFMP for any year is under constant modification. The process of changing unit assignments and deployments is called the orders book process, and it involves presenting the secretary with potential changes to the GFMP that allow the joint force to meet new and emerging challenges.

improvised explosive device (IED): An IED can be buried, vehicle-borne, or carried by a person. It can be detonated by pressure or by command from a distance.

intelligence community (IC): The body of organizations, military and civilian, that comprise the intelligence collection and analysis component of the nation.

The Interagency: The group of agencies that collaborate to process and deliver options to senior decision-makers. This is a broad term, and agencies may drop in and out as necessary. In the national security realm, the Department of State and Department of Defense are always represented, and many others may participate as needed.

Joint Chiefs of Staff (JCS): These are the service chiefs of the Army, Marine Corps, Navy, Air Force, Space Force, and the chief of the National Guard Bureau. The chairman and the vice chairman are also members of the JCS. The service chiefs wear two hats: as the heads of their respective services and as members of the Joint Chiefs of Staff. Like the chairman, they exercise no command authority and are not in the chain of command.

Joint Staff (JS): This is the nation's senior military staff. Joint in nature, with a strength of around 1,600 personnel, it supports the secretary of defense, the chairman, and the joint chiefs in the execution of their responsibilities.

It is often confused with the Joint Chiefs of Staff, but the Joint Staff is a separate entity.

Joint Staff directorates: In the U.S. system, the organization of a staff is designed along Napoleonic lines. The J-1 is responsible for personnel, the J-2 for intelligence, the J-3 for operations, the J-4 for logistics, the J-5 for strategy, policy, and plans, the J-6 for communications, the J-7 for training and force development, and the J-8 for fiscal matters and programming.

Marine Expeditionary Unit (MEU): The smallest of the Marine Corps' air-ground task forces. It is forward-deployed on Navy ships and can rapidly react to crisis situations. It is composed of about 2,000 Marines.

MQ-9 Reaper: The ubiquitous long-range propeller-driven uncrewed drone employed by U.S. forces around the world. Built by General Atomics, the Reaper combines long range and flexibility. It flies at medium to low altitudes. The platform can be used for surveillance or strike.

National Security Council (NSC), Principal Committee (PC), Deputy Committee (DC): The series of committees that formulate national security policy for the United States. In the simplest terms, if the president is in the room, it is an NSC meeting. When cabinet officers are present without the president, it is a PC, and when their deputies are present, it becomes a DC. Theoretically, PCs and DCs generate recommendations, and NSCs generate decisions.

National Security Strategy (NSS), National Defense Strategy (NDS), National Military Strategy (NMS): The hierarchical set of statutorily mandated documents that should outline the strategic objectives of the United States. The NSS marshals all of the resources of the nation, while the NDS and NMS are internal Department of Defense documents. In theory, they nest within each other, with the NSS at the top.

Office of the Secretary of Defense (OSD): The collective term for the deputy secretary, the under secretaries, and their many assistants that comprise the civilian leadership of the Department of Defense. Like the Joint Staff, with the exception of the secretary, these organizations are not in the chain of command.

Patriot: The name for the U.S. surface-to-air missile system. It is the most effective weapon of its type in the world. It has been widely exported and is used by many friendly nations. The Patriot system has the ability to share information across a vast network, creating a common operational picture that allows rapid sharing of data.

RQ-4: A high-altitude jet-powered intelligence collection platform. Uncrewed, it has extremely long-range capabilities. It is a pure intelligence-gatherer, with no strike capabilities.

Tomahawk land attack cruise missile (TLAM): The Navy's TLAM is a long-range jet propelled cruise missile of exceptional accuracy that can be fired from ships or submarines. Policymakers like it because of its accuracy and ability to strike targets with no risk to U.S. servicemembers.

uncrewed aerial vehicle, uncrewed aerial system (UAV, UAS): Typically, these terms refer to air-breathing platforms, not missiles or rockets.

NOTES

Chapter 2. Central Command

1. Much of this chapter is based on David Crist's definitive history of the United States and Iran, *The Twilight War: The Secret History of America's Thirty-Year Conflict with Iran* (New York: Penguin, 2013), which is unsurpassed in the depth of its analysis, the magisterial synthesis of its judgments, and the elegance of its style. This book remains the single irreplaceable work on the United States and Iran.
2. Jimmy Carter, Presidential Directive/NSC-18, "U.S. National Strategy," August 24, 1977, 4–5.
3. A named operation or campaign is an operation that has a formal name assigned to it and, more importantly, typically provides directive guidance to the services about how to fund it. Typically, these are long-term events. It is an important bureaucratic point with the Pentagon.

Chapter 3. Confronting Iran

1. There was lots of coverage of this message. Typical was Rebecca Falconer, "Bolton: U.S. Sending Navy Strike Group to Iran to Send 'Clear Message,'" *Axios*, May 7, 2019.
2. Thomas Friedman, "Biden Made Sure 'Trump Is Not Going to Be President for Four More Years,'" *New York Times*, December 2, 2020, https://www.nytimes.com/2020/12/02/opinion/biden-interview-mcconnell-china-iran.html.
3. Reuters, "Iran's Missile Programme Is Non-Negotiable, Says Rouhani," Reuters, December 14, 2020, https://www.reuters.com/article/iran-nuclear-usa-int-idUSKBN28O1KU/.
4. See two pieces by Uzi Ruin, the former head of Israel's missile defense program, claiming that precision strike systems such as these are true weapons of mass disruption and destruction and might be war-winners: "Israel and the Precision-Guided Missile Threat," Perspectives Paper 1607, Begin-Sadat Center for Strategic Studies, June 16, 2020, https://besacenter.org/israel-precision-guided-missiles/; and "The New Day After: Accurate Missiles in the Middle East," presentation, Nonproliferation Policy Education Center, April 22, 2021, https://npolicy.org/the-new-day-after-accurate-missiles-in-the-middle-east/.

Chapter 5. Soleimani

1. Defense Intelligence Agency, *Iran: Military Power, Ensuring Regime Survival, and Ensuring Regional Dominance* (Washington, DC: Government Publishing Office, 2019), 57–58.
2. Defense Intelligence Agency, 57.
3. Adam Entous and Evan Osnos, "Qassem Suleimani and How Nations Decide to Kill," *New Yorker*, February 10, 2020.

Chapter 6. Aftermath

1. Farnaz Fassihi, "Iranian Diplomat Says Tehran's Military Leaders Thwart Diplomacy," *New York Times*, April 26, 2021, A8.

Chapter 8. Drawing Down the Long War in Afghanistan

1. Mark Esper, *A Sacred Oath: Memoirs of a Secretary of Defense during Extraordinary Times* (New York: William Morrow, 2022), 385–87.
2. Winston Churchill, *The World Crisis: Volume III* (New York: Bloomsbury, 2015), 71.
3. From T. S. Eliot, "The Love Song of J. Alfred Prufrock," 1915.
4. Senate Committee on Armed Services testimony of CJCS Gen. Mark Milley, September 28, 2021.

Chapter 9. A Long December

1. Katie Bo Williams, "Outgoing Syria Envoy Admits Hiding U.S. Troop Numbers; Praises Trump's Mideast Record," Defense One, November 12, 2020.
2. Farnaz Fassifi, David E. Sanger, Eric Schmitt, and Ronen Bergman, "Iran's Top Scientist Killed in Ambush, State Media Say," *New York Times*, November 27, 2020.
3. See Zach Dorfman, "Frustrated with CIA, Trump Administration Turned to Pentagon for Shadow War with Iran," Yahoo News, November 23, 2021.
4. Sir William Slim, *Unofficial History* (London: Cassell, 1959).
5. President of the United States, Tweet, 1647, December 23, 2020.
6. U.S. Central Command, statement on December 20, 2020, rocket attack, released December 23, 2020.
7. Esper, *Sacred Oath*, 185–86.

Chapter 10. Cleansing the Temple

1. See Kenneth F. McKenzie Jr., "Assessing Risk: Enabling Sound Defense Decisions," chapter seven, in *QDR 2001: Strategy-Driven Choices for America's Security*, ed. Michéle A. Flournoy (Washington, DC: NDU Press, 2001).
2. This quote is modeled on Ernest K. Gann's "Rule books are paper—they will not soften a sudden meeting of stone and metal."
3. Lytton Strachey, *Eminent Victorians, The Illustrated Edition* (London: Bloomsbury Publishing, 1988), 46.

Chapter 11. The Noose Tightens in Afghanistan

1. Michael R. Gordon, Gordon Lubold, Vivian Salama, and Jessica Donati, "Inside Biden's Afghanistan Withdrawal Plan: Warnings, Doubts, but Little Change," *Wall Street Journal*, September 5, 2021.

Chapter 12. An Inconvenient Truth

1. See Adam Roston and Nandita Bose, "Exclusive: Before Afghan Collapse, Biden Pressed Ghani to 'Change Perception,'" Reuters, August 31, 2021.
2. Roston and Bose.
3. Helmuth von Moltke, *Moltke on the Art of War: Selected Writings*, ed. Daniel J. Hughes (Novato, CA: Presidio Press, 1993), 45.

Chapter 13. No Safety or Surprise

1. Michael Herr, *Dispatches* (New York: Alfred A. Knopf, 1977), 260.

Chapter 14. Accountability

1. Commander, CENTCOM, press conference, April 22, 2021.

Chapter 15. Iran, Iraq, Syria

1. Robin Wright, "The Looming Threat of a Nuclear Crisis with Iran," *New Yorker*, December 27, 2021.
2. Michael R. Gordon and David S. Cloud, "U.S. Held Secret Meeting with Israeli, Arab Military Chiefs to Counter Iran Air Threat," *Wall Street Journal*, June 26, 2022.

Chapter 16. Considering Phlebas

1. I wrote about this in "Beyond Luddites and Magicians: Examining the Military Technical Revolution," *Parameters* 25, no. 1 (1995).
2. Among many articles on this subject, see Alice Hunt Friend and Mara Karlin, "Towards a Concept of Good Civilian Guidance," *War on the Rocks*, May 29, 2020.
3. Eliot A. Cohen, *Supreme Command: Soldiers, Statesmen, and Leadership in Wartime* (New York: Free Press, 2002), 11, but also throughout the rest of this excellent book.
4. Peter Feaver, *Armed Servants: Agency, Oversight, and Civil-Military Relations* (Cambridge, MA: Harvard University Press, 2003), 65.
5. Joint Service Committee on Military Justice, *Manual for Courts-Martial* (Washington, DC: The Joint Staff, 2019).
6. General Mattis thoughtfully left a copy of this book, with an inscription for future CENTCOM commanders, in his old office. I found the book insightful and useful. It's still there.

INDEX

ABOUT THE AUTHOR

Gen. Kenneth F. McKenzie Jr., USMC (Ret.), served as Commander, United States Central Command from March 2019 to April 2022. Prior to that, he spent almost two years as Director for Strategy, Plans, and Policy on the Joint Staff and then served almost two years as Director of the Joint Staff. He has commanded at the platoon, company, battalion, Marine Expeditionary Unit (MEU), and component levels. General McKenzie is an honors graduate of the Armor Officer Advanced Course, Marine Corps Command and Staff College, and the School of Advanced Warfighting. He served as a Senior Military Fellow within the Institute for National Strategic Studies at the National Defense University. He has a master's degree in teaching with a concentration in history. After graduating from The Citadel, he was commissioned into the Marine Corps and trained as an infantry officer. He resides in Tampa, Florida.

The **Naval Institute Press** is the book-publishing arm of the U.S. Naval Institute, a private, nonprofit, membership society for sea service professionals and others who share an interest in naval and maritime affairs. Established in 1873 at the U.S. Naval Academy in Annapolis, Maryland, where its offices remain today, the Naval Institute has members worldwide.

Members of the Naval Institute support the education programs of the society and receive the influential monthly magazine *Proceedings* or the colorful bimonthly magazine *Naval History* and discounts on fine nautical prints and on ship and aircraft photos. They also have access to the transcripts of the Institute's Oral History Program and get discounted admission to any of the Institute-sponsored seminars offered around the country.

The Naval Institute's book-publishing program, begun in 1898 with basic guides to naval practices, has broadened its scope to include books of more general interest. Now the Naval Institute Press publishes about seventy titles each year, ranging from how-to books on boating and navigation to battle histories, biographies, ship and aircraft guides, and novels. Institute members receive significant discounts on the Press' more than eight hundred books in print.

Full-time students are eligible for special half-price membership rates. Life memberships are also available.

For more information about Naval Institute Press books that are currently available, visit www.usni.org/press/books. To learn about joining the U.S. Naval Institute, please write to:

Member Services
U.S. Naval Institute
291 Wood Road
Annapolis, MD 21402-5034
Telephone: (800) 233-8764
Fax: (410) 571-1703
Web address: www.usni.org